"The field of philanthropy has such a pressing need for stories and examples of how funders can use their limited resources to take meaningful steps towards a more just world. I am so pleased that *Change Philanthropy* is providing us with accounts of approaches and strategies of foundations working towards this goal."

—*Susan Sandler, philanthropist*

"This volume arrives at just the right time. Poised as we are between a paradigm-shifting recession and the trend towards a gloriously diverse American demographics, these case studies prod philanthropy to fulfill its commitments to grow our democracy towards justice."

—*Erica Hunt, president,*
Twenty-First Century Foundation

"I would strongly encourage philanthropists and funders from large and small institutions to read this book. The Center for Community Change brings together its expertise in social change and access to the funding community in this unique and much-needed book."

—*Rusty M. Stahl, executive director,*
Emerging Practitioners in Philanthropy

CHANGE
Philanthropy

The Chardon Press Series

Fundamental social change happens when people come together to organize, advocate, and create solutions to injustice. Chardon Press recognizes that communities working for social justice need tools to create and sustain healthy organizations. In an effort to support these organizations, Chardon Press produces materials on fundraising, community organizing, and organizational development. These resources are specifically designed to meet the needs of grassroots nonprofits—organizations that face the unique challenge of promoting change with limited staff, funding, and other resources. We at Chardon Press have adapted traditional techniques to the circumstances of grassroots nonprofits. Chardon Press and Jossey-Bass hope these works help people committed to social justice to build mission-driven organizations that are strong, financially secure, and effective.

Kim Klein, Series Editor

Additional titles from Chardon Press

Working Across Generations: Defining the Future of Nonprofit Leadership, *Frances Kunreuther, Helen Kim, Robby Rodriguez*

Inspired Philanthropy: Your Step-by-Step Guide to Creating a Giving Plan and Leaving a Legacy, Third Edition, *Tracy Gary with Nancy Adess*

Tools for Radical Democracy: How to Organize for Power in Your Community, *Joan Minieri, Paul Getsos*

Level Best: How Small and Grassroots Nonprofits Can Tackle Evaluation and Talk Results, *Marcia Festen, Marianne Philbin*

Fundraising for Social Change, Fifth Edition, Revised and Expanded, *Kim Klein*

The Accidental Fundraiser: A Step-by-Step Guide to Raising Money for Your Cause, *Stephanie Roth, Mimi Ho*

Grassroots Grants: An Activist's Guide to Grantseeking, Second Edition, *Andy Robinson*

Fundraising in Times of Crisis, *Kim Klein*

The Nonprofit Membership Toolkit, *Ellis M. M. Robinson*

Stir It Up: Lessons in Community Organizing and Advocacy, *Rinku Sen*

Selling Social Change (Without Selling Out): Earned Income Strategies for Nonprofits, *Andy Robinson*

Raise More Money: The Best of the Grassroots Fundraising Journal, *Kim Klein, Stephanie Roth, Editors*

Fundraising for the Long Haul, *Kim Klein*

Ask and You Shall Receive: A Fundraising Training Program for Religious Organizations and Projects, Leader Manual, *Kim Klein*

Ask and You Shall Receive: A Fundraising Training Program for Religious Organizations and Projects, Participant Manual, *Kim Klein*

Making Policy Making Change: How Communities Are Taking Law into Their Own Hands, *Makani N. Themba*

Roots of Justice: Stories of Organizing in Communities of Color, *Larry R. Salomon*

CHANGE
Philanthropy

Candid Stories

of FOUNDATIONS MAXIMIZING

RESULTS

Through SOCIAL JUSTICE

ALICIA EPSTEIN KORTEN

FOREWORD BY CHRISTOPHER HARRIS AND
DEEPAK BHARGAVA

PROJECT DIRECTOR MARJORIE FINE

SPONSORED BY THE CENTER FOR COMMUNITY CHANGE

JB JOSSEY-BASS
A Wiley Imprint
www.josseybass.com

Published by Jossey-Bass
A Wiley Imprint
989 Market Street, San Francisco, CA 94103-1741—www.josseybass.com

Library of Congress Cataloging-in-Publication Data

Korten, Alicia Epstein, date.
Change philanthropy: candid stories of foundations maximizing results through social justice/Alicia
Epstein Korten; foreword by Christopher Harris and Deepak Bhargava.—1st ed.
    p. cm.—(The Chardon Press series)
  Includes bibliographical references and index.
    ISBN 978-0-470-43516-8 (cloth)
  1. Charities. 2. Social justice. 3. Social change. I. Title.
  HV25.K67 2009
  361.7'632—dc22
                                                                    2009021649

Printed in the United States of America
FIRST EDITION
HB Printing   10 9 8 7 6 5 4 3 2 1

Contents

PART ONE
Securing Success with Campaigns   1

1   Strengthening Unusual Alliances for Living Wages   3

The Case of the Discount Foundation

The Discount Foundation's name is a reference to its small grantmaking budget (roughly $550,000 annually). By positioning itself to influence other funders in the field, this small foundation has played an instrumental role in strengthening labor, community, and faith partnerships that have championed one of the most successful economic justice campaigns in the United States.

2   Supporting Citizen Action and Litigation for Education Reform   22

The Case of the Schott Foundation

Concerned that funding direct school services, such as tutoring and counseling, for public school students was not fully leveraging their money in support of low-income communities, the Leeds and Jobin-Leeds families created the Caroline and Sigmund Schott Foundation—and later supported the emergence of the Schott Foundation for Public Education—to reach a much greater number of children. Supporting a three-pronged strategy—citizen action, litigation, and advocacy—led to historic increases in education funding in New York.

PART TWO
Influencing Market Forces in Support of People and the Planet   43

3   Using an Endowment to Build the Field of Socially Responsible Investing   45

The Case of the Needmor Fund

The Stranahans provide a rare glimpse into the dynamics of a family of wealth as they bridge their differences to position their family foundation, the Needmor Fund, as a leader in the world of socially responsible investing. Reaching beyond their grantmaking, they discovered the impact that they can have by using their endowment funds to generate change.

4   Transforming Business Structures for Communities   65

The Case of the Jacobs Family Foundation and Jacobs Center for Neighborhood Innovation

In this chapter, the staff and founders of the Jacobs Family Foundation and its sister operating foundation, the Jacobs Center for Neighborhood Innovation, share their soul-searching journey to meet the needs of underinvested communities. Beginning by writing blueprints for these communities, the Jacobs Foundations were confronted by the need to bring community members into their decision-making processes. The result was a community-owned marketplace in San Diego and two foundations that aim to go out of business within the next two decades, transferring all assets—including JCNI's share in the marketplace—to the residents working to strengthen their neighborhoods.

PART THREE
Aiding an Identity-Based Movement   89

5   Supporting the Development of an Immigrant Rights Field   91

The Case of the Ford Foundation

During a Ford Foundation leadership transition in the late 1970s and early 1980s, staff members proposed an expansion of their support for immigrants. The resulting program helped grantees build an immigration field in the United States.

6   Maturing an Immigrant Movement   104

The Case of the Open Society Institute

After reading about the devastating impact the 1996 welfare reform laws would have for immigrant families, George Soros decided to commit $50 million to support immigrants in the United States. Revitalizing a beleaguered field, this money helped organizers lay the groundwork for the marches of millions of immigrants in the United States in 2006.

Foreword

We see a growing hunger and passion among donors and foundation staff for effective, long-term strategies to address critical social problems—and *Change Philanthropy* provides a unique and practical road map for the field. The book is a critical contribution to the debate about the role of philanthropy at a time of global economic turmoil, declining foundation assets, and increasing need and suffering in the United States and around the world.

Marjorie Fine brings extensive experience to her role as director of the book project. She was the former executive director of the Unitarian Universalist Veatch Program at Shelter Rock—a remarkable model of social justice philanthropy. In addition, for the past several years she has been director of The Linchpin Campaign, a special project of the Center for Community Change that (1) seeks to educate and engage donors and foundations about community organizing and (2) prepares organizers to communicate effectively to donors about the power of their work. *Change Philanthropy*, an initiative of The Linchpin Campaign, is one vehicle for realizing that broader goal.

Alicia Korten also brings unique and important qualifications to the task at hand. She consults with foundations and public agencies with grantmaking programs, including institutions as varied as the Ford Foundation, United Nations, World Resource Institute, and Inter-American Development Bank. She also worked with indigenous peoples in Panama for many years, helping them secure participation in publicly funded development projects.

• • •

The debate about the future of philanthropy is playing out in a larger social context. The twenty-first century is already shaping up to be a critical one for the future of humanity and the earth. In our increasingly interconnected world, goods, ideas, and elements of culture are moving across the globe with greater ease, but we are also experiencing unprecedented inequality, increasing poverty, forced migrations, and public health crises that spill across borders. We share a climate and an environment that are at serious risk unless we make dramatic shifts in how we organize our economies and live our lives. Patterns of structural racial inequality are deeply entrenched and are contributing to extreme suffering and erosion of rights and civil liberties for many, particularly people of color.

All these challenges to human welfare have invigorated social change movements. A new immigrant rights movement has brought millions of people to civic life. Young people are enlivening politics. New thinking in women's rights and racial justice is prompting deeper reflection about both what changes we should seek and how we should push for them. Movements to fight climate change, create green jobs, and increase access to health care are gaining steam. All this new activism and thinking is heartening because great social progress has always been brought about through such large-scale democratic practice.

Change Philanthropy is a timely entry in a lively debate about how philanthropy can address these challenges of our times. The topic is particularly important, as one of the great paradoxes of rising inequality is that it is fueling an unprecedented increase in the scale and scope of organized philanthropy.

Change Philanthropy represents one effort to show the power of moving beyond alleviating symptoms of inequality to aiming funding at changing the underlying structural arrangements that result in those symptoms. Although most foundations share a commitment to the public good, few have made the explicit decision to identify and work on these deeply entrenched and frequently unspoken challenges.

Advocates of a social justice approach are pointing to a path beyond inherited orthodoxies to structural solutions that get at the underlying causes of poverty, inequality, racial and gender disparities, and the erosion of rights and civil liberties. Policies need to change, as do the way those policies are implemented.

For example, a foundation can support computers in schools in poor neighborhoods, but absent a challenge to the design of public financing for education by property taxes, it permits the continuation of an unequal funding formula that ensures that those schools remain underfunded.

Large numbers of people working together as part of dynamic social movements—with leadership from and by those directly affected by injustice—are needed to provide the ideas and muscle to overcome entrenched interests. Finally, a number of strategies need to be pursued in concert—including community organizing, civic participation, strategic communications, advocacy, and policy development and analysis—to achieve large-scale social change.

Philanthropy has a critical role to play in supporting grantees as they move social change forward. Yet the ferment and creativity in the social change sector has not, for the most part, been matched by resources or commitment from philanthropy.

We believe that foundations' efforts to fund grantees in meeting people's immediate needs through charity are important, particularly during times of crisis. However, we also note that foundations can never match the relative resources and power of the state (local, state, or national) to solve such problems or regulate the inequitable effects of markets.

We know that giving to address issues of structural injustice can be "risky" or "political." Yet we believe that the risk is offset by the long-term payoff, as such giving enables grantees to have impact on a much larger scale.

In our work, we continuously meet funders who are seeking ways to increase their effectiveness in addressing injustice yet who note the lack of literature, tools, and training opportunities for such work. What seminars offer experience in matching effective grant strategies to the rights of LGBT teenagers, or to deep chronic poverty, or to the racial basis of the subprime mortgage crisis?

This book offers interested grantmakers a glimpse into how several funders have supported social justice, and provides a tool for helping readers rethink their own work. First, each chapter shows how the family, program officer, chief executive, or others in the foundation made use of a structural analysis of the injustice they wanted to resolve, though many of them would not call it this and had to come to such an analysis by trial and error. (Maya Wiley's

Afterword on structural racism in this book is a provocative and helpful reflection on this subject.) Second, the chapters show how the foundations learned to craft grant strategies that were strong enough to support grantees in having impact on the targets of that analysis.

• • •

Social justice philanthropy helps people gain the ability to change their own lives. In so doing, the field helps realize the democratic promise of this country and beyond. That is funding for a more lasting public good.

Alicia Korten and Marjorie Fine have done a great service to the field of philanthropy by providing us with stories of how others have changed their thinking and their grantmaking to important effect. The debate about the role of philanthropy in social change is important not so much for its own sake but for its deep relevance to the much larger question as to whether we can address the great social challenges of this century with wisdom, strategic insight, and compassion.

June 2009

DEEPAK BHARGAVA
Executive Director
Center for Community Change

CHRISTOPHER HARRIS
Senior Program Officer
Ford Foundation

Acknowledgments

First and foremost, I thank the Center for Community Change (CCC) for having contracted me to write this book.

Marjorie Fine, who heads The Linchpin Campaign, and the others at the Center worked tirelessly to bring *Change Philanthropy* to fruition. As director of the book project, Marjorie, with her decades of experience in the foundation world, recruited a host of top-caliber people, opened countless doors, and carefully edited and reviewed every chapter. She was often on the phone with me several times a week. Her thoughts and insights are reflected throughout the book.

Deepak Bhargava and Seth Borgos brought their intellectual firepower to the endeavor, including helping choose the cases in this volume. Seth Borgos, together with Julia Paik, also provided essential administrative support. Lynn Kanter brought her tremendous writing skills to bear in helping develop proposals and project reports for the initiative and helped locate appropriate resource people. John Pomeranz also provided invaluable input into the manuscript.

Heartfelt appreciation goes to the Ford Foundation, which provided funding to the Center for this project.

The book also had a first-rate advisory team of social justice leaders. Christopher Harris, Robert Bray, Maya Wiley, Christine Doby, Leroy Johnson, Michael Edwards, Kim Klein, Peter Pennekamp, Barbara Taveras, and Luz Vega-Marquis each brought to bear his or her wealth of experience in choosing the case studies in this volume and determining key messages. Particular thanks go to Robert Bray, who generously extended his extensive marketing skills to the endeavor, and to Kim Klein, who provided substantial support and guidance.

The editorial team at Jossey-Bass—David Harris, Allison Brunner, Lindsay Morton, and Xenia Lisanevich—have been a tremendous support. They have been deeply generous with their time, lending both their experience and good humor to shepherding the book through to publication.

Many other individuals supported the work along the way. David Lerner, Anthony Barnett, Bill Hamilton, and Rochelle Lefkowitz helped brainstorm ways to market the book upon its release. Eleanor Bader, Ignatius Bau, Myra Bicknell, Heidi Binko, Millie Buchanan, Jim Casey, Diana Cohn, Aaron Dorfman, Frank Farrow, Deanne Feeney, Janice Fine, David Foster, Bob Haas, Jan Jaffe, Avila Kilmurray, Lance Lindblom, Laura Livoti, May Louie, Chag Lowry, Nicky McIntyre, Anita Nager, Bill Roberts, Janet Shenk, Peter Teague, Ken Wilson, Emily Young, and Jim Young all gave their time either to review the manuscript or to discuss ideas and possible cases.

A final thanks must go to the foundation trustees and staff interviewed in this book. Many are sharing never-before-told stories in the hopes that their successes and failures will help support colleagues and the philanthropic and not-for-profit field more broadly.

June 2009   ALICIA EPSTEIN KORTEN
                                                   Arlington, Virginia

Introduction

As I was writing this book, I explained to a business colleague of my husband that I was working on a publication about social justice philanthropy. "What's to write?" he asked me. "Seems easy enough. You have money, and you give it to organizations you believe in." Yet mounting an effective funding program, particularly one that seeks to achieve large-scale impact in support of equity and justice, is an art. Defining a strategy for maximum impact, working to develop buy-in within a foundation for a course of action, and identifying grantees and building their trust are but a few of the challenges funders face.

This book is designed for you if you are a foundation trustee, executive director, or program staff person struggling with how to leverage your limited resources to address the enormous social and environmental challenges in the United States and abroad. This book is also designed for you if you are seeking ways to reach a greater number of people than your foundation currently serves. If you are with a nonprofit that partners with foundations to address such issues, you may also find the insider perspective this book offers extremely useful.

The publication includes the inside stories of ten founda-tions that have leveraged their grant dollars, and in many cases endowments and influence, to transform systems—whether in the government, for-profit, or even nonprofit sectors—that strip people of dignity and economic opportunity.

How Can Philanthropy Enhance Its Relevance?

According to the Foundation Center, foundations gave an esti-mated $42.9 billion in 2007.[1] But most of these philanthropic dollars fund direct services, such as hospitals, university endowments, disaster relief, and soup kitchens. Such funding provides important services to many people, particularly when it targets low-income populations, and especially in times of societal crisis and economic downturns.

Yet foundations and nonprofit organizations alone can never provide all the services needed by citizens of any society. Ultimately governments and businesses—with their vastly superior resources—must play a role. Total expenditures for the U.S. federal government in 2007 were just over $3 trillion, and state and local expenditures were just over $2 trillion, dwarfing annual philanthropic grantmaking.[2] And whereas foundations held assets of $670 billion in 2007, the largest fifty companies alone held assets of $16.7 trillion that same year.[3]

With limited funds, organized philanthropy faces a fundamental question: How can foundations best leverage their assets to be more effective agents of social change in support of equity and justice in the twenty-first century? Following the economic turmoil in 2008 and 2009, this question becomes even more important as assets of many foundations shrink, while needs increase.

The question of how foundations use their assets is also a critical one at this time because new money has poured into the field over the last two decades, even as some foundations have lost assets. In 1985, foundations operating in the United States gave away only $6 billion, with assets at roughly $102 billion.[4] By 2007, just before the economic downturn, assets had swelled to over six times that amount.[5] Warren Buffet's projected $31 billion transfer of wealth to the Gates Foundation is one striking example of the scale of money that is influencing philanthropy at this time. As new money comes in, philanthropy is in a state of flux, as recently established foundations determine how these dollars will be used.

This book argues that one critical way for foundations to become even more relevant is to improve the balance between funding services that ameliorate symptoms of societal ills and addressing the root causes of those ills. In 2006, only 12 percent of grantmaking supported systems change for equity and justice, leaving the vast majority of money for services, according to a study by the Foundation Center and Independent Sector.[6]

This funding imbalance—between social justice and services—inhibits foundations from realizing their full potential in addressing societal ills.

Giving for social justice helps ensure that a much greater number of people can enjoy a society's resources and opportunities. By harnessing the power of all sectors of society and more fully recognizing the defining roles government and business play in people's lives, foundations can more effectively help societies meet the multifold needs of the twenty-first century.

The independent nature of many foundations positions them well to take on the role of funding grantees who are challenging societal institutions to be more fair and sustainable. "One of the attributes of foundations has been their ability to take on sensitive issues that other public and private institutions can't take on. [In part because so many have their own endowments,] they can afford to take on risk and fail. They can stick with things for a long time. They can do demonstration and pilot projects to test out new ideas and innovations," notes Barry Gaberman, former senior vice president at the Ford Foundation. Foundations are protected from the cyclical forces that often keep governments from being effective; and because they do not have shareholders demanding a quarterly return, they can focus on long-term results more easily than can publicly traded companies.

WHAT IS SOCIAL JUSTICE PHILANTHROPY?

Social justice actors seek to help citizens transform systems, institutions, and cultures to ensure that all citizens can participate fully in the social, spiritual, economic, and political life of a country, regardless of their position or station in life. The aim of social justice is not to ensure that all people live the same lives or earn the same amount of money. However, a basic tenet is that all have the opportunity to meet their basic needs, to engage freely with one another across differences, and to define and build the institutions that shape their lives.

There is a famous adage that says, "Give a [person] a fish and you have fed him [or her] for a day. Teach a [person] to fish and you have fed him [or her] for a lifetime."

Systems change in support of low-income people takes this saying one step further, acknowledging that many low-income people living by water already know how to fish. Often what they need is support in protecting their right to fish as industrial fisheries take away their access to the water. Or they are fighting to protect their rivers from industrial waste that has poisoned fishing stocks.

In response to homelessness, a traditional philanthropist might fund a homeless shelter. A funder of social justice, in contrast, would ask, "Why are people homeless?" and use the answer to guide his or her grantmaking. Such a strategy might include empowering low-income communities to advocate for policies that prevent homelessness—such as subsidized housing, fairer credit opportunities, and a living wage.

The Leeds family (founders of the Schott Foundation) embarked on just such a journey of transformation, which is highlighted in Chapter Two of this book. Initially, the family funded an education institute to service a handful of children left behind by New York's decaying public school system. Over time, however, the family came to question why so many public schools in New York were failing. As a result, they decided to found the Schott Foundation and put their dollars to work supporting grantees in their efforts to transform the larger New York public school system so as to reach a much broader number of children.

Note: Definition written by Maya Wiley and Alicia Korten.

The Inside Stories of Ten Foundations

This book highlights ten foundations that have moved beyond a focus solely on services, such as homeless shelters and hospitals, to one aimed at helping people influence the context in which they live. Through often lengthy journeys of trial and error, each foundation has chosen to address root causes of problems by asking such questions as "Why does poverty exist?"

The chapters offer a rare glimpse into the often soundproof halls of the funding world as foundations make decisions regarding why and how to support social justice. The stories detail the internal learning processes that helped foundations understand how better to help grantees build the kind of power needed to move systems much larger than themselves. Several show how community organizing grantees—with their focus on building citizens' ability to engage in collective action—have been critical in building that power and shifting systems that had appeared immovable. Each includes the voices of champions inside and outside these foundations as they share their experiences in influencing their own institutions and in working with grantees. Some cases show how those within the foundation addressed the emotional fallout that can occur with change. Yet others depict the risks associated with such grantmaking, and how challenges have been managed. A few of the foundations demonstrate how sharing their decision-making authority with grantees enhanced their ability to provide strategic grants.

Clear themes emerge across the cases with regard to effective strategies for achieving large-scale change in support of equity and justice. Almost all the foundations (and collaboratives) found a clear and limited point of focus. Most concentrated their efforts on helping grantees build strong organizations, including increasing their membership base so that these members could effectively pressure targeted institutions to change. Many emphasized the importance of choosing strong grantees and then giving them enough room to make their own choices by providing general operating support rather than specific project support. Several foundations also developed methods for evaluating their funding strategies, including finding benchmarks that could help measure whether grantees were succeeding over time and switching directions if they weren't. Most reached beyond their own foundations, finding such mechanisms as collaboratives and affinity groups to increase support for an issue or for a type of grantee from other foundations.

A Snapshot of the Stories Highlighted

A team under the direction of Marjorie Fine of the Center for Community Change (formerly head of the Unitarian Universalist Veatch Program at Shelter Rock, a national faith-based grantmaking program) helped choose the cases highlighted in this book. In addition to myself, this team included others at the Center, as well as a nine-person advisory team of funders and nonprofit organization representatives, who thoroughly surveyed the philanthropic land-scape for what we felt were compelling, high-impact stories of change in the sector.

- The Discount Foundation leveraged its very limited resources to support a living-wage movement that led to the first increase in the federal minimum wage in a decade.
- The Schott Foundation is a leader recognized by its peers for supporting grantees' efforts to help change the New York State educational funding formula and increase funding for public schools in New York.
- The Needmor Fund became an early adopter of socially responsible investing, and played a role in helping legitimize that field.
- The Jacobs Family Foundation and the Jacobs Center for Neighborhood Revitalization were able to do what few foundations supporting neighborhood revitalization have: play a pivotal role in transforming a blighted, drug-infested community into a vibrant neighborhood with reduced gang violence and increased economic opportunity. They also helped bring communities into partnership with business, by pioneering the first community-owned initial public stock offering.
- The Liberty Hill Foundation supported the emergence of democratic organizations in Los Angeles that are helping change how that city does business.
- The Charles Stewart Mott Foundation supported grantees in building community organizing infrastructure across the United States, which is helping communities secure important gains with respect to education, wages, health care, housing, and other issues that affect the quality of life of low-income and other citizens.
- The Ford Foundation aided grantees in establishing the field of immigrant rights. Together with the Open Society Institute and others, they supported immigrant leaders and their allies as they transformed this field into a full-fledged social movement.
- The Open Society Institute supported organizations growing the immigrant rights movement, which helped roll back some of the aspects of welfare reform that most negatively affected immigrants.

- The Global Fund for Women helped strengthen women's rights infrastructure around the globe. Its grantees are playing a critical role in supporting women to lead democracy and human rights movements in Nepal, South Africa, Mexico, and other countries.
- The Gulf Coast Fund, created in 2005 following Hurricane Katrina to address the needs of those in the Gulf, strengthened efforts to rebuild these areas in an equitable and sustainable way and to raise awareness nationally regarding positive ways to address global warming.

We also chose foundations that we felt would represent the diversity of the philanthropic world so that you could find yourself and your concerns within these pages. If your private foundation is a household name and is resting on a multibillion-dollar endowment, your concerns may not be the same as those of a small public foundation raising a few hundred thousand dollars a year to give away. Hence the book highlights a mix of national, regional, and smaller family foundations, as well public charities and private independent foundations.

The ten cases also demonstrate a variety of ways in which grantees are using foundation funding for achieving change. These include community organizing, advocacy and public education, sustainable business initiatives, and judicial strategies.

There are ways, however, in which we fell short of reflecting the full diversity of foundations. Only two foundations plan to sunset. There is no case about a community foundation, despite the important work of these foundations across the country. Most of the cases are located in the foundation-dense East and West Coasts in the United States. The book does not begin to capture the range of foundations in other countries, though it does explore the creation of two foundations abroad, one in Nepal and one in Mexico, both influenced by the U.S.-based Global Fund for Women.

While all the highlighted foundations and collaboratives attempt to attack root causes of societal problems, in some respects the book does not move as far "upstream" as we might have liked. The large systems that shape inequality across the globe, such as a narrowly focused U.S. foreign policy, monopolistic public media, and financial systems that concentrate wealth in the hands of a few, were not among the social challenges addressed by the cases.

We chose institutions where we had a rich amount of data to depict the story and the change process within the foundation.

How to Use This Book

You do not need to read this book cover to cover. Each chapter stands alone to allow you to spend time only on the stories most relevant to your particular challenges.

To guide you toward the particular chapters that will address your needs, the book is divided into five parts, each highlighting different funder concerns and goals: (1) securing success with campaigns, (2) influencing market forces in support of people and the planet, (3) catalyzing an identity-based national movement, (4) creating community organizing infrastructure, and (5) transforming funder-grantee power relationships through creative foundation structures.

The following are additional insights into which chapters might be relevant to your needs:

• If you are seeking ways to build support for social justice within your foundation, you may want to read the chapters on the Open Society Institute and the Needmor Fund. In the chapter on the Open Society Institute, you will see how change agents played critical roles in helping the foundation include not only a service-oriented approach to immigrants but also a strategy for changing the circumstances that gave rise to the need for the services. The chapter on the Needmor Fund describes how a family member introduced a social justice lens to its approach to financial investments.

• If you are interested in systems or policies (such as health care or education) in the United States or abroad, you might start with the chapters on the Schott Foundation and the Discount Foundation. Each of these foundations supported grantees with specific policy objectives.

• If you are interested in how your foundation might leverage the power of the business sector for change, the Jacobs Center for Neighborhood Innovation and the Needmor Fund are rich with insights. Both foundations found creative ways to partner with, support, and hold businesses accountable to the needs of low-income communities and the environment.

- If you are a local foundation focused only on your surrounding area, the chapters on the Liberty Hill Foundation and the Jacobs Family Foundation would be the best places to start. Both are place-based funders that have become national models for how to create change at the neighborhood and city levels.

- If you are finding it difficult to build consensus among your trustees because they have such divergent political views, the chapters on the Needmor Fund and the Jacobs Family Foundation both tell stories of how family members were able to bridge their political differences in support of social justice.

- If you want to broaden your impact beyond your grantmaking, the chapters about the Discount Foundation, the Needmor Fund, and the Jacobs Family Foundation will be particularly instructive. The Needmor Fund and the Jacobs Family Foundation leveraged their entire endowment for change; the Discount Foundation used its position as a funder to encourage often larger investments from other foundations in support of living-wage campaigns and labor-community-faith alliances.

- If you are concerned with the power dynamics that plague grantee-funder relationships, the Gulf Coast Fund, the Liberty Hill Foundation, and the Global Fund for Women are all examples of how to build more authentic partnerships with community leaders and neighborhood organizations. Each foundation enhanced its grantmaking by sharing decision-making power with activists.

- If you are interested in supporting a field or a large-scale movement, you may want to read the chapters on the Ford Foundation, the Open Society Institute, and the Mott Foundation. Each of these foundations supported grantees in building the strength of disenfranchised groups, which helped them actively participate in political life in the United States and beyond.

- If you are wondering how to evaluate social justice grantmaking, the chapters on the Schott Foundation and the Open

Society Institute both detail the benchmarks these foundations learned to use to evaluate their long-term justice efforts.

- If you are looking for ways to combine a service approach with a social justice agenda, the chapters on the Open Society Institute and the Liberty Hill Foundation are good places to begin. The Open Society Institute chapter describes how foundations funded critical services, such as helping immigrants file applications for citizenship, in a time of great crisis. The chapter also emphasizes that those services would likely have been ineffective without funding support for policy work that helped move applications through government bureaucracies. The Liberty Hill Foundation chapter also emphasizes how services can play an important role in organizing people who then become active in social justice work.

For those readers who are funders, we hope this book helps you become a more effective grantmaker and find ways to move farther upstream with your giving. By leveraging your resources to address root causes, you join the growing number of funders helping create systems that support a more level playing field for all people, as well as a healthy planet for future generations. We also acknowledge the many foundations, both those we highlighted and those we were not able to fit within these pages, that are already out there doing such work.

We also encourage you to consult with appropriate tax advisers and legal counsel to determine a strategy that is appropriate for your type of foundation. Tax codes are complex and subject to change, and your foundation needs to be up-to-date as you shape your giving strategy. This book is not intended to provide legal or tax advice.

For those readers in nonprofit organizations and in the public and business sectors, we hope that this book enhances your ability to partner effectively with foundations. Our wish is that the book helps foundations more effectively support nonprofits and community-based organizations—as the players on the frontlines of change—so that funding can play an increasingly strategic role in creating a more just and sustainable future for all.

This book is dedicated to the individuals, communities, and organizations that have given of themselves to create a fairer, more sustainable world, as well as to the foundations that have courageously supported those on the front lines of change.

PART
ONE

Securing Success with Campaigns

Foundations working to catalyze change in support of equity and justice most commonly focus their giving on specific issues, such as education, health care, or the environment.

In some instances, such funders become close partners with grantees. By building relationships with the players and paying close attention to campaign details, they are often able to provide funding to grantees at crucial moments.

If you are passionate about a particular issue and would like to support campaign work, the cases of the Discount Foundation and the Schott Foundation will be of particular interest. Through a journey of trial and error, the Discount Foundation came to fund living-wage campaigns and played a role in the success of these campaigns around the country.

The Schott Foundation supported partners who secured historic public funding increases for the New York education system.

The lessons they learned are relevant for all funders, regardless of the area of focus. Along the way, each discovered that limiting the scope of its work and then focusing on ways to support grantees as they built the power to influence targeted issues and constituencies were key ingredients of success.

Strengthening Unusual Alliances for Living Wages

The Case of the Discount Foundation

The Discount Foundation's name is a reference to its small grant-making budget (roughly $550,000 annually). By positioning itself to influence other funders in the field, this small foundation has played an instrumental role in strengthening labor, community, and faith partnerships that have championed one of the most successful economic justice campaigns in the United States.

"Attending college in Los Angeles, I'd walk out the door and see the class differences," recalled Jeff Zinsmeyer, founder of the Discount Foundation. "I'd grown up believing that I lived in a country of opportunity for all. This was the image that a fifteen-year-old raised in the suburbs had, who looked around him and saw everything right. Then I got out into the world and saw that this was not so."

Coming of age during the era of the civil rights movement, Jeff saw how others were fighting to create a fairer society and began to feel that he had a role to play in addressing the inequities he saw. "At some point I asked myself: What is a meaningful life? It seemed to me that what added meaning was working to change that injustice."

When Jeff received an inheritance in the early 1970s, he sought ways to use it to support this goal. "I'd reached the decision that inherited wealth didn't fit with my democratic ideals." Already working for the Center for Community Change (CCC), which helped low-income people build community organizations, he recalled, "I asked my accountant about the maximum amount of money I could contribute for the greatest tax shield, and then somehow I ended up in front of Margery Tabankin, who headed the Youth Project [a CCC-incubated program], asking, 'Where should I put this before year end?'"

Margery remembered, "A guy with long hair walked into my office and said he was interested in giving away a large sum of money anonymously. I got to be close friends with him. I learned more about his interests and how he wanted them to be realized."

In 1977, with Margery's guidance, Jeff decided that with his remaining inheritance he would establish a foundation focused on grassroots organizing.[1] In explaining why he chose to concentrate efforts here, he noted, "I wanted to support organizations that were shifting the maldistribution of wealth and power in our country. Through work I had done on redlining,[2] and then later with CCC, I learned the tremendous leverage that could be achieved through agitation and mobilization rather than direct service. Through my work with CCC, I worked with some of the most exciting community organizations of that period, learning about their struggles for better housing and access to credit."

Discount Foundation Snapshot

Type: Private foundation

Year founded: 1977

Grant range (1977): $10,000–$20,000

Grant range (2007): $15,000–$25,000

Total grants awarded (2007): $550,000

Asset base (2007): $10.3 million

Geographic focus: National

Primary funding areas: Living wage, minimum wage, and building political power of working poor

Staff size (2007): One half-time executive director

Location: Boston

Note: Snapshot information for each chapter varies depending on data available. Dates refer to either the calendar year or the end of the fiscal cycle. For snapshot sources, refer to the Notes section at the end of the book.[3]

In setting up the Discount Foundation (so named because of its small size and even smaller grants), Jeff—together with Margery Tabankin and her husband at the time, Tom Asher—sought out board members with shared values and synergistic chemistry. "We created a board that enjoyed working together in a way that transcended the traditional board. We developed a deep level of trust," Jeff explained, adding that both Margery and Tom became board members.

Further, Jeff sought board members with experience in community organizing. In explaining why this was important, he said, "We had no staff, so we felt individuals who were active in the field could both provide firsthand knowledge of groups as well as spot promising opportunities. We also felt community experience indicated commitment."

For over a decade, the board ran the foundation with no staff. "We did all the work ourselves on top of our full-time jobs," noted Jeff, who worked at FleetBoston Financial's Community Investment Group at the time. "I remember getting calls from grassroots organizers while in my banker's suit working on leveraged buyouts."

During that time, the foundation chose to divide its limited funds among a few grassroots organizations. "We were essentially giving block grants," Jeff recalled. "We'd divide the money equally between groups we felt were doing good grassroots work."

Changing the Foundation's Direction

By the mid-1980s, the board decided to evaluate the foundation's impact. "We were thinking about hiring a staff person, so we felt it made sense to assess our work to see what kind of impact we'd had to date," explained Jeff, "but the evaluator told us, 'Look, what you've done is really interesting, and clearly you are doing God's work, but it's really hard to evaluate something when you aren't clear on what you are setting out to do. I can't evaluate you because you don't have clear objectives.'"

"He was right. We were following a 'thousand flowers bloom' strategy. Our strategy had been to look at all proposals and ask, 'Where's the good organizing?' But there was no clear focus."

Margery elaborated, "While there were a lot of important things happening out there, we realized that the only way we were going to leverage our tiny resources for large-scale impact was to focus."

Thus, in the mid-1980s the board commissioned a series of issue papers and then called a strategy meeting. "I remember it clearly," Jeff noted. "We held it at a hotel outside of Washington, DC, because we wanted to draw from nearby policy expertise."

By the meeting's end, the board had decided to focus on low-income housing. "What was interesting about housing was that there was a myriad of grassroots organizing efforts, but the end results didn't measure up," Jeff explained. "On a federal level, no major housing legislation for low-income people had been passed in a long time. We looked at health care, but decided there were already a lot of resources moving into that area. But we didn't see any funders supporting grantees in pulling together a national housing movement. So we decided that would be our political objective."

In 1988, the board hired Sue Chinn to run the foundation and implement the strategy, despite the fact that she had no foundation experience. "Our most important criterion was getting someone who knew how to organize communities," Jeff recalled. "We felt that if you took a good organizer, they'd organize. If they needed to organize in a local community, they'd do that. If it was the funding community, they'd figure out how to network out and build relationships there; that's what good organizers do. I remember when we interviewed Sue I was thinking, 'If we can find someone who can work by themselves, is motivated, can set up the office, knows all the players, and thinks strategically—those are the key skill sets.'"

As executive director, Sue began working on housing, but found that the foundation's grants were not creating significant results. "Sue went along with our decision for a while, but we slowly began to realize that our efforts to support a national housing movement were not coming together," Jeff recalled. "We were just too small—and the political climate wasn't right—to support grantees in building the constituency needed for comprehensive national housing policy changes."

"We faced the danger of getting too self-important and losing the bumper sticker statement. In a period in which lower-income constituencies were losing political power, a national housing agenda, which required such tremendous amounts of government money, was really hard to pursue. We worked on this objective for eight years and weren't seeing enough progress. We realized we needed to change course."

Identifying New Opportunities

In the mid-1990s, as Sue began to scan the landscape for new strategic opportunities, she sought possibilities that addressed a trend that disturbed her. "I saw the economic tide in the country lifting a lot of boats, but profits weren't trickling down to low-income folks," she explained.

At the same time, Sue was watching transformations occurring within the labor movement. A new focus among unions on "improving conditions for low-wage and immigrant workers allowed the interests of labor and philanthropy to converge," explained Janet Shenk, senior program officer at the Panta Rhea Foundation and formerly a special assistant to John Sweeney, former president of the AFL-CIO.

Sue Chinn had what she described as an "aha" moment at a meeting organized by Baltimoreans United in Leadership Development (BUILD), which was attended by the mayor of Baltimore. Listening to the speakers talk about what they called a living wage, Sue remembered thinking, "this was a concrete tool for dealing with the fact that low-income people just weren't making enough money."

BUILD had teamed up with the American Federation of State, County, and Municipal Employees (AFSCME) and, in 1994, won a living-wage ordinance in Baltimore, one of the first in the country.[4] The ordinance required Baltimore's city service contractors to pay their four thousand workers over 40 percent more than the minimum wage, which was $4.25 an hour at the time.[5] The increase would place those working a forty-hour workweek just above the poverty line.

Sue was excited not only by the concept but also by the partnerships that had formed to pass the ordinance. BUILD was a local affiliate of the Industrial Areas Foundation (IAF), a national membership organization of faith institutions, unions, schools, and community-based organizations.

THE BIRTH OF A SUCCESSFUL CAMPAIGN STRATEGY

BUILD developed the living-wage campaign concept through speaking with people who were using members' church-based feeding programs. "We found that people were using the feeding programs to supplement their low wages," explained Arnie Graf, member of the Industrial Areas Foundation executive team and former BUILD lead organizer.

> So we started doing research to find out how much taxpayer money was encouraging development projects that created these jobs, jobs where a person needed to use the church to supplement their income. Was this really what Baltimoreans thought we were voting for?

> We began to ask ourselves: Why is the minimum wage called a minimum wage? Shouldn't people who worked a forty-hour workweek be able to earn enough to support their family? Through house meetings and church meetings we came up with the idea of a "living wage" and that it should be pegged at a certain percentage above the poverty line.

To reduce opposition to the campaign, BUILD ultimately decided to target services that could not leave the city due to increased wages. "Municipal services weren't businesses that could pick up and go somewhere else," Arnie explained. "The garbage still needed to be collected. The school buses still needed to take people to school."

The fresh frame, combined with smart organizing strategies, proved a potent combination. "A living wage sounded so much stronger than minimum wage," Discount Foundation board member Margery Tabankin reflected. "It felt fair, moral. Who could argue that people working hard didn't deserve to be able to take care of their families' basic needs? This combined with a strong faith-labor-community alliance won that campaign."

When Sue Chinn came back to the Discount Foundation with her new insights, the board was excited. Jeff Zinsmeyer recalled, "This was when we began to see how lucky we had been in hiring a community organizer who was also a strategic thinker. She was able to spot opportunities that were emerging on the ground."

In the next two years, living-wage campaigns began to sprout across the country, spurred by labor, the IAF, ACORN, and others. By 1996, Santa Clara County (in California), Milwaukee, New York City, Portland, and Jersey City had also passed living-wage ordinances.[6] This growing momentum spurred a *New York Times* reporter to write a front-page article on the victories.[7] "When that article ran, next day we started getting calls from around the country from people wanting to know how we had done it," Arnie Graf, IAF executive team member and former BUILD lead organizer, recalled.

With these new developments, Sue felt increasingly optimistic about the opportunities the emerging living-wage movement presented. "I let the board know I wanted to explore living wages as a core strategy for the foundation, and asked them, 'Is this all right with you?' I told them I wanted to take a pass on a grant cycle so I could thoroughly investigate the issue. I thought it was important to take our time in making the transition."

With their approval, Sue slowed the foundation's grantmaking and dedicated her time to research. Among the questions she set out to answer were these:

How do you help grantees build sufficient power to change public policy in support of the working poor?

What stakeholders and allies could help expand the power base of the working poor?

Could living-wage campaigns help build a broader movement?

Could the Discount Foundation's annual payout of roughly a half-million dollars make a difference in increasing low-income wages? If so, what would the foundation's value-added benefit be?

Could the Discount Foundation funding help act as glue between stakeholders and allies of the working poor?

What other foundations were currently involved in efforts to increase low-income wages?

As she did her research, Sue also sought to educate the board by bringing in grassroots organizers, labor leaders, and a host of other individuals to their meetings.

"We took our time and tried to learn what others were doing in the field," Sue explained. She also used several creative tools to educate the board, including a mock docket showcasing the kinds of grantees the foundation might highlight as part of its strategy.

Through the meetings, the board and Sue came to a common vision of how to create change in the United States. "Our board was made up of community organizers," Sue explained. "They understood that to create significant change in our society, you needed to have power. And to have power, people needed to be organized." In their discussions, Sue and the board came to the conclusion that labor, community groups, and faith communities were building blocks for this power. Much of their strategy discussions centered on the importance of labor as one of the "three legs of this stool," Sue recalled.

"Looking at the history of this country, when the lower half has gotten redress, organized labor has usually been involved. There have been dozens of innovations—from the forty-hour workweek to social security—that we probably would not have if it weren't for organized labor," Jeff noted.

In an April 1997 strategy paper to the board, Sue wrote, "despite the best intentions of community groups, churches, and thoughtful academics, there is not enough power to deliver real change—on wages, decent jobs, or welfare—without the 16 million members and resources of the American labor movement."[8]

Although the Discount Foundation did not fund labor unions, John Pomeranz of the firm Harmon, Curran, Spielberg & Eisenberg and attorney for the Center for Community Change notes that mostly foundations can fund unions for their 501(c)(3)-permissible work if proper steps are taken to ensure that the funding meets legal requirements.[9] Foundations and other nonprofits should monitor policy changes, and consult with a knowledgeable lawyer to determine specific requirements for their institutions.

Consolidating Strategy

In 1997, the board announced its new direction. The living-wage campaigns formed the centerpiece of the foundation's strategy, in large part due to their ability to appeal to faith, labor, and community organizations. Another related program area was to protect workers' right to join a union. To support its efforts, the foundation would provide larger, often multiyear grants to fewer organizations.[10]

At the same time, the foundation began to phase out its housing grants. "We gave lots of advance notice," Sue explained. "I don't think anyone was caught off guard. The housing people weren't happy, of course. But people were seeing that the root of the problem was income inequality, particularly in a time of economic boom."

Interestingly, the reasons the foundation chose to highlight living wages stood in stark contrast to those that compelled it to support low-income housing in the late 1980s. It had chosen housing in large part because of what wasn't happening in the field: there was a lack of both funding and a national housing movement. In contrast, the foundation's interest in the living-wage campaigns stemmed from its excitement about what was happening on the ground—namely, successful faith, labor, and community alliances and campaigns.

By 1998, the Discount Foundation was funding promising grantees throughout the country. "We supported some real local initiatives, and also national organizations that had local presence," Margery Tabankin noted. Discount Foundation grantee American Institute for Social Justice (an affiliate of ACORN), for example, created the national Living Wage Resource Center to foster local efforts by providing groups with technical assistance and research support, and helping them build partnerships by sponsoring national conferences.

Further, with the understanding that opposition to living wages was often fueled by financial concerns, the foundation commissioned the Economic Policy Institute to write a report on the financial impact of Baltimore's living wage law. The study showed that the aggregate cost increase for twenty-six living-wage contracts was only 1.2 percent, or less than the rate of inflation, and that the higher wages actually benefited the city by creating a more reliable workforce.[11] Grantees in different areas of the country were then able to use the research results as talking points in their efforts.

Building Philanthropic Interest in Labor

The Discount Foundation also began to look for ways to leverage other foundation dollars. "Once we got involved, there were all kinds of things that began to move," Jeff Zinsmeyer remembered. "Almost immediately, the new focus allowed Sue to get out in front of the funding community."

Sue Chinn recalled, "I went to a funders' conference on jobs, and there was no discussion of unions. I thought 'Gee, this is an important sector. Funders should at least be aware of what they are doing.' This was another 'aha' moment for me," Sue explained, noting, "I realized I needed to help open relationships between funders and unions, given this big shift [to support low-income and immigrant workers] in the labor movement." Sue saw this as fundamental to supporting both living-wage campaigns and the larger Discount Foundation goal of building faith-labor-community partnerships.

To develop these new relationships, Sue began to seek allies from within the funding community. The Unitarian Universalist Veatch Program at Shelter Rock, the Needmor Fund, and other allies were already supporting similar work. Others, such as the Hyams Foundation and the Ms. Foundation for Women, were fairly new to the opportunities labor presented, but were excited by this funding strategy.[12]

By 1997, Sue, together with Henry Allen (who was with the Hyams Foundation at the time and later became the executive director of the Discount Foundation), decided to form a funder affinity group called the Working Group on Labor and Community, under the auspices of the Neighborhood Funders Group. "There was a great deal of excitement and sense that there were real opportunities on the ground," Henry noted. He explained that many members were inspired to join as a result of the growing success of the living-wage campaigns, which "provided concrete examples of the impact of these faith-labor-community partnerships."

Despite the excitement, the Working Group faced significant hurdles in strengthening foundation support for union-community-faith coalitions and workers' rights. "This work was daring and edgy," Henry underlined.

"Before Henry and Sue began the working group, it was virtually unheard of for a union leader to speak at a funder event," Janet Shenk (at the time, special assistant to John Sweeney, president of the AFL-CIO) recalled. Henry Allen continued,

> There were so many negative opinions and attitudes you needed to break through to help foundations understand the diversity within the union movement. We'd get people asking, "What do unions have to do with philanthropy? Isn't this just a special interest group?" Corporate foundations felt that unions went against their own interests. Many people thought organized labor was corrupt and self-serving. Most funders weren't aware that many unions shared their commitment to health care, housing, education, and a range of other critical issues related to social and economic justice. They also were unaware of the profound changes taking place within the union movement to face up to many of its shortcomings, particularly in terms of actively organizing low-wage workers, especially immigrants and other people of color.

Data from the Bureau of Labor Statistics showed that in 2007,[13]

- A worker who was a member of a union or was represented by a union earned about 13 percent more than a comparable worker who was not unionized.
- African Americans in unions earned roughly 17 percent more than those who were not unionized.
- Hispanics in unions earned roughly 34 percent more than those who were not unionized.

To bridge the divide, the Working Group on Labor and Community began to organize opportunities for funders, labor union members, and labor advocates to meet. "We organized many standing-room-only workshops at funder conferences," Henry said. "We had the most impact when we brought people from the field who could speak powerfully about organizing and building power to advance real social and economic justice for working people. We brought in dynamic union organizers, rank-and-file members, and elected local and national labor leaders, and sought opportunities to highlight the extraordinary collaboration between unions and community- and faith-based organizing groups."

"The stories of rank-and-file members were especially compelling," Janet Shenk remarked. "People found it hard to believe that being part of a union organizing drive meant risking your job, perhaps your ability to stay in the U.S. They were amazed that the legal penalties for violating our country's labor laws were so paltry. So we combined the testimonies of workers with presentations by academics and highly credible human rights organizations."

"When Human Rights Watch did a special report—'Unfair Advantage'—on the erosion of workers' freedom of association in the United States," Janet continued, "we brought in the authors to speak to foundation audiences. Slowly, people began to shift away from the 'unions are dinosaurs' analysis to genuine concern about the erosion of labor standards and fundamental rights. High-profile campaigns, such as [Service Employees International Union's] Justice for Janitors, also generated a lot of sympathy for these janitors and admiration for a union putting so many resources into organizing new sectors."

By 2001, the Working Group also had organized many funder site visits, often as an add-on to funder conferences. Funders visited New Orleans, Seattle, Los Angeles, Philadelphia, Tucson, Omaha, Las Vegas, and other cities to see unions, their community partners, and living-wage and other campaigns in action.

SITE VISIT ACTS AS A POWERFUL TOOL

Regina McGraw, executive director of the Wieboldt Foundation and member of the Working Group on Labor and

Community, recounts how a site visit awakened her interest in labor:

> The Working Group on Labor and Community was extremely important for me in learning how unions had changed since the sixties and seventies. I didn't grow up in a pro-union household. My father was an editor, and he edited a column for a guy named Victor Riesel, who wrote about corruption within the unions. Soon after, Victor was walking down a New York street when someone threw sulfuric acid in his face. He was permanently blinded. I grew up in a home where, when unions came up, my dad would say, "Look what happened to Victor."

> This was my only experience with unions until Henry [Allen] and Sue [Chinn] recruited me to join the Working Group. A seminal moment for me was the 2001 Las Vegas site visit [organized by both the Working Group on Labor and Community and Grantmakers Concerned with Immigrants and Refugees].

> Vegas really showed me what could happen in a community when jobs actually paid living wages. People had good housing and education. Who knew that "Sin City" was such a fountain of good practices?

> It all started when the cab picked me up from the airport. The driver's wife had a union job in the service industry. They'd bought a house, and they liked the school that their kid went to. They seemed to have a good quality of life.

> As part of the site visit, we went to a room attendants' training where HERE [Hotel Employees and Restaurant Employees] had created a training center replicating real hotel rooms and women were learning how to make beds and fluff the foofy towels, knowing that after this training they would get living-wage jobs. It was a friendly, professional atmosphere. We stayed at the Monte Carlo, and the manager gave us a tour of the hotel. She talked about how great HERE was for them. The hotel was able to get well-trained workers, and turnover was low because the people who applied knew what to expect and were ready to work.

> The site visit also showed me that Las Vegas didn't get there magically. It was a place where community groups, unions, and faith communities (particularly the African American ministerial community) had created pressure to make this happen.

> In no way did I come back to the Wieboldt Foundation from the site visit and say to the board of this roughly ninety-year-old foundation,

"Now we are going to fund labor-community partnerships." That would not have worked. The transition happened over time. But I started to look for more opportunities to fund these alliances after the site visit. Then about four years ago, a board member said in a presentation, "Our foundation has a special niche in labor-community partnerships." I thought that was really amusing because I thought I had snuck those grants in."

The Working Group provided an organizing platform for foundations interested in the living-wage campaigns. "We shared grant lists and our thinking about how to move forward together," Henry Allen said. Sandra Davis, formerly a member of the Working Group when she was with the Tides Foundation, added, "The Working Group members, particularly the Discount Foundation, were an inspiration. The Discount Foundation's Web site and list of grantees really opened things up for me."

The Working Group allowed each foundation to complement one another's work more easily. The Tides Foundation, for example, noticed that no foundation was comprehensively addressing communications strategies for the campaigns. "We realized the campaigns that were having the most trouble often had difficulty controlling the debate," Sandra recalled. "The strongest campaigns had communications plans and strong relationships with the media."

In response, the Tides Foundation funded a media consultancy group called the SPIN Project to create a media kit tailored to the topic of living wages. The Tides Foundation was then able to encourage other Working Group members to support complementary programs. Foundations began funding training, peer learning, and the SPIN Academy, a multiday media training for living-wage campaign advocates. "This was the kind of kit that would sit there unless we made it real for people," explained SPIN Project founder Robert Bray.

THE VEATCH PROGRAM SUPPORTS ANCHOR ORGANIZATIONS

The Unitarian Universalist Veatch Program at Shelter Rock, a congregation-based giving program, played a crucial role in supporting some of the organizational infrastructure important for the living-wage movement. "Our goal was to support [base-building] organizations that could help build social movements," Victor Quintana, Veatch program officer, explained. Funding, including general support grants, helped these groups organize and mobilize large numbers of people, who were then in place to catalyze action on many issues, including living wages.

The early and continued funding from the Veatch Program and several other key funders helped the Los Angeles Alliance for a New Economy (LAANE) build the membership that supported several wage-related victories. "The Veatch Program has been a consistent funder since our founding [in 1993] and has been crucial to our success," affirmed Madeline Janis, LAANE director.

In 2001, this membership base helped LAANE—together with Strategic Action for a Just Economy (SAJE) and other partners—successfully pressure real estate developers investing $1 billion in a downtown Los Angeles development to commit not only to living wages but also to affordable housing, local hiring, and green spaces.[14] The agreement, called a Community Benefits Agreement, was the first of its kind in the United States.[15]

The Veatch Program's funding also helped establish the SPIN Project, which developed media strategies for many living-wage campaigns. "Victor Quintana and [former Veatch Program executive director] Marjorie Fine understood that grantees needed resources to embed communications in every strategy—whether organizing, advocacy, litigation, or fundraising," SPIN founder Robert Bray noted. When community organizing, they needed messages that turned people out and groups that had the capacity to communicate those messages to targeted audiences. If it was policy, grantees needed messages that targeted policymakers. Yet most funders weren't supporting this. Victor and Margie recommended to their board that the Veatch Program fund the SPIN Project because they realized the field needed a vehicle to help make this happen."

As one of the largest funders of community organizing in the country, with a broad range of relationships in philanthropy and the organizing sector, Veatch was also a valuable asset to the Working Group on Labor and Community. Often cochairing the affinity group, "Veatch was able to publicize the labor-community strategy and elevate the visibility of grantees," former Veatch program officer Seth Borgos noted. "By making significant-sized grants, particularly to risky and innovative projects, we helped signal to the field that these were not marginal efforts."

Securing Big Wins

By 2006, roughly two-thirds of all states in the country had at least one living-wage ordinance. City, town, and county governments and other jurisdictions had passed 140 living-wage ordinances "tying wages and/or benefit requirements to government contract eligibility or financial assistance."[16]

These wins encouraged organizations to find strategies to raise statewide minimum-wage levels. For many, the "key was simply getting on the ballot," noted Brian Kettenring of the Southern Minimum Wage Organizing Project.[17]

Many of these campaigns, which were funded primarily by labor unions, successfully raised their state's minimum wages above the federal level. Whereas in 1997 only five states had taken such action, by 2007 that number had risen to thirty-one states and the District of Columbia.[18] These initiatives, in turn, helped light the fire for an increase in the federal minimum wage. In May 2007, President Bush signed the first increase in the minimum wage since 1997: from $5.15 to $7.25 by 2009.[19]

Reflecting on the bottom-up strategic progression of the campaigns, Garland Yates, a member of the Discount Foundation board, observed, "There had been a lot of unsuccessful attempts to raise the minimum wage nationally, but when it looked like the federal environment wasn't going anywhere, the local and then state initiatives began to emerge. As these succeeded, then those involved had an opportunity to push this back into the national arena."

The living-wage campaigns had repercussions far greater than the increases in wages themselves. The initiatives strengthened the position of low-income people within the country in other ways as well.

The campaigns catalyzed the forging of long-term faith, labor, and community partnerships that worked in support of low-income communities. "We now have low-income citizen organizations that have real seats at the table with some of these labor

unions," Margery Tabankin, board member of Discount Foundation, noted. "Once these groups had worked together on those
campaigns, they began to reach out to one another for other
initiatives as well."

Living-wage ballot initiatives strengthened the voices of the
working poor in other ways as well. The work helped force a
national dialogue on living wages and also had the unintended
side effect of increasing voter turnout in several states.

In addition, the Working Group on Labor and Community
helped a significant number of foundations feel more comfortable with labor. "The importance of unions is still not widely understood among foundations, but the understanding has certainly
increased," affirmed Madeline Janis of the Los Angeles Alliance
for a New Economy (LAANE). "The Working Group on Labor
and Community played an important role in creating that shift."

Madeline pointed to her own experience as evidence of changing attitudes. "[LAANE works] explicitly with unions, and we've
found it increasingly easy to raise money. Our budget has gone
from nothing to $3 million [since our founding in 1993]. When
speaking with funders, we used to have to say 'leadership development' instead of saying 'unions.' We used to say 'worker education'
and have since been able to say 'labor-community partnerships.'
We've felt a clear shift with even the big foundations now accepting
the fact that unions need to be part of alliances for change."

Discount Foundation board member Deepak Bhargava (also
executive director at CCC) noted that the Working Group's impact
has been important even for funders who have decided not to fund
faith-labor-community alliances. "Even if a foundation doesn't want
to fund these campaigns, they are now often aware that labor is an
important stakeholder in the same way churches, local communities, and others are, and need to be invited to the table."

In 2008, the Discount Foundation continued to build on
successes. "They have a grant with the American Rights at Work
Education Fund to educate the public and policymakers about the
urgent need for labor law reform," Janet Shenk said. "The grant
highlights the Discount Foundation's belief that labor shouldn't
be the only voice out there defending a fundamental right to freedom of association, and that growing the labor movement is one
important pillar of a social justice movement."

Conclusion

In a time of diminishing purchasing power of real wages, living- and minimum-wage initiatives have been among the most successful efforts for economic justice in the country. They have touched roughly two-thirds of the states in the United States and altered how people think about jobs and wages. "The work put the issue of how much jobs pay on the national agenda," Sue Chinn reflected.

Marjorie Fine, former executive director of the Veatch Program, added, "Most people believe that a person working forty hours a week should be able to meet their basic needs, and these campaigns help move the country a little closer toward making that a reality."

The Discount Foundation, a tiny institution with one staff person and just over half a million dollars in annual grantmaking, became a national leader within this movement. By rallying the foundation community, Discount played a strategic role in catalyzing resources in support of the campaigns of diverse constituencies concerned about living wages. "This was particularly important in states like Ohio and Nevada, so the work wasn't only a union effort," Henry Allen noted. "Without broad support from faith groups, small businesses, and community organizations, the work would have been written off as a special interest."

Through a yearlong strategic planning process, the Discount Foundation developed a theory of change that identified faith, labor, and community partnerships as key to building power for the working poor. With this understanding, the Discount Foundation positioned itself as a key leader within the foundation community and catalyzed new funding opportunities for these coalitions.

"Even more than providing funding, the Discount Foundation provided an institutional platform from which to lift up organizations that do model work," Deepak Bhargava stated. "The foundation created a cohort of funders all interested in labor-community partnerships. Sue [Chinn] and others took on an organizing role from the perch of the Discount Foundation to help empower poor communities."

Over time, the Discount Foundation matured into a powerful agent of change within the foundation community and beyond. Through leveraging its resources, the foundation has played a role in helping millions earn a living wage in the United States and contributed to building the power of the working poor.

Lessons Learned

The Discount Foundation and its partners learned how to leverage limited resources to help grantees secure significant successes in support of the working poor. Here are a few insights into how they helped support one of the most successful economic justice campaigns of the decade:

- Focus, focus, focus, and leverage all your resources (staff, reputation, grantmaking, money, and so on).
- Identify sectors with the power and motivation to push successfully for changes sought, and find ways to build alliances between these sectors.
- Define a theory of change (for example, alliances between labor, community, and faith groups are critical to building enough power to secure an agenda for the working poor) and then find entry points for achieving that change (for example, living-wage campaigns).
- Choose a programmatic focus based on real successes occurring on the ground rather than one based on an *absence* of activity or results; this approach enables you to build on the energy that others have already generated.
- Build commitment among other funders by giving them actual contact with exciting grantees—through workshops and site visits—and creating an affinity group that builds and channels funder interest.

Supporting Citizen Action and Litigation for Education Reform

The Case of the Schott Foundation

Concerned that funding direct school services, such as tutoring
and counseling, for public school students was not fully leveraging
their money in support of low-income communities, the Leeds and
Jobin-Leeds families created what is now called the Caroline
and Sigmund Schott Fund—and later supported the emergence
of the Schott Foundation for Public Education—to reach a much
greater number of children. Supporting a three-pronged strategy—
citizen action, litigation, and advocacy—led to historic increases in
education funding in New York.

As immigrants fleeing the Holocaust in 1939, Lilo and Gerry
Leeds understood the importance of a good education. "We
didn't come with much money," Lilo recounted. "But we did come
with an education." By the 1980s, that access to education had
helped make them multimillionaires as CMP Media Inc.—the
company they founded in 1971—grew at an average rate of almost
20 percent per year in sales. In 1991, Lilo and Gerry, together
with their son and daughter-in-law Greg and Maria Jobin-Leeds,

used the money they'd made to launch the Caroline and Sigmund Schott Fund so that low-income and largely African American and Latino families could access a quality education and that same opportunity.[1]

From the outset, there was little question that the foundation would support an education agenda. "Education was an easy point of focus for the family," recounted Cassie Schwerner, current vice president of programs for the Schott Foundation for Public Education, a related public charity founded in 1999. "Lilo and Gerry passed on their belief in the power of education to their children. Greg was a high school teacher. Maria is also an educator. Education is a strong Jewish value."

The family's belief in including those who have been excluded from society came from their early life experiences. "I was born in Nazi Germany," Lilo explained. " 'No Jews allowed.' Then I moved to France: 'Down with the Germans!' Then I moved here, and the drinking fountains said 'No coloreds'! We support diversity."

Greg also learned early on to value inclusion. "My sister signed up for Little League. She went to the first day wearing my baseball cap," he recounted. "We immediately got a telegram saying 'Sorry. There's been a mistake. Girls can't play.' So my mother took them to court. They won the court case. My sister was [one of] the first girls to play in the Little League in New York State. She not only played, she was the first in the family to play on the All-Star Team—in a family where she was the only girl! This was a lesson for me that excellence was a consequence of inclusiveness."

The Caroline and Sigmund Schott Fund (then called the Caroline and Sigmund Schott Foundation), and later the Schott Foundation for Public Education, both named after Lilo's parents, became vehicles to express these deep-seated beliefs.

Caroline and Sigmund Schott Fund Snapshot

Type: Private foundation
Year launched: 1991
Foundation assets (2007): $58 million

Geographic focus: New York, Massachusetts, and national
Primary funding area: Public education
Location: Cambridge, Massachusetts, with an office in New York City

Note: Snapshot information for each chapter varies depending on data available. Dates refer to either the calendar year or the end of the fiscal cycle. For snapshot sources, refer to the Notes section at the end of the book.[2]

Schott Foundation for Public Education Snapshot

Type: Public charity
Year founded: 1999
Grant range (2007): $1,000–$200,000
Total grants awarded (2007): $1.6 million
Geographic focus: New York, Massachusetts, and national
Primary funding area: Public education
Staff size in 2007: Eight
Location: Cambridge, Massachusetts, with an office in New York City

Note: Snapshot Information for each chapter varies depending on data available. Dates refer to either the calendar year or the end of the fiscal cycle. For snapshot sources, refer to the Notes section at the end of the book.[3]

Moving Beyond Service Delivery

The four founders of the Caroline and Sigmund Schott Fund, which has its headquarters in Massachusetts, developed their strategic direction during a moment that has become part of the family lore. "In 1991, they took a walk on the beach and outlined where their dreams would take them," Cassie Schwerner recounted. "They wanted fully funded schools in low-income districts with large concentrations of people of color; universal high-quality child-care pre-kindergarten programs; and fair educational opportunities for girls."

Yet how could they reach the millions of children in the United States that needed support? "Not even Bill Gates had enough money to support the kind of funding this would need," Lilo commented.

"No matter how much money our family poured in, we knew it just wouldn't be enough. We needed to leverage our money, or we wouldn't reach the numbers of people we wanted to reach," Greg affirmed.

The question was a particularly important one, given that the year before their walk on the beach, Gerry and Lilo, with support from Greg, had founded the Institute for Student Achievement (ISA). This organization provided a full package of in-school services, including tutoring and counseling, to targeted public school students who were performing in the bottom 25 percent of the population. Despite the program's success, the family was also aware of its limitations. "This was a school-by-school direct service strategy," Cassie explained. "The family recognized that [the ISA] by itself wasn't a systemic solution. For every kid who was going through the program, there were thousands of kids that weren't."

"We were helping maybe a thousand kids. It wasn't enough. The only way to reach that many kids was through the government," Lilo recalled thinking at the time.

GREG QUESTIONS HOW THE U.S. GOVERNMENT IS USING TAX DOLLARS

Greg learned the importance of government funding for education during his years training teachers in Boston in the late 1980s, during a time of government funding cuts for education. "I was training adult literacy teachers at Roxbury Community College. Huge numbers of adult literacy students were on waiting lists, and the state couldn't afford to give them the education they needed to succeed. I had trained great teachers, but the adult literacy

(Continued)

programs had no money to pay them. At the same time, I was watching the United States use our military dollars to fund a ridiculous war in Nicaragua. And that's when I began to really question how our government was allocating our nation's resources. I realized that no matter how good a job I did training teachers, policymakers were making bigger decisions impacting who received a quality education."

Although the family wanted to enhance education throughout the United States, to achieve this goal they decided to focus first on the educational systems in Massachusetts and New York, their states of residence. "If they were successful in Massachusetts and New York, these states could be models that would influence other states and ultimately national education policy," Cassie explained. It also made sense to focus on the state level because "most, if not all, states have constitutions that guarantee a right to education. The U.S. Constitution doesn't. In 1973, the *San Antonio School District v. Rodriguez* case sought to challenge the notion of fiscal inequity in public education. It made it to the Supreme Court but ultimately didn't prevail, on the grounds that the U.S. Constitution didn't provide for education. So lawyers fighting equity lawsuits then had to turn their focus to the states—where they were having some success."

Identifying Promising Grantees

After a year of researching strategies for New York, Greg met Michael Rebell, a lawyer for the Campaign for Fiscal Equity (CFE), which had filed an education lawsuit against the state of New York in 1993. Michael recalled, "I got a call from out of the blue [from Greg]. After I had spoken for a while, Greg said, 'Wow! It sounds like you are doing really important work. Would more money help your effort?'"

Explaining his enthusiasm, Greg commented, "Michael was very convincing. I had read CFE strategy papers—they seemed clear and thoughtful, and Michael had a track record." However, before deciding to move forward with the grant, Greg did further research. "I called Norm Fruchter, who was at the time with the Aaron Diamond Foundation and had helped me make the initial connection to Michael and also the New York Community Trust. Both were already funding the initiative."

"We gave out six checks of roughly $50,000 each that year," Greg recounted. "CFE was one. I was very nervous about letting the money go. These were our first grants of that size."

Of this initial group of grantees, ultimately the foundation decided to continue funding only CFE. "From business investments, I learned to be able to feel comfortable with failure and to fail fast," Greg explained. "If the investment looked like it wasn't going to pay off for a strategy, we needed to let it go, even if it was good work, . . . and move on."

CAMPAIGN FOR FISCAL EQUITY: FINDING A JUDICIAL STRATEGY WITH LEGS

Michael Rebell and Robert Jackson, founders for the Campaign for Fiscal Equity (CFE), met through their involvement with a community school board in upper Manhattan. Michael explained,

> I was the school board's lawyer, and Robert was chairman of the school board. It was the late 1980s, and education budgets were getting slashed. Bob came into my office and said, "It's cutting us to the bone. You've got to do something." But I told him, "Sorry, someone beat you to it. Long Island already went to the courts to fight for more education funding to poor districts, and they lost. The highest court in the state said it wasn't a constitutional issue. We can't go back with the same case so soon. We'll get fined for bringing forward a frivolous case.

> But Bob wouldn't take no for an answer. So I began looking into it. If we could find an argument different from the one Long Island used, then we could file without being fined. I found that the Long Island case had used an equity argument, which says that the Constitution has been violated when one area in a state got more state funding than another. But I learned Kentucky and Montana had come up with a new argument based on adequacy, which argued simply that every child had the right to an adequate education. I went back to Bob and said, "I've got an argument that at least won't get us fined as a frivolous case."

(Continued)

To provide follow-up, the two cofounded CFE in 1993, and that same year filed a suit against New York claiming that children in New York City were not receiving the adequate education that was their constitutional right.

Coupling Court and Advocacy Strategies

During discussions with the Caroline and Sigmund Schott Fund, CFE began to question whether litigation alone would ensure all New York City's children an adequate education. "You just had to look over at our neighboring state, New Jersey," Greg noted. "Concerned citizens sued the state and won all their court cases, but the governor and legislature refused to act."

"I'd been involved in education legal cases and was concerned about how you would often get huge legal breakthroughs and attorneys celebrating, but if you came back in ten years and asked what difference it made in the kids' lives, more often than not the answer was negative," Michael elaborated.

"People were asking, 'What else would have to happen to change the lives of poor kids across New York?'" Cassie added.

Through focus groups, CFE concluded that it needed to supplement the court strategy with a legislative one. Only the legislature could deliver funding to comply with a positive court ruling. And to win in the legislature, "grantees realized they needed to develop a campaign to increase public will across the state while the case was working its way through the courts," Cassie explained. "If this was considered a New York City issue alone, it was never going anywhere in the legislature because of historic tensions between upstate and downstate New York. Upstate New York and their representatives often felt they were neglected and that New York City had too much power."

Winning in the Courts

As CFE was shaping the new elements of its strategy, an intermediate appeals court held that the case should be dismissed without even going to trial, Cassie recalled. The court cited the Long Island ruling as cause.

When Michael appealed the case with the state's highest court, he had his own theory as to the biggest obstacle to a positive ruling. "I believed the New York courts didn't want to get involved in a mess like New Jersey. The New Jersey legislature and the state courts had had a real confrontation over an education case. At one point the New Jersey courts had to threaten the legislature that they would close down all the schools if they didn't comply [with their ruling]." Michael decided to address this possible concern. "I know our sister state has had some trouble," he told the court. "But we've researched a dozen other cases across the country. What we've found is that cases that are not accompanied by a public engagement campaign to bring along the public have implementation problems. But cases that are coupled with efforts to educate and involve the public in a solution have much greater success. If you bring this case to trial, we will organize such a campaign."

Michael explained what he felt happened next. "Suddenly I saw them all taking notes. They were looking directly at me for the first time, and their body language relaxed. Six months later [in 1995], we got a decision of 6-1 in our favor. This was unbelievable!"

However, although the courts had accepted the case, the actual trial would not begin for over three years.

Opening New Opportunities with a Public Charity

As the case was working its way through the courts, the Caroline and Sigmund Schott Fund was undergoing a planning process to establish itself as a more robust and strategic foundation. The staff and board realized that a considerable portion of foundation money was going toward its New York strategy, so they decided to expand beyond their Massachusetts headquarters and open an office in New York City in 1998. "The foundation wanted to stay attuned to what was happening on the ground," Cassie Schwerner noted. They felt that the office would foster closer relationships between the foundation and its grantees, and keep the staff abreast of the political climate in the state.

In addition, in 1999 a new public charity was created.[4] The public charity, which is currently known as the Schott Foundation for Public Education and is the better known of the two foundations, receives annual grants from a variety of sources, including the private foundation.

The creation of the public charity opened several opportunities. First, the Schott Foundation for Public Education included participation by a much broader swath of people than the private foundation, which had been family controlled. In addition, the public charity could earmark funds for lobbying, something that several organizations funded by the private foundation had requested. (See Appendix A for definitions of *public charity* and *private foundation*.)

The move to create a public charity was unusual. Cassie noted, "The family had to be willing to lose some control of the grantmaking decisions, and bring a majority of nonfamily members onto the board."

LEADERSHIP CHALLENGES WITHIN THE PUBLIC CHARITY

The Schott Foundation for Public Education board and staff worked to build diverse leadership. "We were trying to put power in the hands of marginalized communities through our grantmaking, but hadn't been walking our talk. The first three hires to the private foundation had been Jews from New York and New Jersey," Greg—who was then president of the Schott Foundation for Public Education board—explained. "It was time to go into the less comfortable zone and expand beyond our Rolodex."

As part of a multipronged strategy to include people of color and immigrants, in 1999 the Schott Foundation for Public Education partnered with the Tides Foundation and brought Idelisse Malave, Tides executive director, on to their board. In 2001, the public charity hired Dr. Rosa Smith—an African American who had been a high school principal and superintendent in two U.S. districts—as its president. Speaking of her new job, Rosa reflected,

> It was a struggle—a good struggle. Forming a public charity was a transition. The private foundation had been totally family run, so the change was both hard and also understandable. The biggest

challenge was around diversity of opinion. One of the things I did was to hire a consultant to come in and observe a board meeting and then give us feedback. She came to a meeting and told us exactly what she saw: "Greg did this, and everyone else allowed him to do it. There was a staff member nearly in tears, and you all ignored it." She worked closely with Greg and me. He was a better board chair as a result, and I was a better president. I had to work in a place where I didn't have the kind of autonomy I had before. . . . I started meeting with every board member, and then Greg and I would meet with every board member again before the meetings.

Of the process, she noted that it was worthwhile but "very time consuming." Reflecting on his own role in the new public charity, Greg said, "It was important to more and more diversify decision making."

Creating an Evaluation Model

As part of a larger transition, the Schott Foundation for Public Education staff and trustees began to question whether the foundation was in fact achieving its programmatic goals in New York. "My father asked me, 'Where do you want to be in five years?'" Greg recalled. "I told him we wanted more dollars for schools. Later he asked the same question, and I said the same thing. He said, 'How come you always say the same thing? How do you know you are getting there?' It made me realize that we were unaccountable. As long as our financial investments were doing well, we'd stay in business no matter how ineffective a donor we were."

The interaction led Greg and others at the foundation to find ways to measure the foundation's impact. "With our company we measured sales," Greg noted. "We were growing at a rate of about 20 percent annually. With individual school programs, we measured student improvement and dropout rates. But how could we measure social justice? How could we measure progress on an outcome that might be a decade away? I felt we had to figure this out."

The Schott Foundation for Public Education, with support from partners and a consultant, developed a logic model to help measure impact in New York (see the definition of *logic model* on the next page). This strategic planning tool outlined a strategy with four pillars for helping grantees secure wins in both the courts and the legislature and build a constituency to support education reform over the long term. These pillars were

1. *Shape the media message and strengthen public awareness.* Using the media was a key strategy for increasing public awareness because "there were only so many people we could speak to directly," Michael Rebell (CFE) explained. The campaign "needed the media in order to get that statewide reach."
2. *Mobilize a statewide campaign.* "Schott wanted to help grantees not only to build awareness but also to mobilize parents to action and spark a social movement that would force the legislature to respond," Cassie reflected. Michael noted of grantees' thinking, "We wanted to change a significant institution, so we needed to engage the people involved in that system, or the solution would be limited."
3. *Provide technical assistance and other support for a statewide campaign.* The media and grassroots organizers needed "access to data and technical assistance, so we funded think tanks and organizations that provided training to grantees," Cassie explained.
4. *Organize additional funds for the campaign.* Finally, the foundation realized that funder collaboration was critical. "We knew that the existing money supporting the effort—both from the Schott Foundation as well as others—was not going to adequately fund a statewide movement," Cassie noted.

As part of the logic model, the Schott Foundation for Public Education then outlined activities for implementing these strategies, as well as benchmarks to measure its progress. "If we funded grassroots organizing, then we'd note on the logic model that we should see this many leaders developing," Greg explained. "We learned to measure things like the number of legislators who supported our grantees' work and the number and diversity of people our grantees trained."

WHAT IS A LOGIC MODEL?

The program logic model is a picture [or visual image] of how your organization does its work—the theory and assumptions underlying the program. A program logic model links outcomes (both short- and long-term) with program activities/processes and the theoretical assumptions/principles of the program.[5]

Note: From Annie Casey and W. K. Kellogg foundations (see footnote for full reference).

The Schott Foundation for Public Education and its partners looked toward the media for several benchmarks of grantee effectiveness. "We got very focused on the press, and not just counting any articles as a positive," Greg explained. "An article could be favorable, but if it didn't reflect [grantees' messaging], then we didn't count it as a success. For instance, we wouldn't count an article that stated people should support the campaign because people in the suburbs were receiving too much money, and this money should be given to inner-city schools. We wouldn't count that as a positive because that would create an oppositional force."

"After we created the logic model, I put it on my desk," Greg continued. "Whenever I met with anyone, these outcomes were right there. If someone wanted to launch a new initiative, I pointed to the logic model and said, 'How will this further outcomes?' If it didn't fit into the logic model, then it didn't get money."

Leveraging the Media

Although communications was a key articulated strategy, the Schott Foundation only invested heavily in the media just before the case was to go to trial in 1999. Cassie recounted, "Probably three months before the trial, Lilo looked at Greg and me and said, 'We said we wanted to help grantees change the mind of the public and create a movement, so what is CFE doing with media to raise awareness?' Greg and I looked at each other and said, 'Oh wow! She's right. We need to put our money where our mouth is.'"

Noting Cassie's vital role, Greg added, "Cassie recognized this as a significant opportunity because of her expertise in media and movement building."

Greg and Cassie met with CFE, and shortly thereafter the Schott Foundation wrote CFE a check for $270,000.[6] CFE used the money to hire a prestigious public relations firm and an in-house communications strategist. Both played a critical role in developing the campaign's message, feeding stories to the press and cultivating media contacts before and during the seven-month trial.

With these new communications resources in place, the campaign needed a newsworthy action to attract the press. "Before the trial, I said to Michael, 'You need to put some flavor and color into the story,'" recalled Robert Jackson, CFE cofounder and New York City council member. "So I decided to walk the twelve miles from my house to the courthouse on the day of the trial." Reminiscent of the civil rights movement, the walk quickly became a hundred-person march led by Jackson and his young daughter.

The media groundwork and subsequent action sparked a wave of positive coverage of the campaign. "The next day it was on every paper in the metropolitan area. Russian, Greek, Spanish, English—any newspaper you read in the city had a story on CFE," Robert Jackson recounted.

In addition, most of the 269 stories that ran on the case during the seven-month trial captured CFE's message.[7] "Most of the press prior to the trial had only a word or two about CFE, and then would move immediately to how the case would lead to increased taxes," Cassie noted. Most subsequent articles, in contrast, focused on issues of civil rights and fairness.[8] "What happened was a text-book case of why litigation provides an opportunity to raise public awareness. Each step of the way, there were major decisions that were huge media moments. Eventually the whole state was talking about this," Cassie continued.

In January 2001, the hard work of grantees and others bore fruit. The presiding judge—Justice Leland DeGrasse—ruled in favor of the plaintiffs, stating that "New York State has over the course of many years consistently violated the state constitution by failing to provide the opportunity for a sound basic education to New York City public school students."[9]

WHO ELSE HAS SUPPORTED THE INITIATIVE?

Although the Schott Foundation for Public Education and many other funders provided millions of dollars, the organization that ultimately provided the largest financial and in-kind support was Simpson, Thacher and Bartlett, the leading New York law firm that brought the case to trial. "They gave the equivalent of at least $20 million [in pro bono support]," Michael noted. "Whatever we needed, they gave us. At the height of the trial, we had a total of ten lawyers and four paralegals on the case."

The Donors' Education Collaborative (housed at the New York Community Trust) also played an important role, Cassie noted. This donor collaborative consisting of local, national, and corporate funders became an important source of funding and strategic support for the Campaign for Fiscal Equity and other organizations working on the initiative.[10]

Building Support for Education Throughout the State

As the seven-month trial was unfolding, Cassie and Greg were in dialogue with leaders from across the state discussing ways to help parents accelerate the movement. Simultaneously, other actors were also taking initiative. Most important, several grassroots and policy organizations formed a coalition called the Alliance for Quality Education (AQE) to build capacity for a legislative battle following the court ruling. Founded in 2000, the coalition included the Association of Community Organizations for Reform Now (ACORN) and Citizen Action of New York—a coalition of city and state education advocacy and community-based groups and several unions, including the United Federation of Teachers.[11]

Some within the Schott Foundation viewed the unfolding initiative as a mixed blessing. On the one hand, they had been looking for a coalition with the kind of statewide reach and parent and teacher representation that AQE had. On the other hand, they were concerned that the emerging coalition did not have enough representation from unlikely actors, such as business leaders, the clergy, and pediatricians. "We had wanted to follow both a grassroots and a grasstops model. People within the foundation were worried," Cassie explained.

Eventually, both staff and board members became strong advocates for AQE. They saw the organization as critical to the field, and well positioned to build leadership among people of color. "They have built a tremendous leadership development pipeline," Greg explained.

Funding AQE proved to be a strategic choice. By the early 2000s the coalition, supported by the Schott Foundation for Public Education, New York Community Trust, and others, had opened six offices throughout the state. Critical funding for coalition member Public Policy and Education Fund of New York was provided by the Donors' Education Collaborative (DEC), the Hazen Foundation, the New York Foundation, the Rauch Foundation, and others. "We were organizing parents and other interested parties particularly outside of New York City," Regina Eaton, AQE's first executive director, explained.

The coalition's hardest job involved organizing outside New York City. "We needed to make sure people outside of New York didn't feel threatened," Regina noted. "Our work was to get people thinking that every school in need would get funds, not just those in New York City."

"Our strategy was to build the political pressure throughout New York to have education across the state be taken care of all at once," added Karen Scharff, Citizen Action's executive director.

Supporting Grassroots Organizing

"The Schott Foundation for Public Education was an unusual grantmaker in that they funded lobbying. This was a small but essential part of our work, which most grantmakers were unable or unwilling to fund," Karen Scharff reflected of the public charity's role.

"Schott was also the first funder to support the grassroots organizing upstate," Karen continued. "They led the way in getting other funders to feel comfortable funding organizing. Foundation legal departments often have wanted to err on the side of caution, worrying that organizing and lobbying have been too closely linked. Yet without grassroots organizing, change will not happen."

Cassie Schwerner also noted that the work benefited from a changing philanthropic landscape. "The field of philanthropy was beginning to shift, and more colleagues were willing to talk about advocacy and organizing," she explained.

Keeping Public Attention on Education

With all the major players now in place, appeals, counterappeals, and continual change in the political landscape ensued, turning the campaign into a roller-coaster ride for those involved. "Weathering September 11 was really difficult," Greg recalled. "Just before September 11, CFE had been one of the biggest stories. Then the World Trade Center towers fell, and the conversation changed from rebuilding the schools to rebuilding downtown Manhattan. All the public support shifted. Then there was the stock market correction, and we lost money. Some people would say, 'You've spent millions of dollars and have nothing to show for it. What are you guys doing?'" In 2002, the Appellate Division of the State Supreme Court overturned the original ruling (which had stated that New York City had violated the state constitution by not providing children a sound education) with a statement that students were only entitled to an eighth-grade education.[12] Its argument was that children only needed to be prepared for low-level service jobs. Cassie recounted, "I heard the news as I was going to Spain. I remember sitting at the airport and looking at the TV monitors with my mouth dropped open. I was aghast."

As it turned out, however, the ruling was an unexpected boon for the campaign, bringing the public's attention back to education. "The public thought this was outrageous," Regina Eaton (AQE's first executive director) noted.

"The editorials were so on point," Cassie added. Even Governor Pataki, who had been one of the campaign's primary opponents, distanced himself from the decision, stating, "Anyone who thinks an eighth grade education is adequate is 100 percent wrong."[13]

The campaign players also found other ways to bring education back into the limelight. By a turn of luck, Cynthia Nixon, star of HBO's *Sex and the City*, stumbled across an AQE rally as she was dropping off her child at a public kindergarten, and quickly committed herself to the cause, even engaging in an act of civil disobedience that got her arrested. Moved by her commitment, other celebrities soon joined, including renowned rap mogul Russell Simmons, who then went on to recruit Bruce Willis, Alicia Keys, LL Cool J, and P. Diddy.[14] In 2002, many of these stars staged a massive rally attended by tens of thousands of people.

Robert Jackson, who was elected to New York's city council in 2001, also continued to add zest to the story. "When I heard the ruling that the state was only obligated to give an eighth-grade education, I said to Michael, 'I am going to walk from New York City to Albany,'" Robert recounted. "And that's what I did." For a 2003 appeal of the eighth-grade education ruling, Robert walked the 150 miles to the Albany courthouse where the hearing would take place.[15] Hundreds of others either joined for segments of the walk or greeted the walkers when they arrived at their destination. Outside the courthouse, where Michael Rebell was waiting to present the case, Cassie recalled, "Jackson was introduced to the crowd still in his sweatpants and T-shirt. He got up there and said, 'Michael, we just walked the walk, now you go in there and talk the talk.' It was an incredible moment. There wasn't a dry eye in the crowd."

Again the campaign organizers' stamina and perseverance bore fruit. In June 2003, the Court of Appeals reversed the earlier ruling that an eighth-grade education met the states' obligation to its citizens, and defined a sound basic education to include "a meaningful high school education."[16]

Securing Increased Funding

The next struggle was to ensure that the ruling was backed by adequate funding. Although the courts needed to state how much money would be necessary to provide an adequate education, this fight would eventually be won in the political arena.

To build a case, in March 2004 the American Institutes for Research together with Management Analysis and Planning, Inc., released a study funded by the Atlantic Philanthropies, the Bill and Melinda Gates Foundation, and the Ford Foundation quantifying how much was needed to comply with the court ruling. The report stated that in 2001–2002, New York State had spent $31.71 billion on public schools (excluding transportation and debt service), and that an additional $6.2 to $8.4 billion would have been needed to ensure a full opportunity to meet the regents' learning standards for all students.[17] These findings were widely publicized. "When the *New York Times* asked [New York gubernatorial] candidate Eliot Spitzer how much additional money schools needed, he used the number released by the report and said $8.5 billion.[18] By the time he moved from candidate to governor, his position on school funding was firmly locked in place," Cassie recounted.

However, a ruling by the Court of Appeals on November 20, 2006, fell far short of the targeted amount. The new ruling stated that $1.93 billion would ensure that the state met its constitutional requirement.[19]

Ultimately, funding was secured in the political arena, not in the courts. Weeks before the November ruling, Eliot Spitzer had been elected governor and quickly committed to a historic increase in state education funding. Karen Scharff of Citizen Action noted, "Under his proposal, districts across the state would get a funding increase. We could now show that this would truly help districts across the state, not just New York City."

Soon after, the legislature approved a bill calling for an increase in education spending, which promised to bring $7 billion annually in additional funding by 2010.[20] Governor Spitzer called the increase the "largest infusion of [education] resources in our state's history."

The new legislation secured another key campaign goal by simplifying the state funding formula that determined each school's state funding. "The old formula was so complicated that even New York's education commissioner admitted in court he didn't understand it. It wasn't based on need but on political deal making," Cassie explained.

OTHER ROADS IN SUPPORT OF EDUCATION

In 2006, Greg's brother Dan Leeds created a family of organizations—a public charity, a social welfare lobbying organization, a 527, and a New York State PAC—to build a citizens' movement to hold politicians accountable to an education agenda, as well as to help elect pro-education candidates. The organizations, which

(Continued)

use some form of the key words "education voters" in their names, initially focused on New York State but now operate in five states.

Because many of these organizations were financed with individual donations from family members, they were able to be more politically active than organizations funded solely with foundation funds. "In 2006, Ed Voters 527 ran issue ads in contested districts which alerted people to the funding issue and motivated people to call their state senators to let them know they wanted to see more money for education," Greg explained.

In addition, the Leeds and Jobin-Leeds families began to coordinate their personal political contributions in New York State. "We were each giving small amounts of money to the same candidates. A political consultant told us that we needed to combine these, so instead of each giving our own donation, as a family we started giving a larger amount to the Education Voters New York PAC, which ran two independent expenditure campaigns," Greg elaborated. "It was fascinating. With small amounts of money relative to our philanthropic giving, we were having significant impact and were suddenly major players."

Although the funding increase represented an overwhelming victory, the fifteen-year fight has not yet ended. Grantees and their partners have "leveraged systemic change on a financial basis," Greg affirmed. "But the kids are still no better off."

Added Rosa Smith, who stepped down as president of the Schott Foundation for Public Education in 2007, "Money is important but not enough. There are all kinds of systemic problems that hurt low-income kids. For example, when a child moves, they're not allowed to stay in the same school. Poor people move more often. So New York needs a policy that allows kids to stay in the same school and helps them get to that school. Otherwise you have a system designed to fail low-income kids." In addition, she noted that without policy changes, "the poor kids and kids of color will still get the teachers that no one else wants. They'll get the rotten principals. Black boys will still get sent to the special education system. They are subject to stereotypes more than any other group of children; teachers look at them and say, 'I already know this kid is going to prison.'"

In 2007, there were many competing proposals regarding how to spend the additional funds. For the Schott Foundation and its partners, the key has been to ensure that the money actually improves schooling for low-income and minority children. In addition to supporting policy changes that deal with issues of structural racism, grantees are working to ensure that the money goes to "programs that teachers, parents, and community members have identified as priorities—smaller classes, improving teacher quality, after-school programs, things like that," Regina Eaton underlined.

"If it's spent on charter schools, it won't change the dropout rate for the vast majority of black and Latino kids," Cassie Schwerner of the Schott Foundation noted. "The grantees are all working to make sure that every penny of that $7 billion is well spent."

Conclusion

In 1991, while walking on a beach, four members of the Leeds and Jobin-Leeds families spoke of a dream, and by 2007, important elements of that dream had been realized. New York had become a beacon in the national movement for education reform, affirming the right of every child—rich and poor alike—to have an adequate education. That same year, the Council on Foundations awarded the Schott Foundation the prestigious Critical Impact Award for its work in education.

In reflecting on the campaign's key outcomes, Billy Easton, executive director for AQE, stated, "This was a prolonged battle that played out in almost every arena—from the courts to the schools to the streets to the statehouse—and was ultimately delivered by persistent and prolonged grassroots pressure. While the funding increases were historic, even more important was the fact that there was now an organized parent and community voice across the state that was a power to be reckoned with."

"Some parents send their kids to failing schools because they don't know there is something better out there," reflected Zakiyah Ansari, an education activist and mother of eight. "I don't really know politics at all, but once I realized it played such a crucial role in education, I decided I wanted to learn a little bit more. I learned

I didn't have to settle. We could go to Albany. They're not used to seeing parents up there, particularly parents of color."

"I don't think any of us thought it would take fifteen years," Greg Jobin-Leeds recounted. Yet CFE, AQE, and many partners—persisted through both victories and bitter losses. Even after the fall of the World Trade Center towers, when the state's attention became focused on security issues, campaign advocates persevered, finding a way to bring the political spotlight back to an education agenda. Their dedication resulted in historic wins that have reverberated throughout the country.

Lessons Learned

The Schott Foundation for Public Education and other critical funding partners, such as the Donors Education Collaborative (a fourteen-year-old collaborative of numerous funders focused on education within the state, and housed at the New York Community Trust), supported grantees in helping secure historic increases in education funding in the State of New York. Here are strategies they used that you might consider when funding a campaign:

- When working with limited resources, have a laserlike focus in realizing your grantmaking mission, and build momentum by focusing at the state level, before considering funding grantees engaged in federal campaigns.
- To ensure that a court win translates into actual results, consider supporting not only grantees working on judicial strategies but also those engaged in advocacy.
- Build public support for an issue through funding grantees engaged in grassroots organizing and media campaigns.

Influencing Market Forces in Support of People and the Planet

Recognizing the important role business plays in societies, some foundations are seeking ways to ensure that market forces remain accountable not only to a bottom line but also to communities and the environment. For foundations interested in how to harness the power of business in achieving their mission, the stories of the Needmor Fund and the Jacobs Family Foundation are particularly instructive.

In the chapter on the Needmor Fund, you will learn how the Needmor family came to believe that their traditional financial investing strategy was undermining their mission. Through a sometimes difficult journey, the Needmor Foundation became one of the first funders to embrace socially responsible investing and played a role in building an emerging field. The chapter on the Jacobs Family

Foundation and its sister operating foundation, the Jacobs Center for Neighborhood Innovation, bucked conventional philanthropic wisdom. The Jacobs Center bought a city block in a blighted neighborhood. The foundations worked with residents to open shops on the block and pioneered the country's first community development initial public offering. The novel ownership structure has allowed residents to buy shares in the company that controls the property.

In these two stories, you will also learn how individuals inside these foundations overcame significant obstacles to bridge differences in family members' political beliefs and overcome divides by finding strategies that embraced common values.

3

Using an Endowment to Build the Field of Socially Responsible Investing

The Case of the Needmor Fund

The Stranahans provide a rare glimpse into the dynamics of a family of wealth as they bridge their differences to position their family foundation, the Needmor Fund, as a leader in the world of socially responsible investing. Reaching beyond their grantmaking, they discovered the impact that they can have by using their endowment funds to generate change.

Duane and Virginia Secor Stranahan (first generation, now deceased) founded the Needmor Fund in 1956 with family money earned from the Ohio-based Champion Spark Plug Company. "In the early days, it was Duane and Virginia giving to things they had a passion for," explained Dave Beckwith, the fund's current executive director.

Early on, however, the founders brought in other family voices. "My grandfather did not control the decisions," stated the founders' grandchild Sarah Stranahan (third generation, fifty-two years old). "I was voting on Needmor Fund grants at age nineteen. I didn't think this was unusual at the time, but when

I started talking to other family foundations, I realized this was really remarkable."

"My grandfather Duane had this amazing, quiet, intrinsic faith in understanding that every generation had to figure out their own way to get things done," Daniel Stranahan (third generation, thirty-eight) added.[1]

"We were very inclusive of children at these meetings," recalled Duane and Virginia's daughter Mary Stranahan (second generation, sixty-two). "There would be kids underneath the tables playing with all this stuff, and actually adults too. We created quite a few really good doodles, and really good villages of clay creatures. . . . What happened was by letting kids play while we were doing the work, slowly but surely they started listening."[2]

"I think it really delighted Duane what we'd done. We could always count on him to kick in at the last minute, when we were out of money and there was one final project that needed funding. He'd say, 'Well, I'll tell you what . . .' It almost didn't really matter what was funded. Just the fact that an organization was out there doing good and his children and grandchildren were having a vital part of it," Ann Stranahan, wife of Steve Stranahan (second generation, seventy-three), continued.

Family Values That Infused the Foundation

For a family with six children and many more grandchildren, this inclusionary spirit meant that the family needed to find ways to bridge the many conflicting opinions among them—differences that often split along gender and age lines. "There was a seventeen-year difference between my brothers and me," Mary explained. "My sister and I were involved in the 1960s antiwar movement when my older brothers were off having children and working to support them. You can imagine we didn't always have the same views."

Needmor Fund Snapshot

Type: Private family foundation
Year founded: 1956

Grant range (1968): $200–$28,000 (earliest available data)

Assets (1968): $2.8 million

Total grants (1968): $315,500

Grant range (2007): $20,000–$45,000

Total grants awarded (2007): $2.25 million

Total assets (2007): $29.4 million

Geographic focus: Domestic

Primary funding area: Community organizing

Staff size (2007): Four

Location: Toledo, Ohio

Note: Snapshot information for each chapter varies depending on data available. Dates refer to either the calendar year or the end of the fiscal cycle. For snapshot sources, refer to the Notes section at the end of the book.[3]

Duane and Virginia's two younger daughters, Mary and Dinny (second generation, now deceased), learned from their mother to challenge the status quo. "My mother was an Eleanor Roosevelt fan," Mary explained. "Right from the time we were in diapers we understood a little about fairness and the inequities occurring within society."

"My mother grew up in a household very interested in women's rights. She did a lot of what in those days were men's kinds of things like downhill skiing and golf. She was extremely independent," Mary's brother Steve elaborated.

Their father instilled in the family, as well as the foundation, values that helped bridge family differences. "He created a culture of tolerance, openness, and confidence that allowed us to work together with different points of view," Sarah explained.

"His greatest gift was trusting us," Ann added.[4]

Unlike Virginia, Duane did not have the same passion for challenging the status quo. "He didn't feel he needed to solve the world's problems," Sarah explained. "He followed the basic Judeo-Christian tenet, 'If you have the ability and you see someone in need, you have the responsibility to help.' He was not into fancy talk and analysis. If there was a hurricane, it was obvious to him that we needed to help." Elaborating on the family's reaction to this view, she said, "Many of us would say to him, 'We don't really want to fund Band-Aids. We want to fund root problems.' We wanted to get the biggest bang for our buck. So he would have to fund it out of his own pocket. He had a heartfelt concern for helping people who were suffering." In these interactions, the family struggled with how to address the immediate needs of those who were suffering, while also finding ways to address the systems that had helped further people's plight.

An Introduction to Shareholder Activism

The values of independence, compassion, challenging authority, and inclusion served as a platform from which the foundation could build its destiny. Granddaughter Sarah Stranahan became one of several family members who pushed the Needmor Fund in new directions.

"It must have been 1984," Sarah recalled. "I was living at my father Pat's house writing my thesis when I saw in the mail the announcement for the Champion Spark Plug annual meeting, and read that one of Champion's major shareholders, the New York State Employees' Retirement Pension Fund, was sponsoring a shareholder resolution. The resolution stated that [given that Champion had a factory in South Africa manufacturing spark plugs for the African market] the company should adopt the Sullivan Principles."

Sarah explained that these principles "set new standards for factories in South Africa. The belief was that apartheid laws were wrong, so companies needed to create a higher standard." Developed by Reverend Leon Sullivan, a board member of General Motors, in 1977, the principles included such measures as "non-segregation of the races in all eating, comfort and work facilities."[5] "I asked my father about it, and he said, 'Oh that's not interesting and it won't pass,' and I said, 'Oh . . . I think it's interesting,' and I went to the shareholders' meeting."

At the meeting, after it became clear that the resolution would not pass, Sarah asked the individual moving the resolution to bring it back to Champion for another vote the following year. She then spent months neglecting her thesis and preparing for a Needmor Fund board meeting where she hoped to convince the fund's board to vote their shares in favor of the resolution. As part of her preparations, "I called the Interfaith Center on Corporate Responsibility [ICCR] and spoke with Tim Smith, who has become one of the most respected people in the field, and he sent me a huge cardboard box of materials," she recalled.

Debating Whether to Promote Shareholder Activism

At the Needmor Fund board meeting, Sarah gave a presentation on mission-related investing. "Then I got nervous," she recounted. "You could have heard a pin drop, because it was not something that anybody wanted to talk about. I suddenly realized this was not going to be as simple for others as it was for me. The next ten hours were awful. We stayed up 'til about two in the morning. It nearly killed us."

As was historically true within the family, the arguments divided roughly along gender lines. "The men in the family served on the corporate board, and they were working very hard to keep the foundation alive," recalled Sarah. "It was a terrible time for the auto industry. There was a lot of pressure to shut down unionized plants in order to compete with low-cost Japanese cars. The family had agreed not to pay dividends so the company could invest in modernization. Champion was struggling to modernize and was under a lot of pressure. My grandfather; my father, Pat; and my uncle Steve said, 'We have been working so hard to make this all work, and you don't appreciate how hard we work for you. We have been running one of the best plants in South Africa. Don't come in here and tell us what to do.'"

One concern family members raised had to do with independent monitoring, which the company would need to agree to if it signed on to the Sullivan Principles. Sarah's cousin Molly (third generation, fifty-three) noted, "Several people felt we were already doing this, so why did we have to pay for someone to come and monitor our practices?"

Molly recalled how Sarah addressed this argument. "Sarah said, 'OK, maybe we have been doing good things, but other companies haven't. If we want to get other companies to do it, then shouldn't we sign on and open ourselves to an audit too? It's in the interest of transparency and openness. Let us show them our policies. Let us show them what we are doing with housing. Let us show them how many black South Africans we have in management positions. All this needs to be transparent.'"

Reflecting on Sarah's position, Molly recalled feeling a sense of awe. "Sarah was really courageous to take this stand. Here she was challenging her father, her uncle, her grandfather, and the family business that supported Needmor. We owned 16 percent of the company, and all the assets we had at that time were in trusts that were controlled by Steve, Pat, and her grandfather. This was an amazing position to take."

Molly also noted, however, that although several family members resisted the proposal, Sarah's position on this issue was fundamentally aligned with values held by the entire family. "We cared about Champion's impact on workers and their families, so why didn't we care about other companies' impact on workers? That's when things went 'click' for some of us at the meeting. As stockholders we were part owners of these companies, and we had a responsibility."

Steve, however, remained concerned. "I didn't feel we as minority stakeholders should have that kind of influence over the company. To what extent should the family force management to take an action when management was responsible not only to the family but also to other shareholders? To what extent was that responsible?" he asked. "It was great to deal with social inequality, but there was a limit to what the fund could and should do."

The family did not come to agreement that night. The debate had touched such sensitive chords that the members needed time to reflect on all the issues raised. The Sullivan Principles appeared to threaten core sources of their family power—their money and their company. At the same time, the debate challenged their image of themselves as socially responsible leaders in the world of business.

In between these family discussions, Sarah went to speak to the public relations staff at Champion. "They told me, 'Champion does not take political sides.' They disapproved of the idea that shareholders with 'political views,' as they called them, should influence what the company did. They felt the company's job was not to resolve apartheid—it was to be good employers."

Hollow Victory

In a later meeting, the family decided that it would not be possible to reach consensus and instead brought the issue to a vote. The majority ruled in favor of supporting the Sullivan Principles. "The guys felt personally hurt and disrespected," Sarah recalled.

In reflecting back on how she broached mission-related investing with her family, Sarah noted, "In hindsight I could have been more gracious. I could have spoken with individual family members one-on-one before taking it to the board, so people didn't feel sprung on. The way I confronted people, I could have really damaged relationships. Our family did weather it well, but it could have blown up in our faces."

Despite the Needmor Fund's position and Stranahan family votes, the resolution did not pass with a 50 percent vote at Champion's next shareholder meeting.

"Resolutions such as this rarely passed, but often still had significant impact within companies," Tim Smith (of ICCR) explained. "Shareholder pressure convinced many companies to adopt the resolution and even to withdraw from South Africa."

In fact, in 1985, Champion did decide to sign the Sullivan Principles.[6]

The decision, however, proved to be too little too late. "The divestment movement had already moved on to a new strategy," Sarah explained. "Reverend Sullivan was asking corporations to pull out of South Africa. In addition, some apartheid campaigners were saying to shareholders of companies in South Africa, 'Sell all your shares.'"

DEFINITIONS

Mission or program(-related) investing: A foundation uses its portfolio to further its mission as well as protect the principal invested or earn financial returns. The following are five mission-related investing strategies:

(Continued)

Screening: A foundation uses social or environmental criteria as "screens" to align its investments with its mission. Screens can be negative (for example, avoid investing in tobacco companies or major polluters) or positive (focus investments on green companies).

Ranking or rating: A foundation chooses the best-in-class companies within a sector with respect to social and environmental criteria.

Shareholder activity and proxy voting: A foundation uses its investments as a tool to engage in shareholder advocacy—through dialogue with corporate management, shareholder resolutions, and proxy voting—to influence a corporation's behavior on issues relevant to the foundation's mission.

Proactive mission(-related) investing: A foundation decides to invest in a company with a specific social mission or with an identified social or environmental impact—for example, as an angel investor, as a venture investor, or through buying private equity.

Community development investing: A foundation invests money focused on community development and empowering low-income communities—for example, through a certificate of deposit in a community bank, or a loan fund that provides low-interest loans to individuals or businesses in disadvantaged areas.

Note: Definitions are adapted from Sarah Cooch and Mark Kramer (see the Notes section at the end of the book for full reference).[7]

Screening Stocks

The meetings regarding the Sullivan Principles sparked a related debate within the Needmor Fund. "When Sarah brought these issues up, we started flipping through our stock portfolios at one of the meetings," Molly recalled. Sarah explained what happened next. "My uncle Steve turned to me and said, 'What I don't understand is why you are picking on Champion. Look at all the terrible stocks we own. We own defense stocks and mining stocks. We even own Kerr-McGee stocks.[8] Why don't you go after them?'" Sarah continued, "And I looked at him and said, 'You know, that's a great idea.'"

"I invited Amy Domini to come talk to us about [mission-related] investing so we could get educated," recounted Sarah. "Amy hadn't founded Domini Social Investments yet, but she had written a book on the topic. She said we could align our portfolio with our values and that she believed we could make competitive returns doing this. Remember this was the mid-1980s—there was only a limited track record for screened returns." Steve added, "I gave a lot of arguments against this approach. [Mission-related] investing eliminated whole chunks of investment possibilities." Mary explained that "Steve was very concerned we would lose money on the corpus and lose our value."

Sarah recalled, "In the end we agreed to invest a small amount in a screened portfolio. We agreed to run a 'horse race' to see if the experimental screened portfolio's returns would be competitive."

BRIDGING POLITICAL DIFFERENCES

Deciding whether to pursue mission-related investing was not the only time that family differences emerged within the Needmor Fund. "We had executive directors pushing us to focus," Mary recounted. "But how were we going to do that with a family spanning a 180-degree political spectrum?"

The family found their answer to this dilemma at a board meeting. "They had a proposal from women fighting for jobs in the coal fields," recalled Dave Beckwith, Needmor executive director. "Some of them said, 'This is terrible. We've been funding groups fighting coal mines and saying how miserable these jobs are. Now we're going to help women fight to get these terrible jobs? And someone at the table said, 'It's not up to us to decide what they want. It's up to us to decide whether we are with them.'"

Beckwith described this as an "aha" moment for the family. "The dialogue shifted from one person saying, 'I think they are right' and another person saying 'I think they are wrong.'"

"We realized we all believed that people should have the right to participate in democracy," Molly continued.

"The core value that allowed family members with very different political opinions to come together was that we all believed in full political participation—that this was fundamental to

(Continued)

democracy. Immigrants, for example, should be able to organize and advocate even if we didn't think the policies they were advocating were fair. We realized we wanted to fund community organizing," Sarah elaborated.

However, the new focus on community organizing did not sit well with some family members. "One family member eventually decided to leave the Needmor Fund," Beckwith noted.

Reflecting on this event, Molly commented, "It's important to be able to let people go. There is sadness in this, but if we just tried to force consensus, no one would be excited about what we were doing. We're more lively at the edges."

Since 1994, the Needmor Fund has dedicated all of its grant monies to community organizing.

Implementing Strategy to Invest in Values

Next the board developed a mission-related investment statement. "We brought in an investment manager from Franklin Research and Development [now known as Trillium Asset Management]. We learned the first classic step in this type of investing was to eliminate tobacco, alcohol and weapons," Molly continued. "But in our case there were people who enjoyed alcohol and my father started a brewery. There were family members making money from this. So we decided not to screen out alcohol."

Of the process, Molly noted, "I called it values congruent investing rather than socially responsible investing because it really was looking at our values, and making sure we weren't making money in violation of those values. One of the concerns about the phrase 'socially responsible investing' was that it was as if everyone would have the same standard about what was socially responsible. And of course, it depended on each of our values."[9]

After the board finalized the statement, Steve led the effort to develop their strategy for the experimental fund. "We took about a year looking at different investing mechanisms and interviewing different management companies," he explained.

Ultimately, "The stocks did really well," Sarah recalled. "So some of us said, 'Let's screen the rest of our money!'"

Treading New Ground

The family agreed to go to their investment firm Neuberger Berman to request that the firm develop a portfolio aligned with the family's new investment policy. "Neuberger was a big old investment firm in New York, quite a large firm," Sarah explained. "Eventually we told them if we weren't going to be able to screen our portfolio that we would be moving it. Neuberger kind of begrudgingly said, 'Well, there's a woman who's kind of interested in that and her name's Joyce Haboucha and we'll give her this assignment.'"[10]

Joyce Haboucha, Neuberger Berman portfolio manager at the time, recalled, "They told Neuberger that the firm would be given a chance to develop a product. The firm wanted to retain the business. There was fear that if Needmor left, then the family members would leave—that there would be an exodus. The soil was also receptive because the firm's founding partners had a tradition of philanthropy. So Neuberger asked me to develop a social investment product. The company put a lot of resources into this."

Of their holdings, Sarah noted, "About a third of the Needmor Fund holdings were with Neuberger Berman—about $4.5 million. Our endowment was small. Most of the money was going to grants. Our family had a lot of personal money with Neuberger Berman, though—much more than the Needmor Fund."

Given the relative newness of the field, there were very few models of how to use social criteria to choose companies for a portfolio. "There was very little going on. You couldn't buy this kind of research," Joyce explained. "We decided on a methodology that looked at what companies were doing to change things. We wanted not just to avoid certain companies but to look inside the company to see if there were leaders and change agents working to change it. We were looking at processes, not just absolutes."

Neuberger Berman and the Needmor Fund both approved the approach, and Neuberger Berman began to build its expertise in the field. By the late 1980s, the firm was attracting other high-net-worth individuals interested in socially screening their investments.

The success of these individual accounts then led them to develop a socially responsive mutual fund in 1994. Ingrid Dyott, managing director for the socially responsive investing team in

2008, said, "What differentiated Neuberger Berman's socially responsive investing fund was that the professionals at the company in charge of picking stocks were also involved in social and environmental research. Since the fund's inception, financial analysis and social research have been conducted in-house."

Neuberger Berman's expanded focus, in turn, played an important role in moving the field of socially responsible investing toward the mainstream. "The work brought another voice into the mix. When you had a well-established traditional investment firm like ours calling these companies and asking them questions about their environmental and social impact, then you really began to have influence," explained Joyce Haboucha.

"Neuberger really developed a social research expertise. They were the first mainstream investment firm to develop a [comprehensive team]—not just provide one individual. This was significant," Amy Domini (founder of Domini Social Investments) elaborated.

By 2006, Neuberger Berman's socially screened investments included over $2 billion in assets.[11] In addition, the methodology pioneered by Joyce Haboucha and team partner Janet Prindle had "become a standard in the industry," Joyce stated.

Further, "Joyce turned out to be one of the superstars of social investment. [In 2008] she ran a huge department at Rockefeller Financial Services," Sarah added.[12]

Growing Socially Responsible Businesses

The family members also sought other ways outside the Needmor Fund to support the emerging field of mission-related investing. In the mid-1980s, for example, sisters Mary and Dinny Stranahan became early investors in a small startup company by the name of Working Assets Funding Service, a spinoff of the Working Assets Money Market Fund. Created in 1985, the subsidiary offered a credit card that when used for purchases would make a donation to nonprofits "working for peace, human rights, equality, education and the environment."[13]

"They were the first big investors in our company," stated Laura Scher, CEO of Working Assets Funding Service. "Their money was the catalyst for other investors. Not only did they make an investment, they let us use their name to secure a line of credit."

Company president Michael Kieschnick added, "I honestly do not think Working Assets would exist without their investment." By 2006, Working Assets had revenues of $91.7 million and included a staff of eighty-three people.[14]

WORKING ASSETS: MULTIMILLION-DOLLAR COMPANY

By the end of 2008 Working Assets will have given away over $60 million in general support to organizations supporting human rights, environmental sustainability, and economic justice. Working Assets had also launched many long-term campaigns, including helping customers generate millions of faxes and letters to influence policymakers on important legislation.

In describing the company's impact, founder and CEO Laura Scher listed a series of campaign victories for which Working Assets had mobilized constituents. "There's still no drilling in the Arctic. General Motors has stopped asking women if they were pregnant before hiring them in plants they set up in Mexico. We helped pressure Mercedes to set up a $2 billion fund to compensate slave laborers in WWII. Our campaign to raise awareness around the military's new policy of recruiting children in schools is one reason why a lot of the public now knows about this policy."

Of Mary and Dinny Stranahan's critical support of the company, Michael Kieschnick, president of the company, noted, "Instead of limiting their work to their own funding capacity, [Mary and Dinny] helped create a whole new revenue source for social change."

Bolstering a Key Investment Fund

In addition, the Needmor Fund sought out fledgling investment firms pioneering mission-related investing. For example, the Needmor Fund purchased $100,000 worth of shares of the Domini

Social Equity Fund (then named the Domini Social Index Trust), shortly after the fund was formed in 1991.[15] "It didn't make or break the fund's success," Amy Domini noted, "but it was a turning point. This was a signal that we were being accepted into the mainstream, that we were a fund appropriate for a foundation."

Amy Domini explained that the success of the Domini Social Equity Fund, in turn, marked a turning point for the entire field of socially responsible investing. She stated that the index provided, for the first time, an easy way for investors to track the performance of screened mutual funds against nonscreened ones. With returns over time cumulatively outperforming the S&P 500 index, the fund helped diffuse the primary fear that kept larger numbers of investors from joining the movement, namely that such investing would sacrifice financial returns.

HOW HAS THE NEEDMOR FUND'S MISSION-RELATED INVESTMENT STRATEGY PERFORMED?

According to Dave Beckwith, by the late 1990s, the Needmor Fund had become one of the few foundations to have invested all its assets in ways that supported and were consistent with its mission. In doing so, the fund helped challenge the prevailing belief that such an investment strategy meant significantly sacrificing returns.

"If you looked at our total portfolio [in 2007]," Beckwith said, "our performance against similar classes of stocks that don't screen—over one year, three years, and five years—has been within 1 percent in every case. Our investment strategy has been to meet a spending formula that was 6 percent of capital and to preserve our capital at a stable level over time. This strategy has worked."

Strengthening Grantee Work Through Shareholder Activism

In the late 1990s, Steve Viederman joined first the Needmor Fund's finance committee and later the board, and he and Sarah quickly became allies. Steve was at the time the president of the Jessie Smith Noyes Foundation and, according to many individuals in philanthropy, was an early leader in the field of shareholder activism.

"He wanted the Needmor Fund to focus on shareholder activism and to keep it grounded in our work with our grantees," Sarah recalled. The finance committee agreed to the proposal, but said they would not provide staff resources to support the effort.

Sarah quickly realized, however, that very little staff time was needed. One of their socially responsible investment firms, Walden Asset Management, provided leadership for clients and support in filing shareholder resolutions. "We got hours and hours of cheerful, wonderful, free support from an expert investment manager," Sarah explained. "Otherwise this would have been cost-prohibitive."

Sarah noted that the Needmor Fund had access to these shareholder activism resources "because we screened our investments. We were already invested at Walden, so we had access to this deep resource base. Because we were already aligned with people in the socially responsible investing field, we just kept meeting the people we needed to meet."

In the early 2000s, Sarah stumbled across an important opportunity to support a grantee by filing a shareholder resolution. "United for a Fair Economy made an announcement at a conference. They were looking for people that could file a resolution against Yum! Corporation on behalf of the Coalition of Immokalee Workers." I said, 'Yes, that's our grantee!'"

Based in southwest Florida, the member-based Coalition of Immokalee Workers (CIW) was leading a labor-related campaign against Taco Bell. It had organized strikes, boycotts, and cross-country tours to pressure Taco Bell, a subsidiary of Yum! Corporation, to pay their suppliers one penny more per pound of tomatoes and to tell their suppliers to pass this money on to their farm workers. The Needmor Fund had already provided grants that supported this campaign.

NEEDMOR ATTRACTS OTHER FUNDERS

"Needmor was an early funder for the Coalition of Immokalee Workers," Frank Sanchez, senior program officer at the Needmor Fund, explained. "This was important because our money sometimes meant three or four more grants [for the coalition]. We were so thorough with our evaluations and site visits that other foundations sometimes saw our name as a seal of approval."

Around 2003, with the approval of the CIW, the Needmor Fund joined investors and filed a shareholder resolution. These included the United Church Foundation; Pension Boards—United Church of Christ; and the Center for Reflection, Education and Action (CREA).[16]

While other filers played more active roles negotiating with Yum! Brands, the Needmor Fund concentrated on lifting the voices of Immokalee workers themselves. "Instead of going to the shareholder meeting to present our own statement, we invited the Immokalee workers to participate as our proxy," Sarah's cousin Daniel recalled. Frank Sanchez (Needmor Fund senior program officer) recounted, "It really caught the corporation off guard. They weren't expecting the farm workers who were striking to show up at their meeting!"

In 2005, the Immokalee workers won a decisive victory. Taco Bell would pay the extra penny per pound, and this would be passed on to the farm workers, as verified by a third-party monitor. In addition, Taco Bell would establish a code of conduct with growers, explicitly prohibiting human rights violations.[17] This was the first time that a major food corporation had created an enforceable code of conduct for agricultural suppliers in the fast-food industry.[18] Of the agreement the U.S. Congressional Hispanic Caucus stated, "This is a truly historic agreement, marking perhaps the single greatest advance for farm workers since the early struggles of the United Farm Workers."[19]

The Taco Bell success led to other victories. In 2007, CIW won a similar agreement with McDonald's.[20] That same year, "Yum! Corporation announced they would extend their agreement to all five of their brands," stated CIW staffer Julia Perkins.

In reflecting on the importance of the resolution in winning the campaign, Perkins noted, "The resolution was instrumental in raising the campaign to a new level of credibility. The fact that we had many people—consumers, workers, and shareholders—all sending the same message really helped in getting Yum! Brands to pay attention to where they purchased their produce."

Sanchez emphasized, however, the importance of the CIW's multistrategy approach. "The Coalition of Immokalee Workers has been a very strong organization. The shareholder resolution was only one tactic within a comprehensive strategy to win benefits for the communities. The strikes and boycott, the CIW's work with students to organize college campuses to block Taco Bell from operating on their campuses, their effectiveness with the media—all this helped to win the campaign."

Following the victory, Steve Viederman helped the Needmor Fund institutionalize shareholder advocacy as a service the fund offered to its grantees. "I recommended that Needmor send letters to all their grantees saying, 'We believe in shareowner activism.[21] Are you part of any campaigns where this might help?'"

SHAREHOLDER ACTIVISM: A POTENT TOOL

Lance Lindblom, president and CEO of the Nathan Cummings Foundation and, according to many, a key foundation leader within the field, explained, "The Nathan Cummings Foundation has found that the filing of shareholder resolutions has been one of the most effective means of bringing issues to the attention of corporate boards."

"As an owner of a company, you have an obligation to tell that company what you think," noted Mindy Lubber, president of Ceres, the largest coalition of investors and environmental and public interest organizations in North America. "That means raising the red flag if a company is about to invest in five coal-powered plants and you think that is energy of the past. That's not a smart investment decision."

As part of its shareholder activism work, the Nathan Cummings Foundation has been an important partner in creating the Investor Network on Climate Risk (INCR), which is coordinated by Ceres. "This is a group of large institutional investors managing more than $7 trillion in assets who all see that issues like climate have a major effect on the bottom line," Mindy continued.

In 2007–2008, the Nathan Cummings Foundation, working with Catholic Health East, filed a shareholder resolution with Centex, one of the largest home builders in the country, on energy usage in homes. The company subsequently committed to improving energy efficiency in its new homes by 30 to 40 percent.[22]

Conclusion

In the mid-1980s, Sarah Stranahan found the courage to challenge her family to align its investment strategies with its values. The Needmor Fund and the Stranahan family rose to the challenge and lent their voice, their power, and their credibility to what was at the time a fledgling mission-related investing field. Their financial pressure persuaded Neuberger Berman to become one of the first traditional investment firms to develop an in-house mission-related investing team. In addition, the Needmor Fund and the Stranahan family provided important early financial support to Working Assets and Domini Social Investments—both of which became significant players in promoting socially responsible business practices worldwide.

"Change happens with innovators," noted mission-related investing strategist Susan Davis. "Among $100 million-plus families, circles are small and news spreads. I consider that the Stranahan family and the Needmor Fund had a major impact. They were a bellwether."

In taking a stand with its financial resources, the Needmor Fund became a pioneer in a field that is redefining business accountability. In 1980, the vast majority of businesses operated on the assumption that their only accountability to their shareholders was financial. By 2007, the dialogue had changed dramatically. "When I was writing *Ethical Investing* [in the early 1980s] I wrote a letter to Boston Investing," Amy Domini recalled. "I said, 'Here are key words, words such as ethical investing and corporate responsibility; what do you have on these?' They had nothing. This was not in the vocabulary of people in this country in 1980. Two years ago, over four thousand companies published corporate responsibility or sustainability reports. In the 1970s and 1980s, there were just a few lone voices speaking about social and environmental accountability. Now you have chambers of commerce meeting about this issue. Socially responsible investing was a major part of making this happen."

Within the field itself, however, there has been debate as to the impact this shift has had for the working class and the environment. "Many companies do report on social and environmental practices, but in an age of outsourcing, these reports are window dressing unless they take into account the practices of their suppliers," commented Joost Douma, secretary general of the Amsterdam-based International Interfaith Investment Group, a network of investment officers from many of the world's largest faith organizations. Such concerns have made campaigns to hold suppliers accountable (such as the CIW campaign) a key strategy for ensuring that corporations protect the environment, workers, and consumers.

Joost also noted that "corporate behavior would be worse without [mission-related] investing, in particular shareholder activism." However, he added, such efforts need to be reinforced with laws that hold corporations accountable to shareholders, communities, and the environment.

Looking back, Sarah Stranahan felt that the combined elements of the Needmor Fund's investing strategy—from screening to shareholder action—secured the relationships that helped them become players in building the field. "We took a chance and found our allies. Then, as we each built our networks, the people we met along the way became strategic partners. Tim Smith just retired from chairing the Social Investment Forum. We met [Amy Domini] when she was still forming a mutual fund, and now she's a leader in the field. What's been most remarkable has been how these relationships have woven in and out over the years."

"The power of strategy can trump the power of money," Daniel Stranahan commented, reflecting on the Needmor Fund's investment strategy. "The Needmor Fund didn't have endless dollars to fund everything we'd like, so we used all our resources—our grants, our intellectual capital, our investments, our shareholder activism, and our influence—to attain our mission." In doing so, the Needmor Fund has pioneered new models for how foundations can leverage their power in support of more just and equitable societies.

Lessons Learned

The Stranahan family and the Needmor Fund leveraged their reputation and combined assets to support the growing field of socially responsible investing. Here are strategies they used to play a role in building greater mechanisms for accountability into the business sector:

- Leverage all your financial assets—not only your grantmaking money but also your endowment—to catalyze change.
- When members of the foundation cannot agree on the foundation's direction, move beyond positions to values.
- Pass the torch to the next generation by inviting children to meetings and giving youth a say in how money is spent.
- Find ways to support the creation of new sources of funding for social change.

Transforming Business Structures for Communities

The Case of the Jacobs Family Foundation and Jacobs Center for Neighborhood Innovation

In this chapter, the staff and founders of the Jacobs Family Foundation and its sister operating foundation, the Jacobs Center for Neighborhood Innovation, share their soul-searching journey to meet the needs of underinvested communities. Beginning with the writing of blueprints for these communities, the Jacobs foundations were confronted by the need to bring community members into their decision-making processes. The result was a community-owned marketplace in San Diego and two foundations that aim to go out of business within a couple of decades, transferring all assets—including JCNI's share in the marketplace—to the residents working to strengthen their neighborhoods.

"I was twenty years old when Jacobs Engineering Group went public [in 1970]," Valerie Jacobs recounted, referring to her father's business.[1] When Joe Jacobs's three daughters, Valerie, Linda, and Meg, discovered he had earned $10 million in stock and cash in the transaction, Valerie recalled saying, "Gee, Dad, you're rich!"

"My dad was shocked by those words," Valerie continued. "He came back to us and said, 'We are going to give this money away.'

[My sisters and I] didn't have any expectation to inherit so we said, 'Great—can we help?'" In response, in 1988 the family set up the Jacobs Family Foundation with the intention of giving away the foundation's assets within the children's lifetimes.

Jacobs Family Foundation and Jacobs Center for Neighborhood Innovation Snapshot

Jacobs Family Foundation

Type: Private family foundation

Year founded: 1988

Grant range (1988): $100–$56,000

Grant range (2008): $300–$2.6 million

Grants awarded (1988): $67,000

Grants awarded (2008): $6.4 million

Assets (1988): $78,242

Geographic focus: Diamond Neighborhoods of southeastern San Diego

Primary funding area: Neighborhood revitalization

Jacobs Center for Neighborhood Innovation (JCNI)

Type: Private operating foundation

Year founded: 1995

Geographic focus and location: Diamond Neighborhoods of southeastern San Diego

Primary funding area: Neighborhood revitalization

Combined Figures for Both Foundations

Staff size (2008): 135 full- and part-time employees (includes subsidiaries of JCNI, such as Diamond Management Inc. and Jacobs Facilities, LLC)

Assets (2008): $171 million

Note: Snapshot information for each chapter varies depending on data available. Dates refer to either the calendar year or the end of the fiscal cycle. For snapshot sources, refer to the Notes section at the end of the book.[2]

Joe invited his daughters to join him in the endeavor and told them that each person would have an equal vote. When the daughters later heard their father mention that he wanted to provide funding to a conservative think tank, they took issue. "We reminded him about what he'd said about everyone having an equal voice," Meg recalled. "We said that if that wasn't going to happen, we didn't think we should be part of the foundation. It wasn't an ultimatum. It was just what we thought was the right thing to do. He thought about it and told us we were right. After that we only gave grants to projects we could all agree on." Valerie added, "He realized that the foundation needed to be reflective of all of our values if we were going to stay involved."

Soon after, the daughters challenged their father, who was chair of the Jacobs Family Foundation, to share leadership positions with them. Meg became the executive director in 1989.

Bridging Political Differences Within the Family

Meg reflected on her biggest challenge as the foundation's new executive director: "How were we going to find things that we all agreed with?" she had wondered at the time.

The three "passionate liberal" daughters were interested in ending domestic violence, upholding women's rights, and alleviating poverty. "I worked as a social worker in the ghettos in Baltimore out of college," Meg explained. "I saw a lot of racism and how hard it was to get a job when you were African American. I saw people get sick and lose their jobs, and institutions impinging on people."

In contrast to his daughters, Joe Jacobs was a staunch conservative whose two books—one of which was *The Compassionate Conservative*—were endorsed by such political figures as George W. Bush and Donald Rumsfeld. He wanted to focus on free market enterprise and entrepreneurism. "My dad felt that charity, giving somebody money and not requiring anything in return, was demeaning," Valerie recalled. "[Welfare, soup kitchens, and the like] took people's incentive away, as well as their dignity."

Despite their differences, Meg was able to find a focus that bridged family values. Valerie recounted, "Everybody was thrilled when she found a group called FINCA that gave business loans to low-income women in Latin America. It brought all our interests together—free markets, poverty, women."

Over time, however, the family grew to believe that their grants were not having significant impact. "The grants to large organizations felt like a drop in the bucket," Meg recalled.

After hiring consultant Jennifer Vanica in 1991, the family decided to address this concern by funding smaller, grassroots organizations. The staff and board of the Jacobs Family Foundation soon realized, however, that these types of organizations sometimes struggled with the management side of their operations.

"We saw how some grantees might be more effective with stronger accounting and business skills," Valerie recalled. "But instead of just giving grantees the money directly, we decided to leverage Jennifer's background in non-profit management and experiment with funder/grantee relationships so that the Foundation could offer technical assistance directly to the grantees."

In 1995 Jennifer became executive director of the Jacobs Family Foundation. That same year, to complement the Jacobs Family Foundation grantmaking and to support non-profit capacity building, the family created what is today called the Jacobs Center for Neighborhood Innovation (JCNI), and structured it as an operating foundation. (See Appendix A for definition.) This legal classification provided the new entity greater flexibility to support communities through direct services and programs, and later to work in partnership with residents to develop property. Jennifer became president and CEO of JCNI in 2002.

Of the work, Valerie noted that the family and staff were bucking conventional wisdom. "Philanthropy was saying 'Stay out of the technical assistance business. The power dynamics between funders and grantees are too hard to overcome.'"

Several nonprofits did not appreciate the approach. Valerie explained how they were able to manage this concern. "We got better at choosing nonprofit partners. The most important thing was that our values matched. We said, in return for sharing with us the parts of your organization that are not working, we will stick with you until you don't need us anymore."

Questioning Impact

Despite these changes, however, the question kept coming up: Are we making a difference? Meg recalled, "We were putting dribs and drabs of money and time here and there—but as the grassroots organizations got stronger, there were no apparent signs that the conditions in their communities were improving."

Jennifer added, "We started feeling like grants and technical assistance alone did not help neighborhoods work."

As they grappled with next steps, Joe Jacobs's third daughter, Linda, wrote a paper on community development, which influenced the family's thinking; it stated that business loans by themselves could not revitalize neighborhoods. For example, how could a woman attract customers to her business when gangs were killing people outside her restaurant? "We realized we needed to be more comprehensive in our approach, and to do that we had to be more microscopic in our geography," Valerie explained. In response, the family decided to choose a limited number of neighborhoods on which to focus its efforts, and work with residents to intervene across a broad spectrum of social and economic issues.

At the same time, the family and staff were also starting to question why their offices were not closer to their grantees. "How could we be up close and personal when our offices were far away?" Valerie questioned.

MAKING COMMUNITY INVOLVEMENT A TOP PRIORITY

A trip to Africa in the mid-1990s stimulated the foundation's interest in making community involvement in projects a top priority, Jennifer recalled. "We saw these large-scale U.S. Agency for International Development projects that had been plopped in the middle of villages and abandoned. When we asked villagers why, they would say that they never wanted the projects in the first place. We thought, 'Wow! We do this all the time. We commission write-ups and then come into communities and tell people what they need.'"

Moving the Foundations' Offices

"We decided we wanted to work in the Diamond Neighborhoods of southeastern San Diego, an area where we had several grantees," Jennifer Vanica explained.

The Diamond Neighborhoods were a network of ten of the most culturally diverse communities in San Diego. The area's eighty-eight thousand residents included those from more than twenty cultures, including African Americans, Samoans, Laotians, Sudanese, Latinos, Filipinos, and Somalis; the median income in the area was $32,000 in 2000.[3]

"Then we had a convergence moment," Jennifer recounted. "During a community meeting, Diamond residents were complaining about a twenty-acre lot that had an abandoned factory on it, that was attracting crime and gang violence. Three hundred kids had to cross the streets bordering the lot after school. The parents and the grandparents were saying, 'Someone has to do something.' At the same time, we were talking about where to move our offices. We realized we shouldn't move to a well-invested area if we were asking businesses to move into disinvested areas. So Joe said, 'Why don't we buy it?'"

In 1997, JCNI bought the property, and that same year hired seasoned community organizer Roque Barros to involve residents in a plan for its development. The first action that residents, working together with Roque, decided on was to invite neighbors into the factory to help pierce the veil of mystery that had shrouded the property. "We did a Halloween carnival in there," Roque recounted. "Thousands of people came, and they all had stories about this factory, and how they'd thought it was contaminated."

Residents also formed an outreach team to ask neighbors what they would like to see on the site. "We went to homes, churches, schools, even a juvenile residence hall," outreach team member Kelly Steppe recalled. "We took a couple kids out of a twenty-four-hour care facility, so they could give a presentation to Joe."

Roque noted that the work was not easy, and in many instances racial tensions needed to be addressed. "We were walking down the street knocking on doors, and on one side of the street there were the Latinos, and on the other side of the street were the Samoans." To address the conflicts, Roque recruited leaders from each ethnicity to the outreach team and, when they suggested throwing a block party, helped make that happen. "Everyone ate together and danced together, and that was the start of repairing those relationships."

Jennifer Vanica also recalled one of her early, more difficult experiences. "In the survey, the need for day care surfaced, so I was going along setting up a day-care center. But we had some community meetings that turned into the most dog-eat-dog meetings I'd ever been part of. The child-care providers hit the roof. They were worried they'd be put out of business. What became clear was that there was a disconnect between supply and demand. Maybe one apartment complex didn't have day care, but another did. What people needed was more decentralized day care. If you lived in the Little Lao apartment complex, you needed day care in that building—not down the street in Little Samoa."

"We realized from that experience we needed to be very careful about interpreting data. It caused a shift in our internal dialogue," Jennifer explained. "We started asking, 'Who is responsible for interpreting information?'"

Supporting Efforts to Involve Youth

As trust grew, Kelly Steppe (outreach team member from the community) decided to ask Roque Barros for help with a problem she was experiencing in the neighborhood. Working for a security firm, Kelly managed security guards that protected property in the neighborhood. "Kids were writing all over the building walls," Kelly noted. "But these were just kids. If I caught them doing graffiti [they could get in serious trouble with the law]. I didn't want to do that. So I said to Roque, 'Hey, we have to do something. These kids are driving me nuts.' And he said, 'Sister, let's get a group of them together.'"

To support the intervention, Roque recruited Victor Ochoa, a well-known Hispanic activist and muralist from the Diamond Neighborhoods, and helped him set up large walls in a nearby lot, easily viewable from one of the neighborhood's main streets. "Roque got some cans of spray paint and got a few kids to start painting the walls," Kelly recalled.

Within the year, roughly 150 teenagers were using the site, and Victor was supervising daily art classes for them. Graffiti in the neighborhood had declined considerably. Explaining her own motivation to keep the effort going, Kelly said, "I wanted young people to be part of making this neighborhood work, rather than the reason it didn't work."

Listening to the Community

Meanwhile, JCNI was moving forward with plans to develop the site—part of which residents later named Market Creek Plaza—as a commercial and cultural center. To support the process, in 1998 they hired an architectural firm, which worked with Roque and the community outreach team.

Recalling his initial visit to the lot, architect Hector Reyes said, "My boss and I arrived in our suits in his brand new Infiniti. When we got out of the car, within two minutes we had cops by us saying, 'Gentleman, do you know where you're going?' That gave us a frame for the kind of community we were working in."

"The community members wanted a movie theater, a super-market, an ice cream store. They wanted all the things that La Jolla—the upscale neighborhood in San Diego—had," Hector explained. "So that's what we created. The design followed the same standards as a typical retail development project. But when the community members—and the local artists were the most vociferous—saw the renderings, they said that it looked like any other project in any other neighborhood, and that it didn't represent their community."

The process quickly turned into a difficult one for all sides. The architectural firm was frustrated with the unusual community-driven approach. JCNI staff also grew concerned. "I was worried it would affect the financial viability of the project if we had to stay at the table too long," Jennifer Vanica recalled.

"Ultimately, I had to put the whole project on hold. I realized that part of the tension was that JCNI had chosen the architectural firm, and we needed a process where the community would be involved in that decision."

Consequently, Jennifer told Hector's architectural firm (Fehlman LaBarre) that JCNI was reopening the bidding process to include other firms. "They were shocked," she recalled. The lead architect refused to continue participating. "My boss almost dropped the project," Hector added.

Hector, however, saw the news as an opportunity. "I told my boss, 'Give me the project. I'll do the competition, and I will win it.'" Hector's boss agreed.

"My father always said keep your friends close and your enemies closer," Hector continued. "So I invited all the artists to my office to get to know them and ask them what they wanted this project to be. The fact that I was up-front with them helped me build trust with them. I said 'let me tell you my background and then hear a little about your background.'"

In addition, Hector, Roque Barros (community organizer), and Victor Ochoa (artist) asked residents to bring "inspiring pieces that came from their culture to a meeting. "We were amazed by what they brought—live plants, tapestries, dresses. We scanned the images of the tapestries on sheets of paper and then Victor asked them, 'Do not identify the image of the object you brought in—but look for another tapestry from your culture here.' They couldn't do it. They couldn't tell which was from their own culture. What they discovered was that the binding glue between them was bold patterns, textures, and colors. This became the guiding force behind the architectural character."

"It was very powerful because up to that point everybody had felt so different," Jennifer affirmed. "But when all these things were laid out on the floor, what you saw was this incredibly powerful human bond."

Ultimately the community members invited back the same architectural firm, with Hector Reyes now the lead architect for the project. "I'm sure they thought we were completely nuts," Jennifer Vanica laughed. "But we really learned as a team, if you disagree, you have to stay at the table and that anytime we were stuck, we needed to bring the critics into the room."

Allowing the community to choose the architectural firm proved to be a turning point. By putting the project on hold, JCNI had empowered new players to come forward and take leadership positions within the project—in particular, architect Hector Reyes and the community artists. In addition, the decision gave the community greater ownership and control over the process, clearing the way for more workable relationships between all parties. "Over time the volatility of the work just went away," Jennifer explained.

The episode also marked a new definition of community participation for JCNI. "Community participation was no longer confined to an advisory team," Meg recalled. "Residents were in on the actual decision making every step of the way. That was a big leap."

The shift was also influenced by a series of site visits by board members and staff in the late 1990s, Meg recalled. "We went to the East Coast and saw projects where residents were not just being asked their opinions, but staying to be a part of the decision making." Seeing a community-driven development effort, such as the Dudley Street Neighborhood initiative based in Boston, "was a pivotal moment in our commitment to resident ownership of the planning, the process, and the assets."

As part of the commitment to community ownership, over time JCNI worked with community members to form resident teams to guide different aspects of the plaza's development. Teams included art and design, construction, business development and leasing, community ownership design, and resource development.

Seeing a Resource, not a Liability

The process continued to be weighed down, however, in part due to a tangle of regulatory issues, which JCNI and the resident teams had to resolve creatively. "Every time we got blocked, we saw incredible innovation. Figuring out how to work with those obstacles led us to amazing outcomes," Jennifer Vanica reflected.

For example, JCNI staff had wanted to pour concrete over a dry creek bed on the property, but then discovered that the creek was a federally protected wetland. The Army Corps of Engineers controlled the creek bed, Jennifer explained, and wouldn't allow them to build a permanent fixture over this piece of the property. To resolve this issue and comply with regulations, JCNI built a floating amphitheatre stage on the dry bed (which turned into a river when it rained), as floating structures would not impede water flow and would have minimal impact on the environment, Hector explained.

In addition, they worked to clean up the dry bed—which had become a community dumping ground for old mattresses, syringes, shopping carts, and other trash. "This was the back-side of the community," Jennifer noted. "There'd been drug deals and squatters here, and all the trash was creating a toxic environment."

Wanting to restore the natural environment, the team then added vegetation and rechannelized the creek bed. "We put in boulders to slow down the water flow. Kids were getting killed in the dry bed when flash floods came through."

As the creek was transformed, the area became a symbol for many community members. "Every culture at some point organized around waterways," Jennifer noted. "They were transportation hubs. Having a performance venue by the creek in the heart of the plaza became very important for the community. Creeks are usually seen as reasons not to develop because regulations make development cost-prohibitive. But we turned it into a way for people to come out and enjoy the outdoors."

Finding Ways to Attract and Grow Businesses

While the art and design team and the construction team focused on the architecture and the creek, the business development and leasing team helped attract businesses into the plaza. "They wanted a blend of local and national businesses—the national businesses to bring living-wage jobs and foot traffic, and the local businesses to stimulate local entrepreneurship," Jennifer Vanica recounted.

"We did an economic leakage study that showed that sixty million retail dollars were being spent outside the community," Jennifer continued. The study got the attention of Food 4 Less—the supermarket chain preferred by a majority of the community members—and by 1999 it had signed an agreement to open a store on the plaza.[4]

The supermarket was "the first major grocery store in the neighborhood in thirty years," Tracey Bryan, communications team member for JCNI, explained. Tracey elaborated that without a grocery store, some residents turned to local liquor and convenience stores to buy food if they didn't have transportation to shop outside the area.

Map of Market Creek Plaza

Once Food 4 Less had committed, other businesses followed. San Diego Gas & Electric decided it would open a hi-tech bill-paying center. The story reached celebrities, and soon Magic Johnson—owner of Urban Coffee Opportunities, a partnership between Magic Johnson Enterprises and Starbucks—had located a Starbucks coffee shop on the plaza.

Meanwhile, community members were opening their own small businesses. Charles and Bessie Johnson, an African American couple, started Magnolias Authentic Southern Dining, the neighborhood's first upscale, sit-down restaurant. A local Hispanic entrepreneur launched El Pollo Grill, which offered Mexican favorites. JCNI began a microentrepreneur development initiative through a multicultural gift shop called Where the World Meets. The store showcased the work of local artisans and artists, as well as items residents imported from their own countries.

The larger national tenants acted as "anchors," helping draw customers to the plaza. Once there, customers also began using the locally owned stores and restaurants.

Financing the Project

"[To finance the project,] JCNI was borrowing against the Jacobs Family Foundation's stock portfolio and had to divide the property in two," Jennifer noted of how the effort was funded. "Development plans for the full twenty acres were too big—$85 million in total. No one wanted to finance the construction. The portion of the land with the stores became Market Creek Plaza. The other portion was planned as office space."

In 2004, Wells Fargo invested $15 million through Clearinghouse Community Development Financial Institution (CDFI) to refinance a portion of the construction costs, under a federal initiative called the New Markets Tax Credit program, and soon opened a branch on the property.[5] The federal program, aimed at stimulating development in underinvested neighborhoods, encouraged lenders to make loans in inner-city and rural areas at low interest rates in exchange for tax credits on their investments.

Other foundations also joined the effort. Rockefeller, F. B. Heron, Annie E. Casey, and Legler Benbough foundations, for example, all provided program-related investments.[6]

Sharing Ownership

Even before development of the property began, Joe Jacobs had planted a seed within the community for an even larger vision. Valerie recalled how at a community dinner in 1998, he had said, 'I'm risking all my money here. How many of you would risk your money and invest in this block?' Pretty much everyone in the room raised their hand, and he said, 'That makes my heart sing.'"

Believing that people shouldn't be given handouts, Joe wanted to offer shares in the plaza to residents.

"When 120 residents showed up to serve on the team to make it happen, that's when we knew it would have to be a public offering," Jennifer recounted.

"When Jennifer Vanica called to ask me about the idea, I told her it would be a lot cheaper to avoid all the attorney fees and just give the property to residents," explained Kurt Kicklighter, a lawyer at Luce, Forward, Hamilton & Scripps, LLP, who became the lead lawyer on the project. "But Jennifer was adamant that Joe said, 'No. People have to invest.'"

Because no legal mechanism existed to limit sales to neighborhood residents, JCNI decided to create one. "It was a monumental undertaking. Usually filing takes ninety days. This took six years," Kurt noted, pointing to both government regulations and the community processes under way as the causes.

To describe the effort, those involved coined the term *community development initial public offering* (CD-IPO). Such a hybrid had never existed before in the United States.

Initially, the community team worked with JCNI to develop an ownership structure and decided that the company would include only Market Creek Plaza and a nearby one-acre tract for future development. The remaining land would continue under the ownership of JCNI.

With respect to division of ownership interests, the resident team, together with JCNI, decided to divide ownership of the limited-liability company into three parts. The community members would invest $500,000 and would own 20 percent of the membership interests. JCNI would maintain ownership of another 60 percent. Finally, the community members, with support from JCNI, created the Neighborhood Unity Foundation (NUF), a new resident-run 501(c)(3) foundation. This entity would buy the final 20 percent of the membership interests with money it raised and matching funds from the Jacobs Family Foundation.[7]

At this point, however, the community participation in the process came to a halt. A core team of lawyers and JCNI staff wrote the legal documents and in 2001 submitted them to the Department of Corporations, which was responsible for approving the permit for the offering.[8] George Harris, JCNI's former director of community ownership (2005–2009), explained that once the filing process began, "Those involved weren't legally allowed to talk to people about the offering."

"It's an issue of 'gun jumping,'" Jennifer Vanica elaborated. "The term comes from track and field. The Department of Corporations doesn't want you to get people hyped up to buy something before it's cleared the permit process."

As a result of this shutdown of communication, JCNI's relationship with the community began to fray. "We were doing the backroom thing, and the community started wondering what we were up to," Jennifer explained.

Further, Kurt Kicklighter reported feeling that the Department of Corporations viewed the application with cynicism. "I could feel the reviewer's eyes rolling in his head. He gave us back eighty-four things that needed to be modified."

One of the reviewer's primary concerns was that the effort was too risky for low-income first-time investors. "The Department of Corporations protects the general public from unscrupulous people who are looking to take people's money," outreach team member Kelly Steppe explained.

Kurt added, "At the time, the project did not look like a worthwhile investment. Businesses were still being set up. This was a huge project, with the Jacobs Family Foundation investing $20 million, and it had almost no cash flow." Jennifer elaborated, "The department wouldn't approve the permit for the offering until we were out of the high-risk stage of development."

Overcoming Roadblocks to Creating an Initial Public Offering

To address the concerns of both the community and the Department of Corporations, in 2003 JCNI found a legal mechanism to include a reconstituted and expanded small resident ownership team in the filing process. Although unable to divulge information to all community members, JCNI staff realized that by asking the ownership team members to provide consulting services and sign confidentiality agreements, they legally became "insiders" who could participate in the development of the offering.

"By reengaging the residents—this is when the magic started to happen," Jennifer Vanica noted.

JCNI also sponsored a series of resident team discussions and training workshops on investing. Its intent was to ensure that a broad range of residents would be able to understand the investment opportunity when it became available.

The community ownership team members who participated in the broader training then needed to reach consensus on the details of the offering—including who would be allowed to invest. Jennifer Vanica explained, "Ultimately, they agreed that investors had to either live or work in the neighborhood and be volunteering to improve the neighborhood in some way."

To increase democratic participation, the team also decided to include a clause stating that every member would receive only one vote, regardless of how much he or she had invested. "We didn't want an economic model where if you invest more you had a greater voice," lawyer Kurt Kicklighter explained.

To support the Jacobs foundations' sunset goals, residents built two exit strategies into the agreement. First, they determined that the NUF would aim to slowly replace the role the Jacobs foundations have played in the neighborhoods. Second, they included a clause allowing investors the option to buy out JCNI in 2018.[9]

Further, the resident ownership team worked with JCNI to make a host of modifications so as to meet California requirements. Kurt pointed to one example: "We had to carve out of the initial public offering the pieces of Market Creek Plaza that weren't profit-generating entities, like the amphitheatre and the creek."

"The biggest issue was not resolved until 2006," Kurt recalled. "It wasn't clear that the Department of Corporations would let us include first-time investors or people who were considered low income. We were ready to bus people up to Sacramento for a fairness hearing over it. But in the summer of 2006, senior officials at the Department of Corporations accepted a plan put forward by the ownership team we called the 10-10-10 plan. The plan said no one could invest more than 10 percent of their net income or 10 percent of their net worth, and the maximum investment would be capped at $10,000. They felt that took enough risk out."

"We also made community members preferred investors," Kurt added of another mechanism used to reduce investor risk. "The Neighborhood Unity Foundation [NUF] was next in line. JCNI wouldn't see a dime until the community members and NUF had been paid a 10 percent annual return of $50,000 each."

Reflecting on the journey, Kurt Kicklighter noted, "It kept me up at night. There were so many areas where we were pushing the envelope. People always say they want to work on something pioneering, but it's frightening, particularly as the legal adviser."

Transferring Ownership of the Plaza

With the plans moving forward, the next big question was, How many community members would actually invest? "Will we be so underwhelmed, no one will show up? Or will be so overwhelmed we have to turn people away?" George Harris recalled.

To generate interest, a team of residents worked to recruit community members. Some expressed immediate interest. Many, however, remained hesitant. Explaining the suspicion, George noted, "There is a history of being let down here. Many folks come to communities like this and make all these promises and then take people's money."

Indeed, at first it appeared that the years of labor spent on the initiative would be for naught. "We started the offering in June, and no one showed up," Valerie Jacobs recalled. By September I thought, 'Oh my gosh, we're going to fail.' We'd set an internal deadline of October 31, and legally we had to sell the shares by January 3, 2007."

The tide was about to turn, however. When children went back to school in September, suddenly mothers had more time to attend community outreach meetings, and the church networks began getting involved. "On October 31, there was a rush," Jennifer said. "We had people lined up down the street to invest their personal money. But we could only take 450 people, or $500,000, whichever came first, so a lot of people weren't able to invest."[10] Investments ranged from as much as $10,000 to as little as $200.

The limited-liability company made a $100,000 profit in the year following the close of the CD-IPO.[11] These profits were based on income from rent, as the company does not share in the profits of individual businesses on the block, Jennifer explained.

Several of the businesses were booming. "The Food 4 Less had become one of the best performing in the San Diego County district and was getting fifteen thousand customers a week," Jennifer noted.

By November 2007, the investors had received their first 10 percent payout. "And this was the most wonderful part," Valerie Jacobs said. "At the meeting, the president of the advisory board stood up and said, 'Here's my check. I'm going to figure out how I'm going to invest this in our community to make more money. Who wants to join me?' Half the people raised their hands. My dad, who had passed away a few years earlier, would have been blown away. They were looking at long-term asset building, which is exactly what he wanted."

Even more than the money, ownership of the development changed residents' self-perceptions. "Sometimes I'll hear my children tell their friends, 'My mom owns all this,'" Bevelynn said. "And the friends ask, 'Does she own the ice cream store too?' And they'll say, 'Yeah, and she can fire people, too.' Then I have to tell them that I can't hire and fire people, but I can have a say in the type of business that comes. And we can't eat ice cream free at Cold Stone. So don't be telling your friends they can eat at Cold Stone for free. But at the end of the year we'll get a return. When I was their age, I was talking about boys, and here they are talking about stocks and ownership."

A Place Called Home

Unlike the national businesses in the plaza, the small businesses have struggled to stay afloat. "It's really hard for local restaurants to compete with fast-food chains that can buy in bulk," Jennifer Vanica explained. "The chains get their inventory at such a discounted rate. They can spread their costs and weather economic storms. They have so much more capital to back them up."

She also noted that JCNI staff has encouraged the local restaurants to carry healthy food options, which have not always tapped well into the neighborhood market. "Demand went down when [local restaurant] Batter Up! switched its bucket of fried fish to a salad with salmon option. We're trying to balance health and demand. It's the conundrum of choosing whether one meets the market where it is or try to shape the market."

"To help them grow, we've given the businesses a lot of support," Jennifer continued. "We've helped with tax returns and financial statements, figuring out how to cut food costs, operational technical assistance, and vendor acquisition."

"Do you let them fold if they aren't successful?" Jennifer asked rhetorically. "It's a challenging question. We let the first business go down. If it's really not a viable business, you let people move to the next thing. But when they are generating substantial amounts of revenue but still not making a profit, do you help them weather economic storms?"

With respect to how much support to provide, Jennifer noted a common double standard. "There are these extremes in our society. Business is business for the little guys. But then we all chip in $700 billion to help the big guys out," she said, referring to the federal government's 2008 bailout of financial institutions.

As for the graffiti artists, they now have their own graffiti park, which is just across the street from the trolley station next to Market Creek Plaza. The towering walls of graffiti are attracting attention worldwide, and the site has been used for MTV, commercials, and photo shoots. The artists are receiving invitations to fly to events around the world—including a personal invitation from the vice president of Guam.[12] And they have established a thriving business painting designs for T-shirts, banners, and even the occasional sneaker. "One guy sent me Air Force One sneakers to paint. He gave them to his best friend, who wore them with his tux to his wedding," graffiti artist Jose Venegas recounted.

For Jose and many other youth, the work has saved their lives. "If not for this, I'd probably be gang banging and shooting people," Jose said.

In addition, residents had developed spaces in Market Creek Plaza to tell their stories through art, including putting their personal paintings in the stores. They also hung larger-than-life portraits of community residents—painted by community artists—on the exterior walls of the grocery store as a tribute to the community's unsung heroes.

In addition to Market Creek Plaza, in 2008 JCNI completed a conference center named the Joe & Vi Jacobs Center, which houses their new offices. On the other side of the twenty-acre property, the building overlooks the dry creek, now lush with native plants. A bucolic bridge arcing over the creek connects the building grounds to Market Creek Plaza.

"That we are here is big," Valerie reflected of the decision to move into the neighborhood back in 1998. "If you have an issue, you can come and talk to us."

Jennifer Vanica agreed, noting that the two foundations' location has been critical to addressing power differentials with community members. "When we first came, there was a feeling that there was a dollar sign plastered on our foreheads. But that's gone away partly because we are neighbors. People know we are here for the long haul."

The team predicts that the Joe & Vi Jacobs Center will generate hundreds of jobs for the community. The grand hall "seats 650 people for a sit-down dinner," Tracey Bryan, communications team member for JCNI, pointed out. The five-thousand-square-foot kitchen also doubles as a culinary academy, training residents for jobs in hospitality. "There is a whole wave of people looking for green and cultural gathering places."

"The response has been off the charts," Jennifer exclaimed. "Since we've opened the Center, the phones have been ringing off the hook. We're booked for six months out and had to put a hold on reservations to catch our breath."

"To make an economy expand, we need to bring outside dollars in and bounce every dollar seven times right here in our community," Jennifer explained of the theory behind the Joe & Vi Jacobs Center and Market Creek Plaza. "Somebody works at Food 4 Less, and they take their paycheck and have dinner at Magnolias. Then Magnolias buys their centerpieces at Where the World Meets, and Where the World Meets buys products from local vendors. Theoretically, if you can keep money in your community, your economy will expand."

Walking into the main lobby of the conference center, guests are greeted with large flags hanging from the cathedral ceilings, painted with vibrantly dressed men and women in national costumes dancing, drumming, and waving. Each flag has the word

"Welcome" written on it in one of the many languages represented in the neighborhood. On one lobby wall is a larger-than-life image of Joe Jacobs and his wife Vi sitting comfortably on a sofa, flashing warm smiles. On closer inspection, one realizes that the portrait is in fact made up of thousands of square-inch photographs of community members. "Joe and Vi were and are humble people. They would not want a tribute just to them," Tracey affirmed.

Future Plans

With these successes in place, JCNI and resident teams have been looking toward other opportunities. For example, many investors in Market Creek Plaza have pooled their profits into a community investment fund, which has locked their money into a certificate of deposit until another investment opportunity in their community emerges.

Jennifer Vanica smiled as she noted how she has come to think like a capitalist. "I think about Bill Gates and how he gained control of so much of the market. And then I start thinking about what we could do if we owned a larger market share—only in terms of social benefits and community control." She explains what she means with an example. "We've been trying to attract a pharmacy to open a branch on the land we are about to develop. But no one wanted to come because they wanted to be located on the main plaza. Then we told them we could give them an exclusive on the block, and suddenly everyone's outcompeting with each other with social benefits—living wages, guarantees on the numbers of residents they'll hire."

The foundations have also made a significant commitment to sharing learnings with other foundations and organizations interested in community empowerment. JCNI receives and helps coordinate tours of the plaza for roughly seven hundred such visitors a year on topics ranging from resident engagement and ownership to social enterprise and physical development.

As for both foundations' plans to sunset, the staff and board still talk about shutting their doors within the next thirty years. "We are a one-generation experiment," Jennifer noted. "We are always refining our exit strategies. We're trying to create community-controlled assets that can leverage future change when we're gone."

The Jacobs foundations see resident training as fundamental to preparing residents for the transfer. "They own the planning, and through that build vision and hope. They own the implementation strategies, which is how they are developing skills. And they own the assets, which is how they will leverage future change. There's that saying, 'Give a person a fish and feed them for a day. Teach them to fish and feed them for a lifetime.' We are teaching them to buy the pond and stock it in order to impact the next generation," Jennifer explained.

"Our job is to put people in the best possible position to make good decisions with their assets," continued George Harris, JCNI's former director of community ownership. "If when we're gone the community decides to sell Market Creek Plaza, then we have to trust it's because they see an opportunity that will provide the community greater value."

The foundations are, however, still far from their sunset goal. Despite risking much of the Jacobs Foundations' endowments to develop the block, and sharing ownership of the development with community members, the Jacobs Foundation and JCNI's assets have grown. Since buying the property in 1998, Joe Jacobs has endowed the foundations with a total of $143 million, including a venture capital firm that will transfer all its assets to the foundations in 2023.[13] Not counting the appreciation of the forty-five acres they've bought, today the two foundations' assets are roughly $171 million.

Conclusion

In 1997, the Jacobs Center for Neighborhood Innovation bought a twenty-acre blighted property for $3.1 million in a long-disinvested neighborhood in the Diamond Neighborhoods of southeastern San Diego.[14] By 2008, Market Creek Plaza was home to almost a dozen shops—both local businesses and franchises—and even an outdoor amphitheatre, and had become a source of wealth for the community. Market Creek Plaza alone had generated roughly two hundred jobs and $8 million in community contracts, and had recaptured $40 million of the previous $60 million in economic leakage from the community.[15]

The Jacobs foundations, together with residents, have also pioneered a community development initial public offering (CD-IPO).

The first of its kind, the CD-IPO has helped residents own a piece of the plaza, an important neighborhood asset.

In working with residents to create Market Creek Plaza, the foundations have been driven by a central question: "How do you take a blighted piece of land that no one believes has any value, give it value, and then keep that value in the community?" George Harris noted. Community control of assets has been a key answer to that question.

"If we'd just focused on constructing buildings, the blight would have likely just moved to the next neighborhood," Jennifer reflected. "But the community teams were solving these problems instead of just displacing them. Instead of just pushing the gangs to the next neighborhood, for example, people were transforming themselves."

Another key ingredient to their success has been a willingness to reject typical foundation wealth management strategies. Instead of focusing on preserving capital and granting out investment income, the Jacobs Family Foundation decided to leverage most of its capital to help residents bring value to a blighted property. An intention to sunset has also spurred the foundations, together with residents, to pioneer ownership mechanisms aimed at keeping wealth in the community.

Continually relearning the importance of building strong partnerships with community members, the foundations have helped residents become authors of a new community story, one far removed from the one of crime and violence that had dominated this neighborhood only a short decade earlier. "We were the forgotten people," Bevelynn recalled. "This was the neighborhood you ended up in if you didn't make it." Today, graffiti is almost nonexistent. Crime is down. Gangs have declared the area neutral territory. Pedestrians who used to shut themselves in their homes by five in the evening to avoid getting caught in gang violence are out at night. Cultural diversity, which had been a source of tension, has become something to be celebrated.

Along the back of the outdoor amphitheatre is a wall with a sculpted copper tree on it. "It's a tree of life," Jennifer explained. Thousands of round tiles adorn its branches, each with a drawing done by a child living in the neighborhood. Asked to draw pictures of what nature meant to them, the children have drawn butterflies, children playing on river banks, smiling suns, and big yellow flowers, which beam out from the tiles. The tree stands tall as a testament to what this community—with support from foundations and others—has accomplished within a decade.

Lessons Learned

The Jacobs Family Foundation and the Jacobs Center for Neighborhood Innovation have worked with residents to successfully transform blighted neighborhoods into a vibrant urban center. The following are a few lessons in how they helped catalyze one of the most remarkable urban neighborhood turnarounds in the country.

- Leverage all your assets, not just a percentage of investment income.
- Instead of simply providing an income source through yearly grants, help nonprofits and residents build their assets, and support initiatives that keep wealth in neighborhoods.
- Build relationships with community residents and give them an opportunity to make core decisions.
- When at an impasse with family members regarding what to fund, identify common values that bridge differences and consider ways to blend divergent interests (such as through aiding business ventures that target low-income communities).
- Strengthen feedback loops and your own accountability to those you're supporting.

PART
THREE

Aiding an Identity-Based Movement

Giving to build the social, economic, and political power of a constituency is another way for foundations to engage in work that can lead to systems change in support of equity and justice. Immigrants, indigenous peoples, youth, and women are all examples of such constituencies.

Funders are attracted to such funding for many reasons. Commonly foundation staff are motivated by a belief in fairness and a desire to redress injustices toward a particular group. Often they also see tremendous innovation and vision emerging from particular constituencies, and want to strengthen this work. Sometimes staff and trustees find that supporting a constituency helps meet their need for program focus, while honoring grantees' desires to determine their own priorities.

If you are concerned about helping particular groups of people become stronger and more active citizens, the stories of the Ford Foundation and the Open Society Institute are particularly relevant. In the 1980s, the Ford Foundation helped support interest among a broad group of professionals in the economic, social, and human rights of immigrants. The Open Society Institute, the Ford Foundation, and others later assisted immigrants themselves to organize in ways that have helped this group influence local, state, and national dialogues.

Both stories also hold many insights if you are seeking ways to encourage your foundation to move beyond a focus largely on humanitarian assistance and services for particular constituencies. For the Ford Foundation, the Indochinese refugee crisis in the 1980s triggered dialogue among board members regarding an appropriate response. Staff then used this interest to move the foundation beyond a focus on largely humanitarian and resettlement assistance, place the refugee crisis within the larger context of rising immigration within the United States, and create a program to respond. The Open Society Institute's initial interest in immigrants also arose from a crisis—the welfare reform laws of 1996 that took away the rights of many legal residents to social services. Staff helped shape that foundation's response to include support not only for grantees helping naturalize these residents, but also for those aiding them to become active and engaged citizens with the organizational capacity to defend their economic, social, and human rights.

5

Supporting the Development of an Immigrant Rights Field

The Case of the Ford Foundation

During a Ford Foundation leadership transition in the late 1970s and early 1980s, staff members proposed an expansion of their support for immigrants. The resulting program helped grantees build an immigration field in the United States.

The Ford Foundation was established in 1936 with a $25,000 initial gift from Edsel Ford, the son of carmaker Henry Ford. Bequests by Edsel and Henry Ford in 1943 and 1947, respectively, made the foundation the largest of its day and catalyzed an expansion of its mandate to operate as an international institution.

As part of this growth, in the early 1950s the foundation began to support refugees fleeing war-torn countries (primarily from World War II).[1]

In the late 1970s, shortly after the fall of Saigon, as part of a crisis-driven approach to refugees, trustees challenged staff to increase their humanitarian and resettlement giving for refugees flowing out of Indochina, recalled Frank Sutton, former deputy vice president for the International Division, who retired from the

Ford Foundation Snapshot

Type: Private foundation

Year founded: 1936

Initial gift to foundation (1936): $25,000

Grant range (2007): $5,000–$8,000,000

Total grants awarded (2007): $655.9 million

Total grants awarded by immigrant rights portfolio (2007, U.S. only): $4.2 million

Foundation investment portfolio (2007): $13.5 billion

Geographic focus: Domestic and International

Primary funding areas: Peace and social justice; asset building and community development; knowledge, creativity, and freedom

Staff (2008): 341

Location: Headquarters in New York, with offices in Brazil, Chile, Mexico, Kenya, Egypt, Indonesia, India, Vietnam, China, Russia, South Africa, and Nigeria.

Note: Snapshot information for each chapter varies depending on data available. Dates refer to either the calendar year or the end of the fiscal cycle. For snapshot sources, refer to the Notes section at the end of the book.[2]

foundation in 1983. "Raiders were coming aboard ships and robbing and raping refugees. The board wanted to do something." Frank recollected that several trustees wanted to give direct assistance to the refugees, including providing them with transportation out of Indochina.

Yet Frank, like several others in the Ford Foundation's International Division, was concerned about becoming too embroiled in the Indochinese refugee situation. "Refugees were a natural thing for the foundation to get engaged in, but we were cautious because we didn't want to get involved with humanitarian assistance to refugees on an ongoing basis," he said. "Generally, we wanted to understand the causes of the disease, not treat the symptoms. We wanted to help people make India function well and bring Indonesia out of the doldrums."

Some staff also felt concerned that the Ford Foundation's existing focus on refugees was too narrow. "The foundation was treating the refugee problem as if it was a sporadic thing, instead of recognizing it as a chronic disease," Frank Sutton noted, pointing to the many refugees and immigrants that had entered the United States during the 1970s. "The idea of continued violence and failed states was not prominent among foundations at the time."

IMMIGRATION GROWTH IN THE UNITED STATES

Immigration in the United States changed dramatically in the late 1970s and beyond, according to Frank Sharry, former executive director of the National Immigration Forum. "Very few refugees were let into the U.S. from the 1920s to the 1960s, but all this changed after that. There was the Mariel boat lift in Cuba in 1980 [when some 125,000 Cubans crossed the Florida Straits to the United States], the wars in Central America, the currency devaluation and rural dislocation in Mexico."

Undocumented immigrant communities were also increasing. According to the Pew Hispanic Center, in 1980 there were an estimated three million undocumented immigrants in the country. By 2005, that number had risen to eleven million.[3]

According to Daranee Petsod, executive director of Grantmakers Concerned with Immigrants and Refugees, "U.S. policies, compounded by globalization and immigration laws, contributed to the large rise in the undocumented immigrant population." Such policies, she noted, included the wars in Southeast Asia, and trade agreements with Mexico, particularly in the 1990s. "Many Mexican farmers lost their lands as cheap food imports flooded their markets, forcing many to migrate to the U.S. to support their families. Although there is high demand for their low-skilled labor, very few avenues exist for them to enter the United States legally."

Creating a Program

Frank Sutton's concerns regarding the trustees' proposals placed him in a difficult position. "The leadership was pushing for some kind of active engagement, and I was a staff guy, and supposed to defer to the trustees. Yet I was trying to push against the impatience of the trustees to do something."

Frank, together with other staff members in the International Division, decided to write a paper to present to the trustees, requesting roughly half a million dollars, in addition to monies that had already been approved, to open an immigration program that looked beyond individual refugee crises toward longer-term solutions.[4] "Barry Gaberman [deputy vice president for U.S. and international affairs in 1984 and senior vice president between 1996 and 2007] needled me for writing a fifty-page paper for such a tiny request," Frank recalled.

"It started with Adam and Eve as the first migrants, which led me to the concern that he might be naming every one since then," Barry joked.

"But the paper had a much larger intention," Frank continued. "It was meant to help create a program. It was a terrible time for foundations because of stagflation. It was very hard to start things because the value of the foundation's corpus kept going down." In fact, between the mid-1970s and early 1980s, foundation presidents McGeorge Bundy and Franklin Thomas reduced staff size by more than half.[5]

The paper was a success, and in 1983, Ford launched a major expansion of its refugee and immigrant work, in part with the intent of supporting the emergence of a stronger immigration field.[6]

"The paper had impact because it was a time of transition," Barry explained. "Frank Sutton wrote it during a two-year period between mid-1979 and mid-1981, when Frank Thomas [who had become the foundation's president in 1979] was coming to grips with the institution and the direction he wanted to go. Generally people are so stretched that the premium is on writing short and analytic pieces. The archives of the foundation are filled with long and wonderful analytical pieces that didn't create change because pieces like these only have impact during an upheaval."

An immigrant and refugee program presented an opportunity to forward another top priority for Frank Thomas: to break down divisions within the foundation, particularly between domestic and international work. "Immigration was an opportunity to break down the silos," Frank Thomas explained. "The international offices were dealing with an issue that had so many domestic implications."

The new immigration work focused on long-term field building, and included a strong focus on immigrant rights. "People were realizing that migration flows would continue, migrants would always be vulnerable, and that lasting protection of immigrant rights needed institutional infrastructure," explained Taryn Higashi, former deputy director of the foundation's human rights unit.

"Internationally we were already starting to shift away from a classic development agenda, such as economic development and agricultural production," Barry Gaberman noted. Foundation staff, he continued,

> were increasingly concerned that, without looking at human rights, the foundation could merrily go along and justify agricultural gains and economic growth without reference to the repressive nature of the regimes we were working with. We could avoid all the data that showed that our work was only reaching the elite in those countries, that foundation support was in fact helping accelerate inequality and concentrating resources in the hands of a few. We could show all sorts of progress in the aggregate. But when we put on a social justice lens, we couldn't just look at the aggregate. We had to also look at the distributional equity of things. This new approach married the development process to the importance of strengthening the rule of law.

With the program and its basic focus established, the Ford Foundation hired three individuals to support the work, including Diana Morris, who joined the foundation in 1982 as part of a wave of new hires under Frank Thomas's leadership and who retired in 1991. Diana's work focused on immigrant rights in the United States, which by the mid-1990s had become the entire focus of the U.S. component of the immigration program.

"The job was really exciting," Diana recounted. "We had been tasked with helping support the emergence of an immigration field."

Developing a Field

Diana Morris focused primarily on supporting a body of profession-als who were interpreting and implementing new legislation in ways that protected immigrant rights. "The 1980s was a time when immi-gration law was being shaped, so it was important for grantees to be able to influence *how* it was interpreted," she recalled, pointing to the passage of the Refugee Act of 1980 (which systematized U.S. immigration). Before we started our funding, there weren't a lot of people concerned with protecting refugees and immigrants that were contributing to the development of the law."

To support the literature, Diana provided funding to lawyers, which allowed them to more easily take time away from their prac-tice to write. Illustrating the types of issues lawyers would address, she noted, "At that time Congress was contemplating giving Central American immigrants temporary status, but not permanent status. So the foundation gave people funding to write about different types of status. The work ensured that there were different ideas out there on how to shape temporary statuses, and this then helped to shape policy."

Diana noted that the research was effective in part because it was conducted not only by academics and policy analysts but also by lawyers who were litigating cases. They'd be doing research one day, and the next day they would be in the courtroom, so they knew what issues were most pertinent, and could use that research to bolster their cases."

The foundation also supported grantees helping key individu-als develop a commitment to immigrants. "Grantees got private-practice lawyers across the country involved in pro bono work helping immigrants in need," Diana said. "The work was really important, not only for providing a direct service but also for rais-ing the consciousness of a lot of lawyers."

"We supported a wide range of people who became very aware of immigrant issues—policy people, academics, lawyers," Diana said. "They were deliberately very diverse." The National Immigra-tion Forum, an important grantee founded in 1982, helped orga-nize many of these diverse groups.[7] Many grants were provided as general operating support.

Securing Important Wins

In the 1980s, as the immigrant rights field continued to build, advocates claimed several victories. These included the landmark 1982 U.S. Supreme Court ruling *Plyler v. Doe*.[8] Filed by foundation grantee Mexican American Legal Defense and Educational Fund (MALDEF), the case guaranteed undocumented children the right to a free public elementary and secondary education. Mary McClymont noted that the immigration program helped support implementation of the ruling. In another important case litigated by MALDEF and others, *Leticia A. v. Board of Regents*, the California courts ruled in 1985 that undocumented immigrants could attend colleges in California.

In addition, President Reagan signed the Immigration Reform and Control Act of 1986 (IRCA), which included provisions to legalize millions of undocumented immigrants.[9] "There would have probably been some form of legalization [if Ford Foundation grantees had not been involved]," reflected Charles Kamasaki, vice president of the National Council of la Raza, "but a lot more people ultimately received legal status than would have without the existence of grantees funded by Ford." The legislation, however, also increased border enforcement and heavily penalized employers who hired undocumented workers, which many individuals felt increased civil rights violations and workplace raids across the country.

Congress did not include proposed language that likely would have required every person authorized to work in the United States to have a national ID card, according to Charles Kamasaki. Senator Alan Simpson (a bill sponsor) and others had advocated for more secure means of verifying immigration status to keep noncitizens from working in the country. "Senator Simpson argued that this was a huge loophole, and there was some merit to his concern," Charles continued.

Weathering Political Storms

As discussions regarding the Immigration Reform and Control Act of 1986 unfolded, several prominent individuals grew uneasy with the foundation's support of some of the organizations working in support of immigrant rights. "There was controversy," Frank Sharry (former executive director of the National Immigration Forum) recalled.

"[At a meeting with Ford Foundation president Frank Thomas] I told them, 'You can be compassionate, but let's not be stupid," recalled former senator Alan Simpson (R-WY)—a sponsor for the Immigration Reform and Control Act of 1986. "Just start giving to the other side too."

"People picketed outside our New York offices [because of the support we were providing]," Mary McClymont added.

Also in the mid-1980s, Congress grew concerned that a couple of immigrant rights groups were not sufficiently aware of restrictions related to using foundation dollars for lobbying purposes. In response, the Ford Foundation held a series of meetings with grantees to ensure that they were adhering to regulations.

Within the context of federal codes limiting lobbying, there are ways for most organizations receiving foundation dollars to lobby while adhering to regulations, explained John Pomeranz of the firm Harmon, Curran, Spielberg & Eisenberg and attorney for the Center for Community Change. Consult with your legal council to determine giving that is appropriate for your foundation or organization.

Of the controversy, Frank Thomas (former Ford Foundation president) recounted, "Some of our staff got upset. But I needed to stay reasonably calm and focused. If I overreacted, I'd have been throwing away the baby with the bathwater. I needed to be able to step back amidst all this heat and say, 'If we can't support these organizations, then who can?' It also meant keeping trustees informed so they weren't blindsided." He added, "Though I probably felt more emotion than I'm remembering."

"What I was always comforted by was that what we were facilitating was in the great spirit and tradition of the United States. When enabling people to do what was in the interest of the country, the fact that we took heat was all part of the process. The key was to stay clear about the larger purpose."

WITHSTANDING CONTROVERSY

With regard to the controversy stirred by the foundation's immigration work, Barry Gaberman reflected, "When we created the program, there were lots of voices that pointed out that this was controversial and risky. But no one that I recall made the argument that because of that we shouldn't be involved. We've taken on many sensitive issues over the years."

Mary McClymont elaborated: "What impressed me so much was that the leadership of Ford stuck with our immigrant rights work despite the constant scrutiny from outside the foundation before and during my tenure."

"One of the attributes of foundations has been their ability to take on sensitive issues that public and private institutions can't take on," Barry continued. "They can afford to take on risk and fail. They can stick with things for a long time. They can support demonstration and pilot projects to test out new ideas and innovations.

"We all know that in reality foundations haven't always done that. They've jumped to follow the new fad. They've avoided sensitive issues. Something that has been rewarding to me about the Ford Foundation has been that it has been fairly true to adhering to those values—of supporting innovation, shouldering risk, and sticking with things."

A Field into a Movement

The controversy did not sway the foundation from its commitment to refugees and immigrants. "We made a very large contribution to support the implementation of [the Immigration Reform and Control Act of 1986 (IRCA)]," noted Mary McClymont, who took over the immigrant rights portfolio from Diana Morris in 1988.[10]

As part of her tenure, Mary deepened work begun by colleagues at the foundation supporting local and state coalitions that were organizing immigrants for action. "We wanted to support organizations that would not only advocate for, but also increase the participation of, immigrants in American society."

Although Mary didn't realize it at the time, she later reflected that grantees and others were helping "create the beginnings of a social movement." The immigrant rights work, up to this point, had been primarily focused on building a field of largely paid professionals who could act as advocates for immigrant rights. As local and state organizations began organizing immigrants themselves, the field began to transform into a movement. Of the distinction between a field and a movement, Mary explained, "a field usually includes research and legal work, and may include community-based organizations. A social movement, however, includes spontaneous action by the grass roots. The immigrant rights movement needed the initial infrastructure to emerge. The spark that then ignited the movement and people mobilizing was the legislation passed in 1986."

Frank Sharry continued, "Ford began to support immigrant rights coalitions in gateway cities for immigrants across the country."

"The public pressure that these coalitions brought to bear was critical. The national groups did do this, but when this was compounded by regional and local groups, the pressure [for policy change] was much greater," Diana Morris added.

"We wanted to ensure that the growing infrastructure had sources of funding," Mary noted. "When I started there were only a few steady funders on immigration issues—Joyce Mertz Gilmore, Rosenberg, and a few others."

To support local organizations, the foundation created funding pools across the country; further, in 1990 Mary teamed up with the Rosenberg, Irvine, Joyce Mertz Gilmore, St. Paul, Hyams, Boston, and Mellon foundations as well as the New York Community Trust and others to create a national affinity group called Grantmakers Concerned with Immigrants and Refugees (GCIR).

By the early 1990s, Mary McClymont had also begun to recommend funding for emerging immigrant leaders who were becoming important players in the movement. "It was important for individuals to speak for themselves," she explained. "They knew their own problems and could best speak about them. Ford believed in people organizing and speaking for their own communities. It was critical to support them as they created their own organizations."

Marjorie Fine, former executive director of the Veatch Program, noted that this shift toward supporting immigrants themselves was reflective of a larger trend in philanthropy happening at the time.

"Philanthropy as a whole was changing, reflecting the backgrounds of people being hired as foundation directors and program officers. They brought with them a greater appreciation of how to effect deep social change by including those most affected in developing and carrying out strategies, so that they could be their own change agents. Advocacy, organizing, and building strong organizations were viewed as central components of an effective philanthropic strategy—not as an add-on."

As immigrant numbers swelled, national anti-immigrant sentiment also grew, and Mary responded by supporting communications trainings for immigrant leaders. "We funded the Communications Consortium Media Center, a public interest media center, and the National Immigration Forum," adding that these organizations worked with a broad range of partners to help develop messaging for the press about why immigrants were "important to our country and what they brought. I think this was groundbreaking in its time to bring together leaders who were both immigrants and American-born to forge common messages."

Thus the foundation moved from initially funding primarily nonimmigrant-led organizations in the 1980s to ones run by immigrants themselves in the 1990s. "We started out with a set of people and built our support from there. There was the first generation, and then the second generation. As the movement grew, it was apparent that there were more and more immigrants that wanted and were able to lead their communities," Mary McClymont recalled.

Rising U.S. Opposition to Immigration

As pro-immigrant organizations grew, so too did groups concerned with the rising tide of immigrants into the country. "In the 1990s, the suburbs became the nontraditional gateway for immigrants," noted Darren Sandow, executive director of the Long Island–based Horace Hagedorn Foundation, a supporter of immigrant rights. "That caused a lot of friction. These usually started as meaningful local concerns—men littering, and urinating in public, and congregating in large numbers at the local 7-11s, and living in overcrowded housing. Then politicians would react by pointing fingers, and meaningful concerns quickly transformed into real tensions."

These would be further enflamed, Darren continued, by national groups organizing local citizens and connecting them to national networks, including "hate groups."

Looking back, Frank Thomas (former foundation president) commented that he wished that Ford had better anticipated the depth of these rising concerns and worked harder to address them. "We probably paid less attention than was needed to helping people communicate with those who would become disaffected by the new arrivals. We needed to be clearer that what was progress by one group of people could have some adverse effects on another group. Maybe we could have supported more of the storytelling—highlighting the examples of the people who were succeeding, and helping others see that this was larger than their experience. Maybe we could have included more development assistance to those who were not at the absolute bottom of the structure, but were also struggling. We were helping those with the greatest need, but there was an accompanying need to better help the larger society understand this and see it as progress and in line with our collective needs and aspirations."

Conclusion

By the mid-1990s, the immigration field was transforming into a movement, with hundreds of immigrant organizations emerging across the country. The Ford, Joyce Mertz Gilmore, Rosenberg, Russell Sage, Andrew W. Mellon, McKnight, and James Irvine foundations; the Carnegie Corporation of New York; and the Veatch Program all supported organizations as they grew and contributed to this shift.

Many believed that the Ford Foundation played a particularly critical role, often through general operating support grants, in helping people develop the infrastructure that supported the movement. "There was a reason that Ford has been subject to such criticism," affirmed Frank Sharry (formerly with the National Immigration Forum). "They had the guts to fund civil rights and litigation efforts, national policy development forums, and—after the Immigration and Control Act of 1986—to invest in small communities and immigrant coalitions in gateway cities."

These organizations in turn helped shape reaction to the increasing flow of immigrants into the country. Lawyers helped ensure that the interpretation of emerging laws recognized the rights of new Americans. Immigrant leaders began to shape public opinion, speaking through the media and other public channels about the contributions this constituency was making to the country. Through immigrant-led organizations, many were also learning about rights and finding a voice in their communities, their states, and their nation.

However, these gains were countered by a growing lobby concerned with the increasing numbers of undocumented immigrants entering the country, and were complicated by globalization, loss of domestic jobs to offshore locations, and a broad recession. Despite significant wins, immigrants and their advocates found that they were fighting against an increasingly strong movement to roll back immigrant rights. Chapter Six examines how the foundation community responded to the growing backlash against immigrants that swept across the country in the mid-1990s and beyond.

Lessons Learned

The Ford Foundation played an instrumental role in supporting critical organizations as they spurred a movement around one of the most controversial topics in the United States—immigrant rights. How might your foundation contribute to growing a movement?

- Choose an area that has a large natural constituency, and then fund not only allies, but the constituency itself.
- If controversy arises, help trustees and staff stay focused on larger goals and values, particularly those shared by critics. Remember that foundations are less vulnerable than most other institutions and therefore better positioned to take risks.
- To prepare for controversy, develop a plan for how to respond, including working with trustees and staff.
- Find ways to support grantees as they build new interest in the constituency or topic, for example among lawyers and researchers.

6

Maturing
an Immigrant Movement

The Case of the Open Society Institute

After reading about the devastating impact the 1996 welfare reform laws would have on immigrant families, George Soros decided to commit $50 million to support immigrants in the United States. Revitalizing a beleaguered field, this money helped organizers lay the groundwork for the marches of millions of immigrants in the United States in 2006.

In 1996, three laws were passed that significantly changed the landscape for the immigrant movement: the Personal Responsibility and Work Opportunity Reconciliation Act, commonly known as the welfare reform law; the Illegal Immigration Reform and Immigrant Responsibility Act; and the Antiterrorism and Effective Death Penalty Act. These laws "dramatically restricted immigrants' due process and other fundamental rights, kept many legal immigrants from accessing public benefits, and made citizenship more central to the receipt of benefits," explained Taryn Higashi, former deputy director of the Ford Foundation's human rights unit and program officer for refugee and immigrant rights. According to

Bill Ong Hing, founder of the Immigrant Legal Resource Center, the welfare reform bill was projected to save $53.4 billion; 44 percent of those savings would come from eliminating immigrants' access to welfare programs.[1]

Taryn commented, "It was a historic and dark moment for both the legal and undocumented immigrant communities, which called for an extraordinary response from the foundation community." The Open Society Institute (OSI), a foundation founded by George Soros in 1993, joined a core group of national, regional, and local foundations and religious institutions already funding immigrant work. These included the Rockefeller, Joyce Mertz-Gilmore, Ford, Abelard, Rosenberg, Otto Bremer, Bush, and Joyce foundations, as well as the Unitarian Universalist Veatch Program, Carnegie Corporation of New York, and several members of the Funding Exchange Network.[2]

Targeting $50 Million to the Immigrant Field

Shortly after the 1996 laws were passed, George Soros read an article in the *New York Times*. "He read that a family of legal residents, who had played by the rules, was going to lose access to benefits because of welfare reform," Antonio Maciel, former director of the OSI's U.S. Justice Fund, recalled.

Moved by the article, Soros, an immigrant himself, "decided to give away a high-profile $50 million over a period of a few years to help," Antonio explained. "He wanted to use the funding to bring attention to the fact that welfare cuts were falling on the backs of immigrants."

"At that time there was maybe $10 million a year going into the [immigration] field," recalled Frank Sharry, former executive director of the National Immigration Forum.

"So when Soros said he was going to create a new $50 million fund, this was very big news. It was a shot in the arm to advocates who were burned out and beleaguered," Antonio added. "[Soros] immediately convened a meeting with leaders in the immigration field. The feeling was that the best way for immigrants to protect their rights and access to public programs was to become citizens, so that became the programmatic focus."

Within two months, Soros had hired Antonio Maciel to run the fund, and had named it the Emma Lazarus Fund. Emma Lazarus was the famous American poet whose sonnet "The New Colossus" began with the famous words "Give me your tired, your poor/Your huddled masses yearning to breathe free." The poem is engraved on the Statue of Liberty, the symbol of hope that had attracted immigrants from so many parts of the world to the United States.

Open Society Institute Snapshot

Type: Private operating foundation

OSI's U.S. programs founding date: 1993

Total grants awarded by OSI's U.S. programs through 2007: $948.1 million

OSI's U.S. programs assets: OSI offices do not have endowments

Primary funding areas for OSI's U.S. programs (2007): Human rights, justice, and equal opportunity

Geographic focus: Domestic

Staff size for OSI's U.S. programs (2007): Sixty-one

Location: New York City; OSI has offices in New York, Budapest, London, and other locations, which provide support to independent OSI Soros foundations in thirty-two countries.

Emma Lazarus Fund grant range (1997–2000): $10,000–$3 million

Total funds awarded by Emma Lazarus Fund (1997–2000): $50 million

OSI immigration program grant range (2001–2007): $25,000–$1.7 million

OSI immigration program grants awarded (2001–2007): $14.3 million

Note: Snapshot information for each chapter varies depending on data available. Dates refer to either the calendar year or the end of the fiscal cycle. For snapshot sources, refer to the Notes section at the end of the book.[3]

Determining the Strategic Focus for the Fund

Antonio immediately found he was at odds with Soros over strategy. "George wanted a lot of the money to pay for filing fees immigrants were paying to apply for citizenship," Antonio recalled. "But I was hoping that as much of the money as possible would go toward supporting immigrants in their efforts to advocate for their rights."

Antonio sought allies for his approach within OSI. "I spoke with Gara LaMarche, director of OSI's U.S. programs at the time, and others who understood that if we weren't supporting immigrants' ability to seek policy changes through collective action, the impact of that money would not go beyond the individuals who were helped. The main question we asked Soros was, 'What was going to be the long-lasting impact? We could help a lot more people by supporting immigrants in their efforts to address the underlying policies that were working against them, particularly those that excluded legal permanent residents from government assistance programs."

"Soros heard this," Antonio recalled. "And he said OK—but that no more than 10 percent of the money could go to advocacy and organizing. I thought that was great; $5 million was a significant number." Antonio noted that most such grants would be provided as general operating support.

With regard to the remaining 90 percent of the funds, Antonio and other staff members also raised concerns that paying for filing fees would not help significant numbers of immigrants become citizens. "Soros wanted to help the individual," explained Antonio. "We convinced him that filing fees were not the main problem. Even low-income individuals could generally afford the then roughly $100 application fee," Antonio noted. "What immigrants needed were advocates who could help them move effectively through an often complicated and confusing maze of government bureaucracies, from figuring out what benefits they were still eligible for, to filling out accurately the application form for naturalization, and submitting it appropriately."

As he thought about how to proceed, Antonio Maciel harbored worries about quickly injecting $50 million into the immigration field. "It was risky, especially for a field like immigration that only

WHY SOME FUNDERS SHY AWAY FROM SOCIAL CHANGE WORK

Antonio Maciel reflected,

> How do you reconcile the desire to help individuals and see the direct results of that help through a direct service with efforts to ensure that immigrants can organize and advocate for their rights? [The latter strategy] also helps the individuals, and has more lasting results, but you can't clearly trace the events that led to that result.
>
> This comes up a lot with new funders, particularly with people who have made their money. They are used to being risk takers in the business setting, and seeing direct financial results from the money they've invested. But when they apply that model to philanthropy, it doesn't always work. The chain doesn't track through that easily. How do you measure results in a long-term advocacy and organizing campaign where results are long in coming? How do you measure something that didn't happen because of an intervention? How do you measure social justice results for someone who's used to counting numbers? The focus on measurable and direct results has perverse results. Many individuals who were risk takers in the business world become very safe funders. To measure social justice you have to use proxies—the number of stories in the media, testimonies filed. Are grantees getting better access to decision makers? Is legislation being passed?

had a few sources of money, and where many of the organizations were so young," he noted. "If we gave a $200,000 organization a $2 million grant, they would build their staff and change their processes to absorb that money. But if our money dried up in two years, what would they do? The infrastructure would either collapse or contract unless they secured new funding sources." In addition, Antonio had seen grantees hastily develop new leadership and accounting mechanisms to accommodate grants too large for their existing capacity. Often these organizations, and their programs, had faltered.

To address his concern that grantees would grow too quickly, Antonio wanted to offer many organizations small grants that they

could easily absorb. "But we didn't have the staff capacity to monitor lots of grants," he noted. "And I couldn't staff up. The board
wanted this program to be as lean as possible."

ASSESSING WHETHER A SMALL GRANTEE CAN ABSORB A LARGE GRANT

Marjorie Fine, former head of the Veatch Program, noted that
funders are often able to make accurate assessments of whether a
small organization can effectively absorb a large grant. "Often it's a
question of assessing whether they have a good plan, good leadership, and whether it is the right moment. Is the group at a particular
place and ready to grow? If they are, you don't want to hold them
back," she noted. "Is the organization already in motion? Do they
have the capacity to move their plan forward? Is it a moment when
a strong infusion of money will help them grow? If you always give
small groups small grants, then they will *stay* small."

Developing a Regranting Strategy

Antonio Maciel needed a plan that would address his concerns
while also working within the OSI board's parameters. In response,
Antonio and his colleagues proposed granting most of the money
to local funders and immigrant networks to regrant. "We also suggested that in most cases we require matching funds," Antonio
recalled.

The intermediary strategy had several advantages. Involving
others built funder commitment toward immigrants, which Antonio hoped would help sustain the new infrastructure developed
with the $50 million fund. By harnessing the knowledge and
expertise of local funders across the country to effectively choose
local grantees, the strategy also saved Antonio from having to hire
staff. Finally, the structure kept most of the money flowing to local
efforts, critical during a time when policy impacts were being felt
so acutely at the local level.

With respect to organizing and advocacy, giving money to intermediaries had another advantage. "Of the $50 million I granted

out, I gave about $5 million in direct grants to policy, advocacy, and organizing groups," Antonio recounted. "But in the $45 million that I gave to intermediaries, I let the intermediaries devote 10 percent of *their* funding for advocacy and organizing. So even though the grants to the intermediary organizations were considered 'service' grants, many of the intermediaries were actually using up to 10 percent of their grant for local organizing and policy work."

To implement the intermediary strategy and gauge funder interest, Antonio flew to Chicago and more than a dozen other cities with high immigrant populations. "I was astounded by how interested local funders in Chicago were," recalled Chicago-based funder Alice Cottingham, who was a member of Grantmakers Concerned with Immigrants and Refugees. "After Antonio spoke to us, one funder said, 'We've talked about creating a pooled fund for a long time and never done it. Now we've got urgency, the opportunity to increase the value of our contribution with national money, and a clear focus.'" In response, in early 1997 a group of Chicago-based funders created a funding collaborative called the Fund for Immigrants and Refugees. "Antonio gave us $1.5 million. We raised an additional $5.3 million [from twenty-seven funders]," noted Alice Cottingham, who became head of the fund.[4]

Funding an Advocacy and Organizing Agenda

As he implemented the citizenship grantmaking strategy, Antonio Maciel also began to shape the program's advocacy and organizing work, which he realized he could frame as part of OSI's efforts to help immigrants become citizens. Encouraged by individuals such as Margie McHugh, former executive director of the New York Immigration Coalition, Antonio began to realize that "we didn't just want them to become citizens. We wanted to give them the tools to be *engaged* citizens." By expanding the definition of what being a citizen meant, Antonio helped encourage Soros to embrace the fund's advocacy and organizing work as an extension of Soros's own desire to help immigrants naturalize.

Antonio began to look toward city and state coalitions across the country to see who was helping immigrants engage in daily political life and had the capacity to absorb up to $1 million, primarily in general operating support grants. Such grants would provide organizations greater flexibility in how they used the money. Grantees included the New York Immigration Coalition, the Coalition for Humane Immigrant Rights of Los Angeles (CHIRLA), and the Illinois Coalition for Immigrant and Refugee Rights (ICRR).

In addition to their city- and state-level work, OSI, the Ford Foundation, and others supported these coalitions' efforts to develop a national agenda. "From the mid-1990s to 2000 or so, [these foundations] made a small investment to allow coalition directors to meet regularly," noted Margie McHugh (New York Immigration Coalition). "This had remarkable payoff."

Added Taryn Higashi (Unbound Philanthropy; formerly with the Ford Foundation), "Politicians began seeing that their local constituents cared about this issue."

In the meetings, coalition directors were able to share their weaknesses and explore where their needs might differ from those of their national counterparts. For example, Margie noted that when welfare reform was taking shape, the local organizations and state coalitions began caucusing to develop responses to the various proposals, well before most national immigrant groups took up the issue.

Internal Tensions

As local and state-level organizations developed their own policy platforms, internal tensions grew within the immigrant movement. "National and local groups were all kisses in the early nineties, but then it was a cold war in the late nineties," Frank Sharry (formerly with the National Immigration Forum) joked.

The rift occurred fundamentally over strategy. "Now that the local groups were a factor, unfortunately there wasn't a lot of realism about what was happening on the Hill," Frank believed. "[With the passing of the Illegal Immigration Reform and Immigrant Responsibility Act of 1996,] we had lost in the Senate by a landslide. So a number of national groups said we needed to take a more pragmatic approach. Many national groups began acknowledging that illegal immigration was a problem and that targeted enforcement was appropriate. Many local groups felt that this was heretical."

One factor that ultimately helped the groups negotiate these tensions was communication. Such foundations and religious institutions as Carnegie Corporation of New York, the Veatch Program, OSI, and others responded to immigrant groups' pleas for funds to support dialogue. As a result, "there became an assumption that there would be regular meetings between local, state, and national groups. This was a major change, as even a few years earlier there was almost no money for this," Margie McHugh (New York Immigration Coalition) noted. "As coalition directors, we helped the national groups understand that they could be more effective when the local groups made a political opening for them through our local activism."

Another factor that helped bridge the conflict, according to Margie, was that the state-level groups had become powerful enough that the national organizations had to engage them seriously in dialogue. "The coalitions had become credible voices and were able to earn their place at the national table," she noted. "They would not have been able to do that without the major investments of the Open Society Institute, the Joyce Mertz Gilmore Foundation, the Ford Foundation, and others." Often such grants were provided as general operating support.

AN IMMIGRANT LEADER'S STORY

Just as state-level immigration coalitions were negotiating their relationships with national organizations, so too were local immigrant leaders. Foundations worked to remain responsive to the needs of these leaders.

One such immigrant leader was Mexican-born Fernando García in El Paso, Texas.

Fernando had been hired in 1998 by a national organization to run an El Paso office providing legal services. His job was to help monitor and handle human rights abuses along the border. Over time, Fernando grew increasingly distressed because human rights violations were on the rise, despite the presence of the office.

Fernando began to feel that monitoring human rights abuses and resolving individual cases were not enough. "We needed to

look at the factors creating the problems. There was no comprehensive strategy in place for enforcing the Constitution. We
needed a political solution, and historically communities have
been the key element to that kind of change—look at the civil
rights movement, the women's movement."

Because his national organization was resistant to change,
Fernando and fellow immigrant leaders decided to create the
Border Network for Human Rights. "We turned everything
upside down. Instead of having lawyers document everything,
we trained community members to do this. Instead of having a
board, we created neighborhood committees to make their own
decisions."

Soon the Border Network grew to include five hundred families, and human rights violations had declined in areas where the
organization had the greatest presence. Members were internal-
izing their rights and placing signs in the windows of their homes
showing that they belonged to the Border Network. Often the
signs themselves were enough to deter inappropriate behavior,
Fernando said. For example, in Vado, New Mexico, with its population of roughly ten thousand people, "human rights violations
dropped almost 90 percent between 2002 and 2003." With time,
the Border Network and the U.S. Border Patrol began cooperat-
ing on initiatives to reduce abuses in the area.

Fernando noted that Taryn Higashi played an important role
in bolstering the Border Network. She committed Ford Foundation dollars at the time when the Border Network, a tiny grassroots
organization with few national allies, was breaking ties with the
larger national group.

Results

Although the Emma Lazarus Fund closed in 2000, OSI continued
supporting immigrant rights work at a reduced level of funding in
the early 2000s. Initially run by Antonio Maciel, the program has
been managed by Maria Teresa Rojas since 2004.

As hoped, an outpouring of immigrants applied for citizenship, though applications did not always result in people becoming

citizens. "Backlogs [within the then U.S. Immigration and Naturalization Service] thwarted much of the effectiveness," Bill Ong Hing lamented. "The longest time was at the Nebraska Service Center where current staffing and pending applications translated to a ridiculous processing time estimate of over 42 years!"[5]

Although dramatic delays persisted, many felt that wait times and human rights concerns would have been worse had it not been for the advocacy and organizing efforts of the immigrant rights groups. "If we had simply paid for filing fees as initially considered, imagine how many fewer immigrants would have actually become citizens," Antonio Maciel noted. "There wouldn't have been the advocacy and pressure on INS headquarters and regional offices to address the backlog and waiting times."

In spite of the obstacles, naturalization increased dramatically in the United States in the mid- to late 1990s. According to a study done by the Urban Institute, "beginning in the mid-1990s, the number of naturalized citizens rose for the first time in decades, from 6.5 million [in 1990] to over 11 million citizens in 2002."[6]

"The Emma Lazarus Fund really changed the landscape with their support of grantees' efforts," Eric Cohen of the Immigrant Legal Resource Center emphasized. "They assisted with an increase in naturalization applications like we have never seen in the history of the United States. Of course there were lots of other factors involved in the rise, but their funding clearly supported grantees in helping many people become enfranchised and voting citizens." Alice Cottingham pointed to her own state of Illinois as one example. "There were tens of thousands of people in Illinois who became citizens. Without the [OSI supported] Fund for Immigrants and Refugees, that number would have been much less."

In addition, the OSI funds—together with funding from many other foundations—helped strengthen a mosaic of local, state, and national organizations, often with general operating support grants, which provided grantees with greater flexibility in how they used the funds. Groups such as the New York Immigration Coalition and the Asian-American Justice Center became major players building the capacity of grassroots organizations across the country.

The work of immigrant rights groups paid off in several important states. In New York, they helped secure up to half a billion dollars in funding for English as a second language and related programs in public schools.[7] Illinois "ended up with very family friendly policies" with respect to implementation of the welfare reform laws, according to Nikki Stein, executive director of the Chicago-based Polk Bros. Foundation. And in California, immigrants and their advocates helped secure more assistance to legal immigrants than virtually any other state.[8]

As more and more voices joined the chorus in support of immigrant rights, the national climate for immigrants also began to shift. As this happened, so too did national policies affecting immigrants and their families. As early as 1998, supported by an initiative organized by the National Asian Pacific American Legal Consortium, the federal government had repealed some elements of the welfare package affecting immigrants. This included reinstating the eligibility of millions of immigrants and refugees for supplemental security income and food stamps benefits, as documented by Bill Ong Hing in a report to OSI.[9]

Growing Pains

As he had hoped, Antonio Maciel was able to avoid some of the pitfalls of injecting large monetary sums into the field by funding intermediaries who could make small grants. However, in the case of advocacy and organizing, Antonio often provided large grants, and he noted that in a few cases recipients did not absorb these easily. "A few organizations experienced growing pains. Growing from budgets of $200,000 to $1 million, they didn't always have the human resources, the financial management capacity, the breadth and depth of partners to manage such large projects. Organizations brought on or promoted leaders and managers who didn't have enough experience." In hindsight, however, Antonio would not have made these advocacy and organizing grants smaller. "There was too much work to be done," he explained.

Antonio noted that he wished the funding community had worked harder to support capacity building of immigrant organizations before the crisis:

With a few exceptions, funders didn't have the foresight several years earlier to step back and say, "What do we need to do to strengthen the field?" We tend to respond to crises and the popular theme of the moment. This is why I've admired the Ford strategy because they stayed with the field and particular organizations over time. When other funders were saying, "Everything is going great, let's move on," they were saying, "Let's take advantage of the fact that there's no crisis to help grantees build institutions and leaders." If more funders had done that, we would have been in a stronger position. By the time 1996 hit, we couldn't afford to put money into leadership-building retreats for the next generation.

Antonio underlined that despite OSI's significant infusion of funding into the field, the money was still small compared to the need.

Building the Financial Base

As hoped, the efforts of OSI also helped strengthen a funding base for the growing immigrant infrastructure. "George Soros' $50 million investment . . . raised the ante . . . and drew new funders into the field," noted Bob Crane, former president of both the Joyce Mertz Gilmore Foundation and the JEHT Foundation.[10] "The funding community and the immigrant rights constituency have grown enormously since then."

Antonio Maciel did note, however, that not all the funding collaboratives were sustained. Despite contributing members' matching funds, several collaboratives folded after spending the Emma Lazarus Fund money. "I think it would have helped if instead of a two-year match, I had done a four-year match. More funders may have institutionalized a long-term funding strategy," he noted. "Collaboratives where we were less strict about matching funds, such as one in Boston, didn't sustain interest once the Emma Lazarus money ended."

The result was that when the Emma Lazarus Fund closed, "organizing suffered," Angela Sanbrano, president of the National Alliance for Latin American and Caribbean Communities, noted. "We didn't have the resources to develop more organizers and build the capacity of literally hundreds of potential leaders we came in contact with."

In addition to bringing new funders into the field, the work helped several foundations more fully embrace grantmaking strategies that supported grantees who were changing systems in support of immigrant rights. These included both the Polk Bros. Foundation in Illinois and, ironically, OSI itself.

Nikki Stein explained how her involvement with the Fund for Immigrants and Refugees in Illinois helped encourage the Polk Bros. Foundation, where she worked to support not only services but also advocacy.

> We'd been doing a fair amount of grantmaking for direct legal services for immigrants and [following the passage of the 1996 laws] were hearing from our providers that they were being swamped. People were being thrown off lists for food stamps and welfare who shouldn't have been. Through the fund, we were all together in the room with the MacArthur Foundation and other national foundations. They helped give us a more national perspective. We began to look at the issues that were right in front of us within this national context: the disproportionate impact of welfare reform on immigrants and possibilities for implementing welfare reform in a more humane way. [Just like the parable about river babies,] they helped us think more deeply about whether to pull babies out of the river or find out who was putting babies in the river. Our focus as a foundation had been local, which may have made us think we didn't need to look at the big picture. But it became clear that this was one example of how what happened elsewhere totally colored what we could do here in Chicago.

Because the Polk Bros. Foundation's endowment was growing at the time, its new focus on policy and advocacy supplemented its existing services portfolio. "If we had simply withdrawn our support for services, we really would have damaged people's lives," Nikki noted.

As immigrants secured policy victories, even George Soros saw the impact advocacy and organizing was having on the issue he cared about most: the dignity of the individual immigrant. "George began to shift away from supporting services when he saw the impact we had with the advocacy and organizing work," Antonio noted. "It was a critical piece in helping him to shift the focus of the Open Society Institute. He would say his focus was still individuals, but what he began to approve was advocacy, organizing, and supporting grantees as they built collective action."

September 11 and the Creation of a Funder Collaborative

In 2001, the momentum developed by immigrants and others helped propel recently elected presidents George Bush and Vincente Fox to make immigration reform a priority. Ongoing dialogue between the two presidents, and a state visit by Mexican president Vicente Fox to the United States in early September, pointed to the possibility of legislative reform that included favorable measures for immigrants and their families.

With the terrorist attacks in New York and Washington, D.C., on September 11, 2001, however, the momentum the immigrant community had helped to build came to an abrupt halt. "There was a political context that just seemed perfect for comprehensive immigration reform. Then 9/11 put a total kibosh on it. Now everyone was thinking within the context of security," Geri Mannion, director of the U.S. democracy program of Carnegie Corporation of New York, explained. "In the years following the terrorist attacks, the government's efforts to tighten security, coupled with the American public's growing fear and suspicions of 'foreigners,' had a devastating impact on immigrant communities. Workplace raids and deportations increased, often as human rights violations."

By 2003, the U.S. Immigration and Naturalization Service had been disbanded and many of its components absorbed into the newly established Department of Homeland Security. The shift symbolized the growing suspicion of the government, as well as of many citizens, toward the immigrant community, as immigration became framed as a national security concern. "In this reorganization many members of the immigrant community fear they are viewed as potential terrorists," wrote Thomas Donovan in his article "The American Immigration System."[11]

"Taryn [Higashi], Antonio [Maciel], Michele Lord, and I spent a whole year trying to figure out what the heck we were going to do in light of the changed political environment," Geri Mannion recalled. "What was supposed to be new funding efforts to support grantees' efforts to advance comprehensive immigration reform and immigrant integration issues instead needed to be rethought within a security frame and with more attention to protecting individual immigrants' rights. To reconsider what could be done as funders, we got this idea to do a convening in the fall of '02. At that meeting, which included representatives from the Joyce Mertz Gilmore Foundation and Public Interest Projects, other funders, as well as several immigrant leaders, we decided to form a funder collaborative, and by 2003 we had created the Four Freedoms Fund." The name referenced a famous State of the Union address by Franklin D. Roosevelt in which he articulated four freedoms: freedom of speech, freedom of religion, freedom from want, and freedom from fear.

As a collaborative, members noted they were able to coordinate grantmaking in a way they would not have been able to do through informal channels. In fact, many funder members granted their money directly to the Four Freedoms Fund, which would then regrant the funds to grantees. Henry Der of the Evelyn and Walter Haas, Jr. Fund noted, "We'd speak to the field and then would draw a matrix with needs for advocacy, organizing, communications strategies with the media, and research. Every funder had constraints. But what one funder couldn't cover, another could." Geri Mannion noted that the forum allowed them not only to organize their funding but also to do grantee oversight and, more important, to make midcourse corrections as needed.

In addition, the collaborative allowed them to establish their own communications unit within the fund to increase the capacity of grantees to work with the media, and to support better coordination among grantees from the local, state, and national levels. Henry Der explained that grantees were seeking ways to communicate with the public to build political will for reform. "As the anti-immigrant lobby stepped up their campaign in the wake of September 11, many groups were under siege, so the initiative gave a lot of training on how to handle those attacks."

Trust and a sense of equality were key ingredients to the members' ability to work with one another. "In those discussions, it wasn't 'We'll do whatever the foundation contributing the most said,'" Henry noted. "There was no pecking order. I've heard that is rare and that often funders hold their cards close to their vest."

Millions Challenge Growing Anti-Immigrant Sentiment

The anti-immigrant sentiment to which the Four Freedoms Fund was responding culminated "in December 2005, with the Sensen-brenner Bill," Angela Sanbrano (National Alliance for Latin American and Caribbean Communities) noted. "This bill called for the criminalization of undocumented immigrants in the United States."

The immigrant movement, however, had the infrastructure in place to respond. Immigrants themselves had local organizations that represented them. Local organizations were often linked together through larger networks. Groups such as the National Immigration Forum allowed for communication between local, state, and national groups.

Angela recalled, "We were under attack, so we left all our differences and prima donna attitudes and historical dislikes behind, and immigrant groups joined forces to push for change."

To raise the profile of immigrants, organizers planned rallies across the country. "Spanish language radio had a big, big role in getting the word out and energizing people to march," Henry noted. "[Four Freedoms Fund grantee] CHIRLA had a very close working relationship with disc jockeys and helped shape what they would say on the air."

Added Angela, "Millions of people listened to the disc jockeys. They amplified our voices." In spring 2006, millions of people marched in cities around the country.

Subsequently, policymakers softened many aspects of the immigration bill and included measures for legalization for many of the estimated 11.5 to 12 million undocumented workers in the country.[12]

Ultimately, however, Congress did not pass the revised bill. While harboring many concerns about the legislation, most within the immigrant community viewed its defeat with grave concern because of the country's critical need for immigration reform.

OSI'S CONTINUED ROLE IN SUPPORT OF IMMIGRANT RIGHTS

Of OSI's role, Maria Teresa Rojas (Open Society Institute) noted,

> In 2007, when the opportunity opened up to achieve comprehensive immigration reform, George Soros stepped up to the plate again and helped leverage other funding to support reform efforts. He was not deterred by the collapse of immigration reform in 2007. Instead, in addition to the $4.5 million he had already committed for the 2007–2009 funding cycle, he approved $15 million to sustain reform efforts over a period of several years if necessary.[13] The funds have focused on advancing sound immigration policy reform and efforts to stem the further erosion of the civil and human rights of immigrants by restoring due process protections and challenging punitive immigration laws that lead to increased immigrant criminalization, detention, and deportation. Grantmaking has encouraged linking immigration to broader national issues and the building of a broad multiethnic, multiconstituent movement for social justice.

Conclusion

In 2006, the nation witnessed a modern immigrant movement in action, as millions of immigrants marched for their rights. In cities across the United States, immigrants poured into the streets in what for some cities were the largest protests of their time.

"There was the myth that these marches were so spontaneous," immigrant leader Angela Sanbrano noted. "In one way they were, but in another way they were a reflection of the grassroots work and organizing that had been happening for twenty years. That level of networking and mobilization wouldn't have happened if we hadn't had strong membership organizations and if we hadn't already been talking to people across the country. These were nationally coordinated actions."

Immigrants led this movement, and funders supported their efforts. In 1983, the Ford Foundation decided to strengthen an emerging immigrant field (see Chapter Five). Aiding grantees as they developed organizational infrastructure, these efforts helped ensure that the field could absorb $50 million of OSI funding beginning in 1996. In turn, OSI's support helped others join the fold. As the Emma Lazarus Fund closed its doors, the Four Freedoms Fund formed to fill the funding vacuum. The Fund has attracted participation from a variety of new funders, including the Bill and Melinda Gates Foundation.

Although the movement has been unable to secure comprehensive reform, immigrant organizations have been critical in amplifying the voices of this vulnerable population. In so doing, they have helped immigrants secure important victories as they have woven themselves more squarely into the democratic fabric of the United States.

Lessons Learned

The Open Society Institute was able to help immigrants as they secured citizenship and new levels of participation in U.S. democratic life. How might your organization support a social movement?

- For maximum impact, react quickly to unfolding national events.
- Build commitment among key players within your foundation— including founders and donors—by communicating with them and helping link social change strategies to their concerns.
- Be aware that some organizations may not be able to handle rapid growth effectively, and also look for indicators that they can.
- Consider giving general operating support grants, which can provide organizations greater flexibility in how they use funds.
- Explore such mechanisms as funder intermediary pools to (1) build long-term funder interest in the issue area, (2) tap into local funders' expertise and knowledge of local grantees, (3) provide greater flexibility to give small grants, (4) reach local and state-level groups, and (5) introduce new funders to social change strategies.

PART
FOUR

Creating Infrastructure for Justice

Many funders prefer to support project initiatives rather than invest in building the organizations that can carry such efforts forward. Wanting to influence education, the media, or housing, funders commonly earmark their support for a particular project that deals with one of these issue areas. Yet such funding can be shortsighted: a considerable number of nonprofits point to the strength of their organizations as the critical factor in positioning them for success in any given initiative. Community-based organizations, for example, need a strong network of citizens, time for leaders and members to develop common platforms, and strong management structures to carry forward initiatives successfully.

The Liberty Hill Foundation and the Charles Stewart Mott Foundation, highlighted in this part of the book, have chosen a different approach. Instead of focusing on projects related to a specific issue, they are funding democratic practices that build the capacity of communities to address the issues of their choice.

Taking a long-term view of societal problems, both foundations see community-based organizations as fundamental to this mission, and are providing general operating support to build their strength. Grantees have used this flexible funding, coupled with research and consultation, to grow their membership base and evolve into high-impact, large-scale organizations. These groups are choosing their own priorities and campaign areas and helping members effectively influence the institutions that affect their lives.

7

Building Community-Based Power in Los Angeles

The Case of the Liberty Hill Foundation

The Liberty Hill Foundation helped pioneer the community funding board, a body within the foundation responsible for all grant-making. The donors and community activists who make up this entity help channel resources to new and promising leaders in Los Angeles, helping them expand organizations that emerge as major players in Los Angeles and beyond.

The year was 1975. Sarah Pillsbury—an heir to the Pillsbury baking fortune—joined friends Win McCormack, Anne Mendel, and Larry Janss to find ways to give back to Los Angeles, their city of residence. In founding the Liberty Hill Foundation with their pooled wealth, Sarah and the other cofounders hoped to "turn philanthropy on its head," recalled Catherine Suitor, former director of development at the foundation.

Sarah wanted to build a foundation kindred in spirit to the Haymarket People's Fund, a Boston-based public foundation founded by her brother George Pillsbury in 1974. Rather than establishing a traditional foundation structure with program

Liberty Hill Foundation Snapshot

Type: Public charity

Year founded: 1976

Grant range (1977): $500–$3,000

Grant range (2008): $200–$50,000

Total grants awarded (1977): $69,900

Total grants awarded (2008): $4.3 million

Liberty Hill Foundation unexpended balance (1977): $40,000

Liberty Hill Foundation unexpended balance (2008): $8.8 million

Total grants awarded since Liberty Hill's inception: $37 million

Geographic focus: Los Angeles County

Primary funding areas: Economic, social and racial equality, and environmental sustainability

Staff size (2008): Twenty-two

Location: Los Angeles

Total grants awarded by Fund for a New Los Angeles (1993): $240,000

Total grants awarded by Fund for a New Los Angeles (2008): $375,000

Note: Snapshot information for each chapter varies depending on data available. Dates refer to either the calendar year or the end of the fiscal cycle. Numbers have been rounded to the nearest whole. For snapshot sources, refer to the Notes section at the end of the book.[1]

officers, her brother had given community members themselves the power to determine who received grant monies. The central principle driving this foundation structure was that in addition to redistributing wealth for social good, the foundation should share the power over how that wealth was distributed.

The foundation represented values that had been instilled into Sarah by her parents and reinforced by her involvement in several movements of the time. Sarah recalled, "My parents were liberal

Republicans who believed in fairness and justice. I was really lucky. I was born into a family that was not only philanthropic but also socially responsible."

Elaborating on her political evolution, she stated, "My values never changed, but my politics did. My oldest brother Charlie, who had worked on the campaigns of Al Lowenstein [former congressman and opposer of apartheid] and Eugene McCarthy, was a strong influence on both George and me. When I got to Yale, I became involved in everything—from the antiwar movement, to open admissions at Yale, to workers' strikes and the first Earth Day."

Through these experiences, Sarah came to believe that the only way to help create a fairer city of Los Angeles was to strengthen the voices of people who had limited access to power and wealth in the city. Michele Prichard, director of Common Agenda for the Liberty Hill Foundation and former executive director of the foundation, noted that Sarah "believed that community organizing was essential. If you could find the people who had no voice and get them to speak out as a collective group, then they could change city hall."

Sarah and the other founders wanted to achieve their vision of a more just society not only through grantmaking but also, as the Haymarket People's Fund had done, by giving community activists power within the foundation itself. Michele recalled, "The founders felt that those who were most affected by inequity probably would have the best ideas for how to shape strategies. The power to decide needed to reside with the community."

In the 1970s, such an approach was rare in the foundation community. By pursuing this vision, Liberty Hill became a vanguard confronting the power dynamics inherent in grantee-grantor relationships. In so doing, the organization helped develop an emerging model for how foundations could reflect values of democratic ideals and partnership within their own institutional structure.

Listening as a First Step

To decide whether and how to develop the foundation, the founders decided to listen to members of the community. They hired

Mary Jo von Mach, who later became the Liberty Hill Foundation's first executive director, to conduct a landscape survey of individuals and organizations working to create a more just and fair Los Angeles. Although Mary Jo's hard skills were important, her soft skills were what compelled the founders to hire her for the job. Sarah recalled, "We hired her because of her warmth and humor and the fact that she's a really good listener. She's the kind of person people trust [which we saw as critical to the work]." She added, "There was a fair amount of mistrust toward outsiders within many low-income communities in the 1970s."

Mary Jo spent several months interviewing activists in the city—in low-income communities, in foundations, and from a pool of potential donors. She noted, "I did these interviews for a long time—starting in September 1975 working all day, every day." Through the interviews, she hoped to determine whether there was a need for such a foundation, and if so, to help determine the appropriate structure and identify individuals from the community who could participate in the foundation's development.[2]

Mary Jo understood the importance of this initial groundwork. "I knew full well that if we had the right structure and the right people, then whatever we set in motion would work. And if not, it would self-destruct."

In winter 1976, on the basis of the results of the interviews, the founders decided to move forward and incorporate the Liberty Hill Foundation.

Including Community Members in Foundation Decision Making

The power-sharing mechanism the founders chose for the new foundation was called a *community funding board*. This body was to become the grantmaking arm of the foundation. Board members would be in charge of interviewing and selecting grant applicants for funding. Although the community funding board model was already being used by the Haymarket People's Fund, Liberty Hill was the first to mix donors and community activists on the same board.

THE FUNDING EXCHANGE NETWORK

In 1979, the Liberty Hill Foundation—together with the Haymarket People's Fund, the Vanguard Foundation, the Bread and Roses Community Fund, the McKenzie River Gathering Foundation, and the North Star Fund—founded the Funding Exchange Network, which in 2008 included fifteen public foundations committed to both social justice philanthropy and activist-led grantmaking strategies. The mission of the Funding Exchange has been to build a permanent institutional and financial base to support social change through fundraising for local, national, and international grantmaking programs.

The idea for creating this mixed model emerged from the interviews. Mary Jo von Mach began to realize that both donors and community activists had a vital role to play in ensuring the model's success.

From the outset, Mary Jo and the founders were clear that the community activists would be "the foundation's boots on the ground," Mary Jo explained. "They were the ones in the neighborhoods encountering daily problems. They would bring the experiences of what worked and what didn't work." She recalled the community activists' surprise when during the interviews she asked their opinions about the idea. "People would say, 'Are you for real? Is there really someone who is going to give us a voice and money?' They were completely amazed."

Less clear in the beginning was the role that the donors would play. "Originally, I was toying with the idea of a completely community activist board," Mary Jo noted. "But in talking with people, I began to realize that donors had an emotional distance from the projects that was useful. And they were more accustomed to looking beyond individual neighborhoods toward trends happening across the city, as well as nationally. Many community activists in L.A. at the time were focused very locally, so this broader perspective turned out to be very important."

Ultimately, Mary Jo and the founders agreed on a community funding board composed of seven activists and two donors, a roughly three-to-one community activist–donor split. Michele noted that they chose this ratio because "they wanted the power to decide to rest with the community. They became clear that donors should be a voice, but that they shouldn't be the majority."

Addressing Conflict of Interest

With the basic structure in place in 1976, the next step was to choose who would sit on the board. Mary Jo wanted to invite individuals who were already working on transforming institutions and systems to support justice and equality, who would get along on a team, and who had the analytical skills to choose strong applicants. Explaining the importance of this step she stated, "I felt many problems would be avoided if we got the right people there to begin with. Many people thought the activists would all promote their own organizations. But I believed if our instincts were right this wouldn't be an issue, and it wasn't." In order to further minimize any conflict of interest, Mary Jo also aimed to choose individuals with a wide array of backgrounds, and who worked with diverse constituencies. She felt that bringing in many voices would ensure a fairer decision-making process.

ADDRESSING CONCERNS ABOUT CRONYISM

A former director of the foundation's board noted how his fears of conflict of interest were assuaged during his tenure. "I was suspicious there would be a lot of cronyism, and was impressed by how much deliberation there was in choosing proposals. I saw people recuse themselves from votes on their own organizations. I saw community funding board members' organizations not get funded, and that told me there was integrity in the process."

"Early on we developed conflict-of-interest policies," Michele Prichard noted. "If you were a board member, community member, or staff for an applying organization, you needed to leave the room when your proposal was being discussed."

Mary Jo realized that recruiting the right initial members would be important for another reason as well. She wanted the board members to help choose their successors. Therefore, a poorly chosen board would likely perpetuate itself.

Over time, as the foundation began to expand, the community funding board members also created a qualified pool from which Liberty Hill drew several key staff members and consultants.

By spring 1976, Mary Jo and the founders had selected the community funding board. They then worked together to create grantmaking guidelines. "We didn't impose the guidelines. We gave the community funding board a range of options we'd pulled from other foundations, and they spent many meetings going through them and figuring out what would work best." The foundation's staff then became responsible for ensuring that rules and guidelines were maintained.

Catherine Suitor, former director of development, explained that the model worked in part because "we had masterful facilitation in the meetings and clear guidelines. We had Liberty Hill staff there who would say 'that proposal is outside our guidelines.'"

Finding High-Potential Grantees

In addition to their own discerning eyes, the board created other mechanisms for distinguishing between a great project and simply a great proposal. First, the board suggested that the staff offer writing support to anyone who wanted to submit a proposal. Mary Jo explained, "We let people come to our offices after work, and we'd help them put forward a proposal that painted the best picture of them. This helped ensure the small group in East L.A. had the same chance of getting funded as a well-established environmental group." And second, they institutionalized the site visit. At least two board members would visit every semifinalist before approving a grant. "Applicants didn't come to Liberty Hill," noted Mary Jo. "We came to them."

The site visits turned out to be essential, not only for helping identify grantees but also for fundraising efforts. "Any donor that sat on the community funding board became a lifer. The donors would read proposals and get so depressed by all that applicants needed to overcome," Sarah Pillsbury recalled. "Then they'd go into neighborhoods they'd never been to and meet people they'd otherwise never meet, and they would leave almost as hopeful as the people they had spoken to." These powerful allies not only increased their giving over time but also introduced new donors to the foundation.

Sarah recalled how important this additional support was: "I had no love of fundraising. I was a scared kid. Getting donors involved was critical to our success."

Supporting "Change, Not Charity"

In these early meetings, the community funding board members affirmed the original vision of the founders: that the foundation should support "change, not charity." "We didn't want to fund after-school programs or homeless shelters," Michele Prichard said. "We wanted to address the systems that created inequality in the first place. Otherwise we would just be feeding the same homeless people when they got hungry again. We wanted to address root causes that led to problems like homelessness, which is caused by things like poor wages, lack of jobs, lack of affordable housing. To do that we needed to fund grantees working on social policy change."

The board decided to make one exception to the "change, not charity" rule: services could be funded if they supported a larger social change agenda. "Services were sometimes a way to organize people," Michele explained. "For example, our grantee El Rescate was providing legal services to immigrants facing deportation. We funded that work because the grantee was connecting it to a larger policy solution. El Rescate was exposing the wars in Central America that caused people to come here. The services helped them to reach out and connect with people and build relationships. Many of the refugees receiving services then became active in talking to churches about their own individual plights. They used their own individual stories to educate the public about the U.S. role in the wars that had dislocated them from their countries of origin."

One debate that consumed the board during these early meetings was whether the foundation should support film projects. As a well-known film producer in Hollywood who produced such blockbusters as *Desperately Seeking Susan,* Sarah felt that film could play an important role in shifting the public's perception of relevant issues. Several board members, however, disagreed, arguing that "film was too amorphous. People were concerned that there were no clear results," Mary Jo noted. Ultimately, they decided that film work would be eligible only if it was linked to a direct organizing strategy.

One of the first films the board supported was the *Song of the Canary,* a movie about workers' exposure to the chemical DBCP. While creating the film, David Davis discovered that every worker involved in producing DBCP in an Occidental Chemical Company plant in California was sterile. Mary Jo recounted, "The film was used by advocacy groups who pushed for a ban on the substance." The national outrage unleashed by the film, combined with follow-up advocacy work, led to the chemical's ban in the United States.[3] The movie, supported in part by a foundation willing to take a risk on an unknown film producer, was nominated for an Emmy and received awards for best documentary film at the Athens, Chicago, and Mannheim film festivals.[4]

The Community Funding Board Model

With respect to grantmaking, the community activists on the board proved skilled at finding potential leaders in communities. "Many of the [organizations they were building] had just barely gotten their 501(c)(3) status. They were meeting in someone's living room," Catherine Suitor (Liberty Hill Foundation) remembered. Yet the board members seemed to have an uncanny ability to discern which of these humble enterprises would become high-impact initiatives. The injections of $500 to $3,000 grants made a tremendous difference to these tiny organizations, many of which had never received monies before.[5]

"One of our first grants was to the Coalition for Economic Survival, [which became an important organization protecting tenants' rights including those related to rent control]," Mary Jo von Mach recalled. "The community funding board could see they were different from most organizations in the city in several ways. This was a group that was multiracial in reality. It wasn't merely a stated goal, as was true with many other organizations. They weren't single issue, and they weren't working in just one neighborhood. You couldn't say there was another group like them in the city at the time. People tended to be single neighborhood and single issue."

Larry Gross, founder and executive director for the Coalition for Economic Survival, explained the importance of the Liberty Hill Foundation's initial support. "When we got the grant from Liberty Hill it was a big deal. Wow! Our first grant! In those days we weren't making payroll. We were on the phones calling the phone company to make sure they didn't cut our lines because we couldn't pay the bill. Liberty Hill provided a small cushion that gave us some breathing room to get up on our feet and develop. We might not have survived without them."

Reflecting on applying for foundation dollars, Larry added, "We were very wary of money, because we were concerned about the strings attached, that it would make us less effective. Initially we thought our members could support our expenses. But that was somewhat idealistic. Growth created more financial needs. Then Liberty Hill came along. We felt that if any foundation would give us flexible funds, Liberty Hill was it. They provided us with general [operating] support and enabled us to fund organizing work that no other foundation would fund."

COALITION FOR ECONOMIC SURVIVAL SECURES IMPORTANT WINS

By 2007, the Coalition for Economic Survival had a membership of five thousand individuals and a budget of roughly half a million dollars. (Funders included California Endowment.) The coalition had won important rent control ordinances in Los Angeles and West Hollywood. To facilitate their passage, "We helped create a city," Larry Gross explained. "[The City of West Hollywood] was one of the only cities in the United States based on rent control."[6]

The community funding board also helped build relationships between disparate communities in Los Angeles. Catherine Suitor noted that the board was "a tremendous movement builder that got people rubbing shoulders across race and class. We'd have people in the same room who would never otherwise interact: a youth from South Central L.A., a tenant organizer from East L.A., and an activist from the gay community. People built relationships that they could take back out into their work."

Former Liberty Hill executive director and board member Torie Osborn explained that meetings "took me out of my world. When I was a board member, we were in the middle of the AIDS epidemic, and my world was all about gays and AIDS. I developed relationships with people outside of my sphere. It enabled me to see AIDS in the broader context of homelessness, lack of health care, and of course race and class issues."

Assuming a Leadership Role in the Philanthropic Community

The power of the community funding board, however, did not fully manifest itself until April 29, 1992—the day that sparked the Rodney King civil disturbances in Los Angeles. The acquittal of four officers involved in the beating of Rodney King was the match that lit a powder keg in many low-income communities of color in Los Angeles. In a three-day period, hundreds of people were killed or injured, and many thousands were arrested.[7] Suddenly the grassroots community voices, which the foundation had worked to make more visible, took on new importance.

People within the funding world who wanted to help rebuild Los Angeles were searching for ways to respond. "We said, 'We have a community funding model that keeps us in touch with the people in those communities, and you are welcome to join,'" Catherine recalled.

Just six months before the civil disturbances, the foundation had organized a conference for roughly one hundred community organizers from across the city of Los Angeles who were aware of growing tensions triggered by increasing disparities between rich and poor in the city. "They feared there would be riots," Torie Osborn recalled. "There was so much despair in the communities—the crack epidemic, the loss of jobs, the destruction of affordable housing, homelessness, the fact that there were hundreds of liquor stores in their communities and no supermarkets. They articulated at that conference the deep racial and class divisions that would soon explode onto the streets."

Within the funding world, Liberty Hill and its grantees were catapulted into a leadership role as people worked to find a way to ease the tensions in the city. Michele Prichard noted that "after the riots many funders looked at Liberty Hill as a small but successful foundation that had actually been able to fund some groups working in the damaged neighborhoods. There was growing acceptance of our credibility in the philanthropic world."

At the same time, members of the philanthropic community in Los Angeles found themselves searching for new grantmaking strategies to address the city's problems. "It was a teachable moment," Michele recalled. "Everyone was open to new ideas. It was so traumatizing, and we all felt that what we had been doing was not enough."

To help find answers, Liberty Hill sponsored a series of panel discussions, retreats, and tours for individual donors and foundation officers to visit grantees in the affected areas. These events created opportunities for people in the city to build new relationships, forge strategy, and find common ground. "They were very important spaces to build a new vision from the ashes through a lens of economic justice," Torie explained.

For several foundations in California, this shift meant moving funds toward more risky ventures. "Before the riots, many funders hadn't wanted to fund anything if they weren't sure their investment was going to pay off," Catherine recalled. "Through the dialogues, people began to realize they wouldn't get to the real issues if they didn't take a chance." Foundations in the area "became more likely to move outside their comfort zone and fund groups that were run by community activists and nontraditional community leaders."

Several foundations and other funding entities felt that Liberty Hill was in a strategic position to address the city's mounting problems. A number began to channel funds through the foundation, feeling that the community funding board would best be able to identify the organizations that could most successfully help rebuild L.A. and heal racial tensions. These included the McKay Foundation, the Jewish Fund for Justice, the Urban Foundation of the United Methodist Church, and Comic Relief, an annual fundraising event featuring Billy Crystal, Robin Williams, and Whoopi Goldberg.[8]

Helping Grantees Build Infrastructure

The civil disturbances also propelled Liberty Hill to further evaluate its own grantmaking strategies, which it had already begun to question before the uprising. "Liberty Hill had been following a strategy of 'let a thousand flowers bloom'—giving money in tiny amounts all over the place," Catherine Suitor (former director of development) recalled.

"We began to feel many of our grantees were working so hard on immediate and urgent issues, but weren't building organizational infrastructure that could endure," Michele Prichard added.

"Our strategy was to fund seed organizations, provide a couple years of support and then move on. We were beginning to question whether this was the best approach," Paula Litt, a former board member and current donor, elaborated.

The discussions fed into a strategic planning process already under way. "The riots got people very clear that these were problems that were not going to be solved by one campaign," Torie Osborn (former executive director) noted.

"We decided we wanted to build long-term institutions that could weather over time and build leadership," Sarah Pillsbury elaborated. "We wanted to build anchor groups in L.A. that were based in communities. [Such organizations would] have enough capacity to provide leadership and assistance to other emerging groups working on similar issues. Some of our groups were really successful. Instead of kicking them out the door because of their success, we decided to support them in becoming even more successful."

The strategic feedback loop created by the board structure helped the foundation develop its vision. "By having community members on the funding board, we were aggregating lessons from the field," Torie explained. "With community activists alongside donors, the aggregate story of how to create a social justice movement in Los Angeles got clearer."

To sharpen its focus on economic and racial justice, in 1993 the Liberty Hill Foundation created a grantmaking program called the Fund for a New Los Angeles. This fund, which allowed Liberty Hill to provide more significant support to anchor organizations in the city, was made possible by a $1 million donation from a wealthy donor and $185,000 from Comic Relief.[9]

The new fund gave larger grants over a longer period of time than Liberty Hill had historically provided. "We started to realize it was OK to provide many years of repeat funding," Paula Litt noted. "This was seen as very unorthodox at the time, but we felt we needed to build these groups' capacity. When we started, if you had said 'We are going to fund these groups for twelve years,' I probably would have said no."

Rebuilding Ravaged Communities

Shortly after the civil disturbances, Liberty Hill graduated several of their most successful grantees to the Fund for a New Los Angeles. "We were looking for organizations that seemed to be moving the ball down the court by using public policy, building new leadership, and organizing people," Michele Prichard explained. Whereas previously these organizations had received seed grants ranging from $500 to $3,000, early grantees of the new fund received as much as $35,000.[10]

One such grantee was the Community Coalition for Substance Abuse Prevention and Treatment (Community Coalition), which was founded in 1990 with an initial seed grant from Liberty Hill.[11] Many funding board members felt that this community organization, based in South L.A., had the dynamic leadership, community connections, and clear analysis needed to support the neighborhoods most affected by the violence.

With its grant funds, the Community Coalition organized a campaign to prevent the rebuilding of liquor stores burned down in the civil disturbances. These stores had become crime magnets for drug trafficking and prostitution. Margarita Ramirez, deputy director of grantmaking at Liberty Hill, recalled that the coalition members "went door to door to door saying, 'Liquor stores have been such a problem. Let's build something in their place that can support our communities.' They wanted to build grocery stores and laundromats instead."

The initiative was a tremendous success and helped reduce crime and stabilize many neighborhoods in the area. The Community Coalition and partners' efforts kept 150 liquor stores from being rebuilt, helped open forty-four community-friendly businesses, and encouraged the L.A. City Council to pass stricter requirements for opening liquor stores in South Los Angeles. By 1994, the coalition had taken its fight to the state level and won "a significant legal decision by the California Supreme Court to [uphold] the power of cities to regulate alcohol-related nuisance businesses."[12]

Today the Community Coalition is a well-established organization. With four thousand members and a 2006 budget of $2.3 million, the organization received funding from twenty sources in 2006.[13]

Conclusion

In 1976, Liberty Hill took a historic leap of faith by giving community activists control over its grantmaking process. In doing so, the foundation helped equalize power relationships between donors and foundation staff and the communities they wanted to serve. The community funding board allowed the founders to embed their social justice values into the very DNA of the foundation.

The impact of the board's structure reached far beyond Liberty Hill's walls. The resulting mix of talent helped the foundation seed anchor organizations that have supported the growth of powerful social movements in Los Angeles. Although there is much work still to do, in many ways Los Angeles today is "ahead of the country by leaps and bounds," Margarita Ramirez (Liberty Hill Foundation) noted. "What makes Los Angeles stand out is the maturity, networking, and depth of the movement."

Community-based organizations and legal centers, often with multimillion-dollar budgets, have sprung up throughout the city. Such organizations that received early and continued funding from Liberty Hill have included the Strategic Concepts in Organizing and Policy Education (SCOPE), the Los Angeles Alliance for a New Economy (LAANE), the Koreatown Immigrant Workers Alliance (KIWA), and the Asian Pacific American Legal Center.

Such groups, working together with their partners, have spearheaded important wins. These have included the first-ever private sector wage agreement in the Korean American community to increase wages in select Korean-owned supermarkets; a $4 million award to seventy-two garment workers engaged in sweatshop labor; and a $10 million workforce development program to place low-income city residents in the entertainment industry.[14]

Michele Prichard (former executive director) explained the importance of the role Liberty Hill has played in nurturing these organizations: "Initiatives are important, but they are the brainchildren of organizations. Initiatives need an institutional base with staff that can survive over the long term."

Further, the community funding board helped build the skills of some of the most promising community activists in the city. Many of these individuals have gone on to become important leaders for social justice in California. For example, California State Assembly member Karen Bass—founder of the Community Coalition—used the skills she developed to make history in 2008 by becoming the first African American woman in the country to serve as speaker of a state legislative assembly.[15] "We have photos of the funding boards, and sometimes we'll look at those photos with a smile because so many of these people have gone on to such influential positions," Margarita noted.

Community-led initiatives represent "a new force in Los Angeles politics, one that exists almost entirely outside traditional power circles," Torie Osborn (former executive director) noted in a *New York Times* op-ed piece.[16] One step at a time, these efforts have indeed been changing Los Angeles.

Peter Teague, a program director at the Nathan Cummings Foundation, noted, "The Liberty Hill Foundation is one of the best examples in the country of philanthropy done right. If every city in the country had a Liberty Hill, what a different country we would be."

Lessons Learned

The Liberty Hill Foundation decided to share power with activists in Los Angeles and as a result was able to identify fledgling organizations that have grown into powerful community-based legal and research organizations. How might your foundation build infrastructure that can help support movements for change?

- Harness the wisdom of activists to help identify the strongest candidates, and embed strong conflict-of-interest rules in the process to avoid cronyism.
- Support organizations—particularly those with a track record of success—for a minimum of twelve years to help grow fledgling organizations into powerful institutions.
- Leverage moments of crisis to help catapult ideas, leaders, and grantees into the limelight. If you have strong grantees addressing the crisis, consider starting a fund to which others can contribute.

8

Strengthening National Community-Based Networks

The Case of the Charles Stewart Mott Foundation

The Charles Stewart Mott Foundation champions community engagement efforts in Flint, Michigan, and nationally. In its early years, such efforts focused primarily on school-based organizing strategies, and over time came to include support for congregation-based networks and other forms of community engagement. By building network capacity, the foundation helps organizations like PICO National Network raise children's health care to the top of the national agenda in the United States and help secure billions more for uninsured kids.

The founder of the Charles Stewart Mott Foundation, C. S. Mott, who made his money from his early investments and subsequent involvement with the General Motors Company, infused the foundation with a belief that communities actively engaging with public institutions were central to a healthy and functioning democracy. "[To understand the Mott Foundation] you have to understand the core of what made this man tick . . . . It was the strength of individuals, and the quality of individuals, and the relationship of one individual to another," stated William S. (Bill) White, president of the Charles Stewart Mott Foundation since 1976.[1]

"It seems to me that every person is always in a kind of informal partnership with his community," founder C. S. Mott reflected. "His own success is dependent, to a large degree, on that community. The community, after all, is the sum total of the individuals who make it up. The institutions of a community, in turn, are the means by which those individuals express their faith, their ideals, and their concerns for fellow men."[2]

The story of the Mott Foundation has been one of finding different ways to manifest this central belief in the strength of the individual and the importance of his or her relationship with community. Sometimes this belief has been expressed through direct funding for services—such as hospitals and universities, which C. S. Mott saw as central to a well-functioning community. Other times the foundation pursued a social justice approach, working to catalyze change in institutions and systems so that they would better serve people (particularly those of low income) and communities.

The following story traces the evolution of the foundation through its quest to bring communities into relationships with the civic institutions that affect their lives. Initially, much of this work focused on helping citizens interact effectively with schools in Flint, Michigan—a manufacturing home for the U.S. car industry through much of the 1900s and the city where C. S. Mott settled. However, over time the Mott Foundation expanded its focus to include the strengthening of congregation-based networks (affiliated churches, synagogues, and other faith-based institutions), neighborhood groups, and other membership organizations working to hold many types of civic institutions accountable to citizens—particularly those who generally don't have a voice.

Some of the strategies the foundation has chosen have focused on building participatory mechanisms for community engagement within public institutions. The foundation's early work with educational systems, for example, focused on bringing parents, teachers, clergy, businesspeople, and others together on school-based councils, which were funded in part with public dollars. Such councils, the defining characteristic of community schools, facilitated a range of activities, from programming after-school activities, to developing school curriculum, to acting as a forum for community members to discuss other neighborhood concerns—such as where to place a stop sign or how to clean up a park. "Weaving the community into schools is critical," one Mott Foundation grantee noted. "You need to be on the inside to make schools work."

Other strategies have focused on building community-based membership organizations that often have a great deal of autonomy from either the private sector or the public sector. Many of the neighborhood organizations and congregation-based networks the foundation has supported fall into this category. With their increased autonomy, these organizations have at times been able to secure fundamental reform of public institutions, including increasing state budgets for health care and education, through such activities as organizing; planning actions to educate lawmakers and the public; and research, media work, and direct lobbying (though lobbying has not been funded by the Mott Foundation).

Several of these congregation-based networks and neighborhood organizations grew out of the legacy of Saul Alinsky, who many credit as the father of modern-day community organizing. This model of community organizing centers on helping people build power through their numbers. The sometimes millions of voices in these networks create a counterbalancing force that helps hold public officials and others accountable to the needs of citizens, rather than moneyed interests.

These strategies demonstrate the diverse ways in which the Mott Foundation has pursued social justice. The journey illustrates a foundation willing to experiment and to embrace new approaches, while staying true to its central belief in the importance of individuals engaging in community life and democratic practice.

Charles Stewart Mott Foundation Snapshot

Type: Private foundation

Year founded: 1926

Grant range (1928): $2–$5,000

Total grants awarded (first grants awarded—1928): $30,192

(Continued)

Total assets in 1926: two thousand shares of General Motors valued at $320,000

Grant range (2007): $10,000–$2.3 million

Total grants awarded (2007): $108.7 million

Total assets (2007): $2.7 billion

Geographic focus: Domestic and international

Primary funding areas: Pathways Out of Poverty, civil society, environment, and Flint area

Staff size (2007): Eighty-six (figure includes "loaned staff" and does not include "contract employees/consultants")

Location: Headquarters in Flint, Michigan, with offices in Troy, Michigan; Johannesburg, South Africa; and London

Total grants awarded by Building Organized Communities grant-making area (1999): $6.4 million

Total grants awarded by Building Organized Communities (2007): $4.83 million

Note: Snapshot information for each chapter varies depending on data available. Dates refer to either the calendar year or the end of the fiscal cycle. For snapshot sources, refer to the Notes section at the end of the book.[3]

Civic Participation in Public Institutions

Even in his early years in Flint, C. S. Mott took an interest in the civic life of this growing town. "Flint was like the gold rush—the American dream," Bill White recounted. "C. S. Mott was Mayor three times in 1912, 1913 and 1918 and saw the need for water, sewer, streets and schools. So he became involved in developing Flint's entire civic structure."

As part of his work helping citizens engage civic institutions, in 1926 C. S. Mott created the Mott Foundation and later became involved in transforming schools into community resources. "You had a population that was coming into factories," Bill explained. "How do you give them extra activities? Build strong neighborhoods and all that? They came up with the idea and I think it's still very valid, that the school is owned by the public. C. S. Mott was a factory man. [He realized that schools could], like a factory, work 24/7. [Schools] needed to have a special position that could help put on the activities that the community wanted." School councils became an institutionalized space for citizens to provide input into this process.

Funded in large part by the Mott Foundation, and pioneered by Frank Manley, the idea of community schools had soon spread across Flint. "In the fifties, if you came into Flint in the evening you'd find these schools lit up," recounted Jeanette Mansour, who has worked with the foundation since 1978 on the program staff and as a consultant. "Whether people were learning sewing, or square dancing—these were active and lively places. Communities coalesced around these schools."

Initially, the school councils provided a space for these groups to program school activities together, but in many cases these councils over time became central meeting areas for community members to discuss other neighborhood concerns. "[It was about] how to empower the parents and how to empower the schools," Bill explained. "The school needs to be part of the community . . . . So here you have distinctly community people coming in and working in the schools." The Mott Foundation *1973 Annual Report* underlined, "Today the Foundation is proving that the school as a resource center can provide a driving force for grappling with the major and crucial problems threatening the very survival of citizens and their community."[4]

The community school—including the school councils—pioneered by the Mott Foundation also influenced education in many parts of the United States. By 1971, "programs were operating successfully in school districts encompassing more than six million people."[5] Many of these districts included minority communities. In the mid-1970s, federal legislation passed providing funding for community school development through the U.S. Office of Education.[6]

Bill noted one mechanism that encouraged the spread of the schools. "There were 10,000 to 12,000 people per year who would come to Flint schools to see them."

Foundation at a Turning Point

The 1970s marked a turning point for the foundation, which included "deep reflection about what direction to take the foundation," explained Cris Doby, program officer for the foundation's Building Organized Communities grantmaking area. During this period, the foundation expanded its national work and institutionalized new systems of decision making. The foundation also began to experiment with new forms of community engagement—including support for neighborhood organizations and congregation-based networks engaged in community organizing work.

Explaining the impetus for the changes, Bill White recalled, "In the 1970s there is a changing of the guard. C. S. Mott passes on. Frank Manley passes on. The 1969 Tax Reform Act is passed, which affects the foundation because you have to separate aspects of family, foundation, and some other things. And I entered the scene, whether you like it or not," Bill joked with regard to his arrival at the Mott Foundation.

After graduating from Dartmouth, Bill White worked on Wall Street and was part of a management consulting firm. He was also married to C. S. Mott's granddaughter Claire Mott, and joined the foundation staff as a consultant to help the foundation address the operating changes required by the 1969 Tax Reform Act. (By 1976 he had become president of the foundation.)

"The world [in the 1960s and early 1970s] was changing also," Bill continued. "We had the Detroit riots of 1967 or so, the Great Society programs, the Vietnam War, racial issues. There is urban unrest in this town, people meeting to try to solve problems."

Initially as a consultant and then as senior staff and trustee, Bill focused on helping the foundation manage the transitions. "[I was] trying to organize the foundation to take advantage of things, that's what was driving me. Build on your legacy and try to take it forward."

Such work included several institutional shifts, largely aimed at increasing the foundation's flexibility to take advantage of new opportunities. Bill convinced C. S. Mott to approve an annual administrative budget, rather than every project put forward, and worked with the board to change its approach to approving grants through more delegated authority. The shifts allowed the board to focus on such big-picture foundation concerns as policy and strategy and gave Bill the flexibility to then determine how to implement these decisions appropriately.

As part of the shift, over the next decade, the foundation decided to slowly phase out funding for existing Flint Board of Education programs. The new philosophy was that if the community believed in the programs, it should pay for them with taxes, fees, and charges, and in many instances communities did vote for increased taxes to maintain them.

School Councils and New Community Organizing Opportunities

Instead of funding the same initiatives, the foundation began to find ways to encourage the school programs they had helped establish to innovate and revitalize themselves. These efforts were instrumental in planting seeds for the foundation's future work supporting community organizing not related to school councils.

In 1975, the foundation launched an initiative challenging "each of the 41 elementary school community advisory councils in Flint to use up to $5,000 toward [largely] community-based improvement projects or processes."[7] The program represented an effort by the foundation to pioneer models by which communities could use the school councils to solve their own problems, not only in schools but also more broadly. "It was a school-based approach to organizing," Bill explained.

By 1976, the program had evolved into a national initiative named Stimulating Neighborhood Action Process (SNAP).[8] This program aimed to expand the scope of school councils nationally.

The foundation also began to encourage community members to run the school councils. "[Someone] said, 'Why do you need a fully certificated community school director who has a master's degree and a big salary running this community school? Why not get someone from the community? Let's emphasize the process side."

As part of this shift, the same individual also convinced the foundation to emphasize the term *community education* over *community school* to support the focus on process over program. Bill reflected on the impact of this shift. "I feel we gave up something ... because you know what you're talking about when you talk about a community school. When you talk about 'community education,' it could be anything, anywhere in the world."

By changing the language, however, the foundation laid the groundwork for expanding its work beyond schools. The fact that community education could describe non-school-related activities ultimately helped open the door for the foundation to support neighborhood organizations and congregation-based networks, as well as other forms of community engagement, such as community development corporations.[9] Suddenly the work of neighborhood organizations, churches, and other membership organizations influencing public institutions from outside these entities began to fit more squarely within the scope of the foundation.

Embracing New Forms of Community Organizing

Also in the 1970s, Bill White sought to develop a more comprehensive foundation strategy to underpin its grantmaking going forward, one that ultimately led the foundation to support new forms of community organizing. "[Senior program executive] Homer Dowdy and I spent three months holed up in an empty room, just writing," Bill continued. The final product was a new plan called Foundation for Living, which built on C. S. Mott's belief in community and worked to create a more explicit foundation approach with respect to supporting the ability of individuals to engage in democracy—in their neighborhoods and beyond.

One program area was community renewal, which focused in part on the effective functioning of community systems. In 1976 Bill hired Bob Nichol, a community organizer who worked in East Harlem, New York, to run this program.

Bob recalled of his new job, "A friend of mine told me if I went to work for a foundation, I'd never have a bad meal and never hear the truth again. It was true. It was a real experience to be taken from a job community organizing in East Harlem and be plopped down in Flint where people kind of fawned over me."

Jon Blyth, another program officer hired at the same time as Bob Nichol, had a different view of those early years. "These were golden jobs," he recalled. "We had an awful lot of freedom. We had a lot of opportunity to create a new image for the foundation."

From his new base in Flint, Bob used some of his freedom to provide funding to neighborhood organizations engaged in community organizing in a variety of low-income neighborhoods, including East Harlem. This organizing was not centered around the schools. Instead the work helped community members develop their own independent organizations that could focus on their issues of choice. Although the foundation had already begun this transition, such work was still significantly different from the approaches the foundation had undertaken to that point.

Unlike the school councils, these organizations often found themselves in opposition to the government. "They pressured local officials to enforce housing codes, build low-income housing units, and increase public funding for schools in their neighborhoods," explained Jack Litzenberg, interim program director for Pathways Out of Poverty and with the foundation since 1984.

"There was a power model to [Bob Nichol's] work," Jack recalled. "One of the many bad things about being low income is that you don't have a voice, so local officials and developers often do not take into account your needs. Bob was supporting grantees as they worked to create change through summing up numbers of people in a community so that their stand would have the most people behind it." By building membership institutions that supported collective action, East Harlem residents could claim a greater share of the city's resources, which flowed disproportionally to wealthier neighborhoods with greater power and influence in New York City.

The strategy Bob was using, however, had some familiarity to the Mott Foundation at the time: "Trustees were used to supporting school councils," Jack recalled. "Mott trustees understood the efficacy of civic engagement. They may not have deployed the word 'power,' but they understood the concept of organizing communities. While Bob was much more focused on building a social movement [that would address inequality in our society], the concept of organizing was not scary to the trustees." Further, some at the foundation were aware that such forms of community-based organizations were emerging around the country, fueled by the movements of the 1960s. Citizens were creating congregation-based and other networks to organize people.

Nevertheless, such grants often met with resistance within the foundation. "It was uncomfortable trying to move these community organizing grants through the system," Bob Nichol recalled.

Impressed by a presentation Bob gave at a retreat, Bill White (president) supported a trustee trip to New York City in August 1977 to see the work Bob was funding. The site visit was one of a series aimed at educating the trustees regarding different forms of community engagement work in which the foundation was involved.

"We took the trustees to the South Bronx to see what organizing in that region of the country was all about," Jon Blyth (former program officer) recalled. "In my view the trustees didn't grasp the full significance of poverty in America until that visit to the South Bronx."

Bob also encouraged the foundation to hire the Center for Community Change (CCC) to evaluate prospects for neighborhood revitalization and organizing in Flint, including the effectiveness of the school councils funded by the Mott Foundation. He hoped that the evaluation would raise questions within the foundation regarding its preferred strategies for change. Presented to the foundation's board of trustees, one of the key recommendations was that the foundation move "beyond school councils to fund and help grow whole neighborhood organizations," recalled Andy Mott (no relation to C. S. Mott), CCC's deputy director at the time.

Although Bob Nichol left the Mott Foundation in 1978 only two years into his tenure, "he lit a match," explained Rob Collier, program officer at the foundation between 1977 and 1983 (and president of the Council of Michigan Foundations in 2008). Bob had educated several program officers who continued to push the foundation to support organizing outside the school system.

"I became passionately involved," explained Jon Blyth. "Bob was a jeans and sneakers guy. I fought with a sport coat and tie. I tried to reach decisions in a compromise way."

Over time the foundation became increasingly open to supporting these non-school-centered approaches to organizing. "Bob opened the door," Jon explained, "but Bill White deserved the credit for permitting his creative program officers to start bringing in grants related to this kind of community organizing. Maryanne Mott, daughter of Charles Stewart Mott and a trustee, provided leadership among trustees in promoting and expanding the foundation's organizing agenda."

"I think that people began to realize that [in some cases] they couldn't make things better, without making things different," added Cris Doby, program officer.

Program officers also sought ways to increase the comfort level of management and trustees toward such forms of community organizing. "We had to be careful in developing new grant strategies and projects with management and trustees," Jon recalled. "Rather than supporting solely community organizing, we decided to fund partnerships of local groups and scientists working with communities at risk. One example was grant support to the Harvard School of Public Health, accompanied by support for a local group in a Boston-area community facing unknown but possibly deadly risks from toxic groundwater contamination. A well-established institution like Harvard made everyone feel comfortable. We weren't fighting industry or jobs. We were promoting good science and a level playing field so the communities with chemical plants in their neighborhoods had access to information."

Lyndon Johnson's War on Poverty, launched in 1964, also influenced the foundation. "All of a sudden you have all these types of agencies coming into local communities, all these federal dollars," Bill recalled. "But [community groups] are not ready. They don't have their organization. They don't have their formal papers so they can't get government money."

These circumstances focused the foundation's attention on the need to support community-based organizations in their efforts to pressure civic institutions to change, as well as to strengthen their capacity to capture federal dollars aimed at providing services to low-income communities. Encouraged in part by CCC to meet these needs, in 1979 the Mott Foundation established what is now called the Intermediary Support Organization (ISO) program. The program funded several intermediary organizations, including CCC and the National Council of la Raza, which provided regranting and technical assistance to emerging neighborhood organizations.[10]

In helping persuade others within the foundation, the community organizing advocates used the school councils as a touchstone. "The school councils were what got management to accept the national ISO program," noted Jack Litzenberg (interim program director). "Through the school councils, management was already familiar with the concept of citizens banding together for social goals."

Supporting Non-School-Centered Community Organizing

In the 1990s, institutional evaluations concluded that the ISO program beneficiaries, particularly when they focused on expanding membership to build power for change, as opposed to simply dispensing direct services, were very successful in achieving policy changes. "A service role would be a program to clean up a burned house, as opposed to going to city hall to make sure city hall had it cleaned up, and to come up with a plan for annual inspection of houses to prevent another fire from happening," Jack Litzenberg explained. Although neighborhood organizations providing services with federal dollars played an important role, they often did not have the kind of independence needed to effectively pressure the government for policy changes.

Then, in 1997 the foundation hired Ron White, a program officer with a long history of supporting such forms of community organizing. Ron articulated the central questions guiding his programming: "Where do we learn the democratic practice of politics? Where were the larger centers of organizing that might impact the country? . . . So I began thinking, 'Wouldn't it be great to fund statewide and national community organizing?'"

Such a strategy would build on the Mott Foundation's support of neighborhood organizations and school councils. However, instead of simply supporting local organizations, Ron wanted to work with entities that were connecting local groups, many of them clusters of activist congregations, together across the country. These organizations were part of a wave of local grassroots groups that were banding together for larger-scale change, and reshaping the landscape of community organizing across the country.

TYPES OF COMMUNITY-BASED MEMBERSHIP ORGANIZATIONS

The following are two types of community-based membership organizations:

Neighborhood organizations typically focus on issues of local scope and impact, such as schools, housing, zoning, commercial development, or public services.

National [Networks] in community organizing range from relatively centralized organizations with local chapters to organizing networks whose affiliates are structurally independent but share a common worldview, methodology, training, system, or policy agenda.

Although each individual organization is different, national groups often have similar strengths and weaknesses. "National organizations have the infrastructure to move things at a larger scale [and thus have greater capacity to shape national dialogue]," reflected Luz Vega-Marquis, president and CEO of the Marguerite Casey Foundation. "But the national networks need to work on better representation from the local affiliates."

To counteract these weaknesses, Ann Bastian at the New World Foundation explained, "Our foundation only funds local chapters of national networks."

Independent and local organizations, in contrast, "are really important for innovation," Luz remarked, noting that such organizations are often well rooted in the local realities of their members. Ann added that the independent organizations are commonly more effective at building coalitions with other membership organizations than are their national counterparts.

Note: From *Funding Community Organizing.* Full reference is in the Notes at the end of the book.[11]

To support this objective, soon after he arrived Ron began funding large regional networks, many of which were congregation based, with grants that often ranged between $150,000 and $300,000. These included the Gamaliel Foundation, PICO National

Network, and Direct Action and Research Training Center (DART), among others. These organizations were some of the largest of the congregation-based networks gaining force around the country. Although congregations also sometimes funded such networks, grants represented important contributions.

"I wanted organizations that were forming leaders, knew how to organize and build power, and that were growing," explained Ron. "People voted with their feet. Did people show up when the organization called a meeting?"

CONGREGATION-BASED ORGANIZING

There are between one and three million people organized under congregation-based community organizing networks, according to the 2001 report "Faith Based Community Organizing: The State of the Field," commissioned by Interfaith Funders.[12]

Expanding Foundation Commitment to Community Participation

Ron White also developed eight training sessions with colleagues to discuss approaches to poverty. Part of a larger strategic planning process for the foundation, the trainings helped increase the number of individuals within the foundation familiar with using organizing to build the power of communities to ensure that public and private institutions remained responsive to community needs and accountable to any promises they made to citizens and others.

In one session, Ron showed colleagues a video on the Dudley Street Neighborhood Initiative, a community-led neighborhood development effort in Boston, which had received funding from the Mott Foundation. The video, called *Holding Ground: The Rebirth of Dudley Street*, began with the original meeting called by the Mabel Louise Riley Foundation to launch this effort. Ron recounted,

> As I remember that video, the Riley Foundation called together the community and said, "This is what we have planned for your community." And in the middle of the meeting a woman stood up and said, "How come those of us who have been living this every day aren't sitting up there where you are?"

I stopped the tape at that point to talk about this woman's role. Some people said, "This is an awful lot of money. Who cares who does it?" Then we had a discussion about who does things, and why that's an important question.

As I remember, every person who had been at the meeting highlighted in the video said afterwards, "If she hadn't done that, we would have made a terrible mistake." The Riley Foundation would have poured millions into this community, and it would have been wasted. The foundation was proposing things that were good for downtown development but not reflective of community needs.

For example, without community control of the development process, development would have likely attracted chain stores, whereas the community wanted to preserve existing small businesses owned by community members. (See Chapter Four for a description of the Jacobs Family Foundation's community-driven development efforts.)

"By the end of the eight sessions, my colleagues were getting pretty excited," Ron recalled. "Some were focusing on economic development. Others on education. But they could all see how these community organizing models could work with their initiatives. Unless a community was organized, a project could not be accountable to that community. It was about 'power before program.'"

Translating Excitement into Action

In 1999, the trustees approved a program area called Pathways Out of Poverty, which built on the foundation's previous grantmaking and interests. One of the four grantmaking areas under this program was Building Organized Communities, which aimed to build the overall infrastructure of organizing by supporting regional and national networks, many of them congregation based. In addition to funding networks directly, the foundation decided to help grow the capacity of local organizations to join larger networks through the ISO program, given the value the foundation was seeing in these larger networks.

The strategy for the grantmaking area was to provide general operating support grants. "We felt, if these networks got some breathing space, they might be able to move in powerful directions. But it was a real step out in trust to say, 'These groups have a track record. Let's trust them with some money to build out in whatever direction they believe they need to go,'" explained Cris Doby, who was hired in 2000 to help support the grantmaking area. "We felt this was a better way to go because it gave the leadership to the grantees rather than the foundation or a consultant deciding what these networks needed to do."

BETTER RESULTS THROUGH COMMUNITY ENGAGEMENT AND ORGANIZING

Educating colleagues regarding the importance of community engagement and neighborhood and congregation-based organizing has been an ongoing process.

Finding colleagues too busy to participate in site visits and trainings, Cris Doby (program officer) found other ways to increase their commitment. "What really helped advance the work was having an organizing grantee supported in another program area's portfolio," Cris explained.

The Environment Program, for instance, was funding the Metropolitan Organizing Strategy Enabling Strength (MOSES)—a congregation-based community organizing group based in Detroit. Cris helped the Mott Foundation environment team see "how MOSES was part of a larger discipline," recalled Linda Helstowski, a consultant to the environment program.

Describing her own transformation, Linda said, "I had a very top-down notion of how to get a solution in place." She recounted a meeting that helped challenge this approach: "Cris took the lead on a meeting with MOSES and let what they wanted to do bubble up. A MOSES spokesperson said, 'We know from our community that transportation is the key issue, so we will need to get these decision-makers around the table and will be targeting these specific goals.' I remember thinking 'Wow! This is really different.' MOSES—as a membership organization controlled by community members themselves—clearly had a pulse on what was happening in the community. I was used to grantees defining the agenda first and then going to rally people in communities."

Cris added, "Many funders and others think that leadership and expertise dwell in think tanks or with academics and policymakers. Organizing insists that leadership and expertise also reside in communities, regardless of income or education."

Building Trust with the Grantees

When Cris Doby took over the full Building Organized Communities portfolio in 2003, strengthening trust became her top priority. "I needed to build trust with my grantees so that I could have meaningful conversations with them about what they needed," Cris underlined. "Ron White had an outstanding relationship with his grantees. [When he left], that trust was not transferred to me." The grantees were saying 'He gets us and she doesn't.' There was one time when a grantee actually drove me to shouting, and I'm a person that doesn't even raise my voice in my own home. They didn't trust me, and they weren't giving me the information I needed. They answered every question with 'Ron said this and Ron did that.' And I finally said, "*Ron is not here anymore!*"

"Trust is not simply transferred between program officers," Cris explained. "The program officer needs to invest the time and develop that trust."

"It was a year of intense travel and relationship building. I felt my job at that point was really, really hard. But I never lost sight of the fact that their jobs were far harder."

Cris listed strategies she used to build trust, many of which she had learned from her colleagues at the Mott Foundation and in the field. With her grantees, she worked to (1) be honest and upfront; (2) ensure they didn't scorn one another in her presence; (3) let them know she was not a judge—her success depended on theirs; (4) support them with proposal development; (5) raise their profiles with other funders, including securing additional funding sources; and (6) use the foundation's convening power, but judiciously, so as not to overburden grantees already stretched for time. Of this final point, Cris noted, I had to be careful when convening grantees, knowing they'd come just because a funder called. Convening them without their buy-in would have been a waste of time."

Over the course of the year, Cris began to see signs of trust emerge. "What shifted as they grew to trust me was something any program officer would want. When things went wrong, they told me immediately. It was important because I needed to tell my superiors. If [the foundation] was going to end up in the news, we needed to know that."

In the last decade there has been growing interest among foundations in supporting congregation-based organizing, noted Kathy Partridge, executive director of Interfaith Funders, a network of funders focused on congregation-based community organizing. The Marguerite Casey, W. K. Kellogg, Annie Casey, Gates, Ford, and Robert Wood Johnson foundations, and the California Endowment, Carnegie Corporation of New York, Jewish Funds for Justice, the Open Society Institute, and dozens of local foundations have all funded congregation-based networks or affiliates (or both).

The biggest funders of congregation-based organizing, however, are faith-based grantmaking programs themselves. "No other organization comes close to the Catholic Campaign for Human Development in funding congregation-based organizing in the last thirty years," Kathy emphasized. The Unitarian Universalist Veatch Program at Shelter Rock has also been a strong and consistent funder of such efforts.

Building Capacity Nationally

The story of the PICO National Network depicts how grantees used Mott dollars to build their capacity and secure wins for low-income communities. A national network of local organizations, PICO was organizing congregations around the country in support of primarily low-income and middle-class communities.

With Ron White's initial grants given even before the Building Organized Communities grantmaking area was approved, Mott funding to PICO between 1998 and 2004 totaled $2.2 million.[13] The general support grants helped solidify PICO local affiliates and state-level networks, and provided a platform from which PICO began to explore a federal-level campaign. Spurred by state-level wins in California, "PICO members began asking, 'If we can [have so much success] in California, imagine if all our organizations across the country came together?'" recounted John Baumann, founder and former executive director for PICO.

In 2005, local affiliates decided to focus on expanding the State Children's Health Insurance Program (SCHIP) as a federal campaign topic. Created in 1997, the federal program supplemented state funding for health care for uninsured children.[14] PICO joined Washington, D.C.–based children's advocates, such as Georgetown Center for Children and Families, First Focus, and the American Academy of Pediatrics, to champion SCHIP, and quickly became indispensable to the campaign.

"Influence in Washington is local. We had to show congress-people that their constituents cared about this issue," recounted Gordon Whitman, PICO's director of public policy and communications. "So PICO affiliates ran a series of state campaigns that added up to one federal campaign. We organized rallies. We ran compassionate Sundays where churches across the country organized actions. We knew when to move things at strategic times based on what was happening in local areas. We coordinated and led the faith community."

In addition, PICO's local affiliates brought a human face to Washington. "We became the 'go-to source' when people needed a parent to speak. There was some unreality in D.C., and so we brought that real experience."

FUNDING CAMPAIGNS

For Cris Doby, witnessing PICO's journey has been a learning experience. "It was quite a challenge to the PICO organizations and organizers," Cris noted, emphasizing that the high-pressure work took a toll on both leaders and affiliates. If I'd known how hard it was going to be for them, I might have helped them structure the money differently. We might have pulled some money to give organizers and key leaders a respite."

"We also should have found more ways to credit PICO," Cris emphasized. "There were several groups that were not generous in

(Continued)

sharing credit, and it undermined the work. We could have been thinking about ways to credential PICO differently [to strengthen its position in Washington]—make introductory calls, introduce them to other funders. Some advocacy groups were smarter about their press relations, so they were better at getting their names associated with the win."

In 2009, the campaign's efforts bore fruit. President Barack Obama signed a bill increasing spending for SCHIP by $32.8 billion and raising tobacco taxes to pay for it.[15] The Congressional Budget Office predicts that the bill will help cover more than "four million children by 2013, while continuing coverage for seven million youngsters."[16] The win came after a defeat in 2007, when President George W. Bush vetoed a similar bill.

For PICO, the initiative has been about, even more than securing a policy victory, rebuilding democracy. Scott Reed, executive director of PICO, recounted a story that motivated him. "Frank Goring, one of PICO's leaders from the Faith Chapel Church of God, went to a DC meeting. It was a fairly intimidating environment. The grand buildings and big doorways could make a person feel small. Frank Goring said he'd been orphaned when he was young, had lived in a series of foster homes, and was told he would never amount to anything. He said, 'Here I am leading a delegation' and broke down in tears."

Of the significance of this moment, Scott explained, "It's been about demystifying Washington for citizens around the country. I've heard this over and over again. It's been a message of hope and transformation. By demystifying what happens in DC, people's imagination can catch fire, and they can see how their creative proposals can lead to significant changes."

"Our organizing model has been values based," John Baumann continued. "Members have been reflecting on those values and how they relate to scripture."

"We helped congregations organize compassion Sabbath to understand the issue of children's health coverage through their own faith values," Gordon Whitman explained. "Pastors prayed for uninsured children and for wisdom among elected officials."

Growth and Impact of National Networks

By 2009, PICO had become one of the largest community-based organizations in the United States, supported by the Mott, Knight, Public Welfare, Marguerite Casey, Nathan Cummings, and Packard foundations and Jewish Funds for Justice, Unitarian Universalist Veatch Program at Shelter Rock, and California Endowment, among others.[17] Through organizing, PICO had grown to include one thousand member institutions representing roughly one million families.

Other major national congregation-based networks and their affiliates funded under Mott's Building Organized Communities program were also experiencing similar growth. By 2008, Direct Action and Research Training Center (DART) had more than doubled in size since 2000 to include roughly four hundred local religious congregations.[18] Gamaliel Foundation experienced similar growth, and in 2008 had a multifaith, multiracial membership base of over one million people.[19]

Reflecting on the growth of congregation-based networks, Kathy Partridge of Interfaith Funders noted, "This is a major movement."

CONGREGATION-BASED NETWORKS

Direct Action and Research Training Center (DART) is a network of religious congregations (including churches, synagogues, mosques, and others) based in six states, working toward local policy changes.

Gamaliel Foundation is a national network of congregation-based organizations focused both on development issues in urban and suburban areas and democracy more broadly. In 2008, the Gamaliel Foundation was in the news in part because President Barack Obama had helped establish a Gamaliel Foundation local affiliate during his days as a community organizer.[20]

Individuals from both DART and the Gamaliel Foundation noted that support from the Mott Foundation has played an important role in growing this movement. "Our success was based on the fact that we really focused on strengthening each affiliate and training our organizers. Mott was the key funder for that," John Calkins of DART explained.

Greg Galluzo, executive director for the Gamaliel Foundation, added, "Gamaliel would have found a way or made a way. That said—that money was some of the best we ever got. It was for general operating support and was predictable, which let us use it to strike at the heart of what organizing has been about—building organizations for power."

An organizer of one community-based organization explained why increasing membership has been so important. "When people have power, they have the ability to give or take away something that a decision maker wants, so it's not just big developers and moneyed interests calling the shots. You see a dramatic difference in how people act when they walk into a room with twenty-five hundred religious folks who all want the same thing." He noted that one effective practice has been to bring policymakers and other decision makers into a room and ask them for specific proposals—such as a tax increase to pay for an education initiative.

As was true for PICO, the affiliates have been making waves. In Polk County, Florida, for example, DART affiliate PEACE was a significant player in helping the county commission pass a sales tax for health care for the uninsured, which in 2006–2007 raised $35.7 million.[21] In Pinellas County, Florida, DART affiliate FAST was instrumental in securing more than $15 million in county funds for affordable housing units.[22]

Many of these congregation-based networks have also been effective in schools (an ongoing priority of the Mott Foundation), in part by building communication channels between parents and school administrators. The Annenberg Institute for School Reform (Brown University) concluded in a study of PICO, DART, and other community organizing groups, "Across multiple data sources, our six-year study found strong and consistent relationships between community organizing and policy and resource decisions, school-level improvements, and student outcomes."[23]

Conclusion

C. S. Mott founded the Charles Stewart Mott Foundation in part to strengthen citizen participation in community life in Flint, Michigan. His passion for ensuring that individuals remained actively engaged in public life led him to support what became his lasting legacy—the growth of community schools first in his hometown and then nationally. In many states, the work has played a role in transforming the school systems in support of equity and justice by changing how these institutions interact with the often low-income communities in which they are situated.

After Mott's passing, the leaders of the Mott Foundation remained true to his original purpose and sought ways to expand on his core beliefs by experimenting with additional forms of community engagement. Reflecting on the variety of models the foundation has pursued, Marilyn Stein LeFeber, vice president of communications, said, "A community should be able to define what those vehicles are. Sometimes they will be through schools. Sometimes independent organizations. Sometimes something else." Bill White (president) agreed: "It is going to vary from community to community to community."

One of a variety of approaches the foundation has pursued has been support for congregation-based networks, and the Mott Foundation's patient capital has been one important factor supporting organizing across the country. Cris Doby noted, "the growth of organizing has been nothing short of phenomenal, with the networks we've supported vastly increasing their capacity." Through these networks citizens have been making their voices heard around the country and beyond—helping channel millions, and in some cases billions, of local, state, and federal dollars into health care, housing, and education for primarily low-income and middle-class citizens. By helping citizens join forces, the Mott Foundation has been supporting efforts to reweave the democratic cloth of the United States.

Lessons Learned

Since its founding, the Mott Foundation has helped strengthen many forms of community engagement, including community organizing. How might you support community engagement—including community organizing—within your foundation? The following are some strategies:

- Consider supporting both insider and outsider strategies. Help catalyze the development of participatory mechanisms within the institutions and agencies that affect people's lives, to ensure their active participation within them, but also support independent membership-based organizations that can pressure such institutions to change from the outside.
- To increase interest in community organizing, (1) give high priority to site visits as a way to engage trustees with new ideas; (2) find grantees in the portfolios of your colleagues and show them how these grantees are part of a larger field; and (3) find ways to show colleagues how community organizing can significantly enhance the results of any issue area (such as education, health care, or housing), constituency, or community).
- When developing a grantmaking strategy, focus on how to help grantees build the power needed to move a group, institution, or policy target. Usually individuals need to be not only educated but also pressured in some way before they will change.

Transforming Funder-Grantee Power Relationships Through Creative Foundation Structures

One important aspect of social justice philanthropy is working to transform inequities in the world outside foundations. Another is helping transform the hierarchies that foundations are often a part of creating.

Money is a source of influence, and how foundations choose to give has impact. Understanding this, a growing number of foundations have challenged the power relationships inherent to grantee-grantor relationships, asking why grantors should be the primary decision makers determining who receives funding and who doesn't.

Leading this movement is a group of fifteen public foundations committed to sharing decision making with activists, particularly as this relates to grantmaking strategies. Part of the Funding Exchange Network, in 2008 these were the Appalachian Community Fund, Bread

& Roses Community Fund, Chinook Fund, Crossroad Fund, Fund
for Santa Barbara, Fund for Southern Communities, Hawai'i People's Fund, Haymarket People's Fund, Headwaters Foundation
for Justice, Liberty Hill Foundation, McKenzie River Gathering
Foundation, North Star Fund, Foundation for Change, Three Rivers Community Foundation, and Wisconsin Community Fund.[1]
Community foundations such as the Humboldt Area Foundation
in California have also found ways to adapt these principles to
their own institutions. Other foundations have embraced a hybrid
approach, mixing activists and family members on their boards.

If you are interested in finding ways to reduce power imbal-
ances with grantees, the cases of the Global Fund for Women and
the Gulf Coast Fund are rich with insight, as is the chapter on the
Liberty Hill Foundation in Part Four.

The Global Fund for Women used an international team of
advisers to help guide grantmaking, and played an important role
in helping women internationally build funds in their own countries, in part to reduce their dependency on U.S. philanthropic
dollars. The Gulf Coast Fund—working to support survivors of
Hurricanes Katrina and Rita in Alabama, Louisiana, Mississippi,
and Texas—chose to create an advisory group of individuals from
the affected regions to choose grantees.

Individuals from both the Global Fund for Women and the
Gulf Coast Fund echoed similar reasons for pursuing such strategies. Both found that participatory structures led to better grantmaking and higher impact. Further, each was concerned with the
power dynamics of race, class, and location—in a system where
philanthropic money was flowing from economically rich areas to
economically disadvantaged ones.

By equalizing power relationships, the foundation and the collaborative helped build vibrant forces for change in the areas in
which they work.

9

Addressing Internationally Women's Needs for Funding

The Case of the Global Fund for Women

Concerned with the dearth of resources available to women's rights organizers, the U.S.-based Global Fund for Women helps women of the "global south" build indigenous sources of funding. The resulting local foundations join forces to strengthen women's voices around the globe.

Frances Kissling, former president of what is now called Catholics for Choice, described the evening when the idea for the Global Fund for Women emerged. "It was early 1987. Anne Firth Murray [with the Hewlett Foundation], Laura Lederer [with the Skaggs Foundation] and I were having drinks at the Council on Foundations' conference."[1]

As the women chatted, the dialogue turned to the many underfunded small women's groups that existed internationally. Having witnessed how pathbreaking many of these women's groups were, the women also noted how difficult they were to fund. They were often small and unknown, and many in the foundation world didn't fully understand the significance of their work.

During the conversation, Anne noted how she had seen these small grassroots organizations run by women as vital to her own family planning portfolio at the Hewlett Foundation, but that the foundation's board had discouraged her from funding them. "The Hewlett Foundation was funding groups that [provided a service—that of distributing] contraceptives," Anne said. "They weren't ready to make the jump over to recognizing how the groups' work empowering women was an important part of [what was at the time called] fertility control." Explaining the foundation's resistance, she noted that in the 1980s, empowering women to have greater control of their lives—including negotiating contraception with sexual partners—was not yet widely viewed by the philanthropic community as critical to family planning or even possible.

Contemplating her approaching departure from the Hewlett Foundation, Anne recalled saying to Laura and Frances that evening, "I really regret that I wasn't able to establish a fund at Hewlett to meet the needs of these small groups of women." Frances remembered responding, "You are the one moving on. Why don't you start a foundation to support women like this?" When Anne protested that foundations were founded by rich people, Frances replied, "'Well, I'd give $500 to a foundation like that, wouldn't you?'" Anne replied with a yes, and the women ordered another bottle of champagne.

"And that was the beginning of the Global Fund for Women," Frances concluded. Explaining why she had asked Anne this fateful question, Frances said, "I was very intrigued with the idea that all women could be philanthropists."

Global Fund for Women Snapshot

Type: Public charity
Year founded: 1987
Grant range (1988): $3,000–$5,000
Grant range (2008): $500–$183,000
Total grants awarded (1988): $22,000

Total grants awarded (2008): $8.7 million

Total assets (1988): $67,000

Total assets (2008): $25 million

Geographic focus: International

Primary current funding areas: Building peace and ending gender-based violence; ensuring economic and environmental justice; advancing health and sexual and reproductive rights; expanding civic and political participation; increasing access to education; and fostering social change philanthropy

Staff size in 2008: Forty-one

Location: Originally in Palo Alto, California; moved to San Francisco, California, in 2000; New York office added in 2007

Note: Snapshot information for each chapter varies depending on data available. Dates refer to either the calendar year or the end of the fiscal cycle. For snapshot sources, refer to the Notes section at the end of the book.[2]

Starting a Fund

"The next morning, I began wandering around the conference—after all, there was a great deal of money at this conference—telling people, 'We're thinking about creating a women's fund,'" Anne recalled. "There were three women who asked how they could support it. I said to them, 'Why don't you give $5,000 and become founding donors?'" Laughing, Anne Firth Murray noted, "I mean, I just made it up. I wish I'd said $10,000."

"By the evening I was saying to people, 'We've created a women's fund,'" Anne continued. "From that day on, I was obsessed."

When Anne went home to Palo Alto, California, she asked the David and Lucile Packard Foundation for a mailbox to receive mail at its address. "I asked executive director [at the time] Cole Wilbur, 'Would you allow us to get our mail here? Would you give us a box?' And he said, 'Why just a box? Why not an office instead?' We were welcomed by the Packard Foundation and occupied an office there for the first year of the life of the Global Fund."

In 1987, the Global Fund incorporated as a public charity. Kavita Ramdas, president and CEO of the Global Fund since 1996, commented of its creation, "The fund was inspired by the feistiness of women and was fueled by the no-holds-barred tradition and entrepreneurial spirit of Silicon Valley."

Although Anne noted that she garnered significant support from people on the East Coast, Frances Kissling pointed to resistance among many East Coast–based funders. "Within the philanthropic community, there were people doing international women's work who were not happy that the Global Fund was starting. They wanted us to work within traditional development assistance channels or international institutions like the UN."

Frances noted that the Global Fund's ability to grow was also based on another ingredient: the reputation of its founders and the access available to them. "Had [someone] with less standing among philanthropists tried to start the fund, it could have been crushed. There's been this myth that territoriality happens only among grantees, but territoriality has been part of the philanthropic world as well. While the Global Fund did not start with a wealthy individual, [despite their working-class backgrounds] Anne and Laura had become part of a network of money and were therefore also allowed to do certain things in our society," Frances continued. "They could not be stopped so easily. Not everyone who started a new foundation got offered free space at the Packard Foundation."

"We made the first set of grants based on the knowledge the early board brought to the Fund," Frances noted. "We were all travelers and knew a lot of people."

"One of the things that quite impressed me, when we were doing the second round of grants [in 1988–1989]," Frances continued, "was speaking to a grantee in the Philippines who had not re-applied. I asked the people who worked there why and they said, 'Because we told somebody else to apply.' There was a way in which people saw this as a community resource. The 'Keep the Resource to Yourself Principle' didn't prevail."

"I think that generosity of spirit came from the fact that the leadership of the fund was clearly more like the grantees than unlike the grantees," Frances continued. "People understood that the money was being raised. It wasn't just some big pot of Microsoft money sitting around. And the money was small. It wasn't enough to be worth not being generous about. It was also easy to get. You could write a two-page proposal in any language, and the next thing you knew you had a $5,000 grant from this new funder."

SMALL GRANTS: A CRITICAL GRANTMAKING TOOL

The Global Fund for Women has been one of a few pioneers that has established small grants as an important vehicle for grassroots change. Others have included the Global Greengrants Fund, Grassroots Grantmakers, First Peoples Worldwide, and the International Development Exchange.

While pointing to the role seed grants play in establishing organizations, most supporters of these grants also caution that larger strategic grants are also crucial, particularly as organizations grow. With this in mind, over time the Global Fund for Women has given increasingly large grants aimed at stabilizing key players within the women's movement worldwide. At the same time, they have continued their small grants program and remain one of the most reliable sources of funding for small startup women's groups.

To support grantmaking, the board created an advisory council to vet proposals and inform potential grantees of the fund's existence. "These were people that we met from around the world that were active in the feminist movement," Frances Kissling noted. In 1990, the council included eighty-three individuals from Africa, Asia, Latin America, Europe, Australia, and the United States.[3]

Although the founders had different recollections of what was funded in the early years, Anne noted, "We were funding groups on the edge that were trying to transform their societies and taking risks to do that. These were often groups that couldn't receive money from other sources because of the nature of the issues they were taking on."

Empowering Grantees with Trust

As the Global Fund staff and board operationalized their ideas, Anne underlined the importance of asking the women grantees themselves for guidance. "The young program officers would say again and again, 'What do we do about this?' and I'd say, 'Why don't we ask the women?'"

Guided by a belief that the women knew best, the Global Fund gave general operating support to its grantees. "From evaluations, we learned the tremendous value of money that was given with trust and that wasn't tied to specific projects," Anne noted, stating that this trust sometimes had a transformational effect on the women. "Many said that this way of operating resulted in their feeling empowered to move out beyond their communities—to become the leading women's center in Harare, for example. I realized that if we did our work in ways that were cognizant of the change we sought— that is, with love—then we would achieve what we sought."

A New Fund in Mexico

Despite the Global Fund's initial success, Anne noted her feelings of unease regarding power dynamics between the "global north" (industrialized northern countries) and the "global south" (the so-called developing countries) that the Global Fund might risk perpetuating. The dynamic was one in which northern countries held the purse strings that determined which organizations thrived in southern countries.

Anne wanted to use the Global Fund to help "eliminate hierarchies between those who had money and those who didn't. [To address this,] our hope was to seed lots of women's funds around the world that could raise their own money," she recalled.

The first pioneers, who were inspired in part by the Global Fund example and propelled by their desire to empower women to have greater control of their lives in Mexico, were Mariclaire Acosta and Sylvia Marcos, Mexican advisers to the Global Fund. After attending a Global Fund board meeting in 1989, they decided to start their own fund in Mexico called Semillas (Seeds),[4] and recruited fellow Mexican feminist Lucero Gonzales to join them. "I ended up being the one to move the project forward," Lucero noted.

To support the organization's early development, Global Fund staff provided Semillas with technical and fundraising support and an initial seed grant of $7,500.[5] "The first computer and fax machine I ever had in my house, the Global Fund staff brought," Lucero recalled. In addition, "the Global Fund introduced us to U.S. funders," she noted, adding that she also brought fundraising experience to the table, having organized a major international women's conference.

"We were pioneers. There was no other women's fund in Mexico," Lucero noted.

Encouraging Other Funds Globally

Excited by the formation of Semillas, Anne found herself encouraging advisers at meetings in other parts of the world to begin their own funds—including in Southeast Asia and Africa. "I admit I had the agenda that they start these funds," Anne recalled, "even though I'd learned very clearly through my years at Hewlett that when the funder tried to initiate something it rarely worked."

Anne's efforts in Southeast Asia and Africa did not initially bear fruit. "In Southeast Asia, they didn't want a fund," Anne recalled. "They said it was too political and that becoming funders would change their relationship to other activists. In Africa, a couple of people wanted to start a fund, but at first it didn't go anywhere. I realized that unless you had someone who felt passionately and would run with the idea on the ground, it wasn't going to work."

When encouraging women to start their own initiatives failed, the Global Fund instead helped women learn about funds and grantmaking, in the hopes that some might become inspired to create foundations and would then have the capacity to do so. Anne recalled, "We decided for our fifth anniversary we would give away $5,000 to ten groups, so that they could in turn give away that money to other groups." The intent behind the effort was to allow grantees to reverse roles and experience what acting as a grantor was like. Another initiative was to conduct workshops at international conferences to train women on how to fundraise. In addition, the fund brought their partners to the Palo Alto office in part to familiarize them with how a fund operated, including through an advisers-in-residence program.

A Nepali Fund

The Global Fund's efforts to transfer skills and knowledge to a broad range of overseas partners touched Rita Thapa, a Nepali working at UNIFEM's office in her home country. Her experience working with the Global Fund's donor circle, combined with her own frustration with her existing job, were two important factors that led her to decide, while at the 1995 Beijing conference for women, to start a fund.

"As soon as I got back from Beijing, I submitted my resignation letter," Rita recounted. Recalling how her boss responded, Rita—whose husband had recently passed away—recounted, "My boss was Nepali and knew me well. She held my hand and said, 'Your two girls need to get married and you have a little son. Don't leave this job. How will you survive?' But I was impregnated, and the seed just grew."

Rita wanted the new entity to challenge north-south funding relationships. Wanting Nepalese women to shape their own priorities, she made a radical commitment. "Rita decided she wouldn't take any money from outside of Nepal—unless there were no strings attached," Anne explained. "This was transformational. Katmandu was filled with every type of international agency, and Rita had all the connections. She could have been funded instantly."

The first grants—although coming from the north—met her initial requirements in that they had very few restrictions. This initial funding came first from the Global Fund for Women ($20,000 in 1995) and was followed soon after by Mama Cash, a women's fund in the Netherlands.[6] "I was assured funding, and that took a huge burden from my head," Rita explained.

Although initial funding came from the north, Rita hoped to build on the philanthropic tradition that existed within Nepal itself. "Giving was inherent to our culture and practice. I wanted to build on that tradition and encourage people to give to women's empowerment rather than just giving money to support the big rituals in the [Hindu and Buddhist] temples [and mosques]."

Kavita Ramdas (president and CEO of the Global Fund for Women) recounted a story that illustrated Rita's tenacity with respect to raising funds. "Rita was speaking to a group of women about this idea and they said, 'This is a good idea for people in

America, but we have no money. Our husbands would never give money to this.'"

"Rita took her gold bracelet off her hand, put it on the table, and said, 'If we really care, we all have resources. Now who will join me?'" Kavita continued. Through such recruiting methods, Rita brought together a group of women determined to ensure that the fund—which they named Tewa (meaning "support" in Nepali)—would succeed.[7]

"Rita involved people that were very diverse," Anne commented. "The people represented on their advisory board [included women from all castes]. I remember at the Beijing conference the Indian women literally almost cringing. The Dalit women (the untouchables) and the upper-class women were not supposed to touch each other. And here Tewa would have meetings with everyone in a circle with pillows on the floor, all speaking. The women said this was revolutionary."

The women's biggest hurdle was to find ways to encourage Nepali citizens, who had little tradition of giving to non-faith-related institutions, to support them. "We couldn't raise the money through e-mail or mail like in the U.S. because there was an absence of trust toward NGOs," Rita explained. Instead the women channeled Nepal's tradition of volunteerism, one in which those without money provided a contribution to their temple through volunteer work. "We mobilized four hundred women volunteers to raise small amounts of money from many people," Rita recalled. "These women reached out to their own families where trust already existed."

The money then went to women's groups across Nepal. "We funded hundreds of women's organizations located in almost every district," Rita noted. "Many of these groups the international aid agencies would never reach. Most women did not have the language or the ability to reach those resources." By 2007 they had given away 257 grants in fifty-three districts in Nepal totaling just over $250,000.[8] Although small by U.S. standards, this amount of money was substantial for the low-income communities that Tewa was reaching.

With respect to their grantmaking strategy, Tewa often chose grantees that were engaged in small income-generating projects; however, the grants had a much larger aim. "Our work appeared to be small," Rita noted, "but when a group of women came together in a village and ran a secretariat, it enhanced their visibility and voice. They might be raising goats or doing vegetable farming—but this translated into power."

To ensure that the work was achieving this goal, Rita noted that Tewa had stringent criteria for choosing its grantees. "We made a distinction between programs that gave women credit to do income-generating projects and women who came together on their own to transform their lives and used income-generating projects to stay organized. These were women who were already organized before they received any money."

To help the women develop a frame for their work, Tewa also held regional workshops. "Women understood what the politics of power were, as they were the most affected by these politics," Rita affirmed. "They saw this the minute they came together and began talking about it more openly."

Growing Women's Funds

As Tewa and Semillas grew, the success of these funds had a ripple effect in other countries. "After Tewa was formed, things started to happen much more quickly," Anne recalled. "There was this cascading effect of women learning about philanthropy as we brought women organizing funds to more and more events," Kavita noted.

Marjan Sax, a founder of Mama Cash, added, "There was a growing consciousness—it wasn't like one person came up with the idea. There has always been a lot of discomfort about the power dynamics of coming to the rich West to ask for money. Women finding ways to raise money themselves and have control of their own money was very empowering."

By 1998, at a meeting organized by Mama Cash, funds from both the north and south decided to form a network, which they called the International Network of Women's Funds. Democratically run by its members, the network established a headquarters in South Africa to provide capacity and relationship building support to member funds. Although the Global Fund for Women and Mama Cash were both members, as an independent entity the network represented the maturing and increasing autonomy of the international funds.

In 2000, Tewa hosted the network's first meeting in Nepal. "There was such a raw emotional quality to it," Kavita Ramdas recalled of this event. We had an amazing march with the women, which ended at a temple where women had not been allowed into before. It had been a forbidden temple! It was the women of Tewa who had persuaded the priest to let women in. They'd said, 'How can you be a temple for all people when it is forbidden to women?' We lit 365 oil lamps to represent that every day should be a day in which women's rights and dignity should be respected around the world."

"At that meeting, Semillas said, 'OK—we'll host the next meeting,'" Kavita recounted. "That was the moment everyone realized—wow!—we are creating a movement."

Increasing Challenges for Funds

As interest in building women's funds around the world grew, however, so too did problems associated with the emergence of such funds. "We were so excited," Kavita recalled. "But we didn't really do anything around feasibility. If people wanted to start a fund, the Global Fund said, 'That's great! Here's the money.' But some of these funds fell apart in a couple years."

"We learned that a 'thousand flowers bloom' strategy could work for our typical grantees—but funds needed more stringent rules because the stakes were higher," Kavita explained. "[Because of their grantmaking function, the funds] were in the national spotlight in a totally different way from our other grantees." They were often the target of public criticism regarding how money was being spent and who was receiving funds. Kavita pointed to a fund in Latin America as an example; it fell apart a few years after its founding due to "lack of capacity and experience and feuding between board members."

In hindsight, Kavita noted, "Would I recommend site visits for every fund we were supporting? Absolutely. For most of our grants, we could rely on advisers on the ground, but for the funds, we needed greater engagement."

Many of the new funds also had difficulties fundraising, Kavita added, noting that unlike the founders of Semillas and Tewa, many had no fundraising experience. "We should have brought all the funds together, so they could say to one another, 'This is really hard to do,' and if you wanted to start a fund, you needed to be able to raise money."

Tina Thiart, who was hired in 2006 as executive director of the International Network of Women's Funds (INWF), recalled one fund's financial crisis and how it was resolved. "One fund was in serious financial distress," she recalled.

"My first reaction was to get them a huge amount of money, so I phoned Mama Cash and Global Fund to consider a grant," Tina continued. "But instead of sending money, they asked me, 'How are INWF members going to mentor this fund to help them recover?'" Then I thought maybe the fund needed a change of leadership. But when I saw how the fund had grown and the executive director had not been able to address the issue of managing the growth, I thought, 'With the right [support], would the executive director be in a different position?'"

Instead of immediately providing money, the INWF helped connect them to other funds that could act as mentors on how to manage growth. "The fund—with its existing director—was able to develop an analysis and a strategic plan to stay ahead of their challenges."

Transforming Power Relations

Kavita Ramdas also observed that grantees did not always feel comfortable with the methods the Global Fund was using to encourage the creation of new foundations. For example, for the Global Fund's tenth anniversary, in 1997 they decided to once again give grantees an opportunity to be grantmakers and picked ten groups to give away $10,000 each. In a follow-up independent evaluation of these partnership grants, Kavita recalled, "Some organizations said, 'We felt we couldn't say no to you when you gave us money [because we were grantees], but we didn't have the capacity to give it away.'"

As a result of this feedback, the Global Fund stopped awarding selected grantees regranting money. "Instead we opened the process and offered groups the opportunity to apply for [this] money," Kavita explained. "It was one thing if an organization had consciously decided that it wanted to be a women's fund. This was very different from saying, 'We've anointed you.'"

Although supportive of the new approach, Frances noted her own view that asking grantees to become funders had some value. "People who got money had all sorts of feelings about the people who gave them the money. They might think, 'I'm taking money from the oppressors in the north.' Then when the grantee becomes the funder, they suddenly think, 'Oh no, I'm taking power. Now I am the dominator.' I wanted people who had these views to deal with those views."

Kavita added, "The fear people held was that—once they had access to resources—they would lose their connection to the ground and the grassroots struggles and become complacent."

In addition, despite a remarkably cooperative spirit between funds that were often sharing the same political space, conflicts over recognition and power did arise. "Now you had new funds that wanted the typical things organizations wanted: identity, public recognition, power, control," Frances recalled. "Sometimes it was unclear whether a fund was independent from the Global Fund [because the Global Fund was its primary funding source or was acting as its fiscal sponsor]. Issues arose like who got on the program for a philanthropic meeting in the [country where a fund was based]—the Global Fund or the sister fund?"

Ana Maria Enriquez, former program officer at the Global Fund and senior philanthropic adviser for Semillas from 2006 to 2007, elaborated, "In a sense these funds were now in competition—they got money from many of the same sources. It was up to us to convey to donors that we weren't duplicating the work of these local funds—that we were an important ally within the U.S. philanthropic community and often provided them critical dollars for general operating support that they couldn't get elsewhere."

Clarifying roles helped reduce the friction. For example, through dialogue, the Global Fund (at the time fiscal sponsor for Semillas) and Semillas decided they would have different foci in Mexico. "Semillas would focus on labor rights, and the Global Fund would focus on reproductive rights," Ana Maria explained. The move also helped encourage U.S.-based grantmakers to begin funding Semillas directly.

Within the Global Fund, friction also developed regarding the allocation of funds to Semillas. "If you asked the Global Fund to give a report on grantmaking—the biggest numbers were to Semillas," Ana Maria recalled.

"These were not huge amounts," Ana Maria added, explaining that the highest annual giving to foundations was $50,000. However, such grants at times represented significant percentages of fund budgets.

To resolve the concern, "we developed the Feminist Budgeting Process," Ana Maria recalled. "The Global Fund was an out-of-the-box place, so we developed an indicator [to determine how to distribute funds between countries] that was grounded in the movement. We came up with an equation that looked at the vibrancy of a movement, the cost of living index (how far did a rupee go versus a peso), and combined this with the human development index of the United Nations."

Kavita Ramdas added, "We tracked numbers of requests from women's groups; public visibility as well as freedom and mobility of women's organizations; legal barriers to organizing for women's rights; existence of supportive laws for the charitable or nonprofit sector; and the level of local, regional, and national gatherings for women."

As a result of this analysis, the Global Fund decided that it was providing Semillas an appropriate level of funding and decided not to reduce its giving.

Transforming Philanthropic Power Dynamics

Over time, new funds continued to be created. By 2007 "there were about twenty in the global south that had received their first grant from the Global Fund and/or Mama Cash. They really were all over—Brazil, South Africa, Mongolia, Hong Kong, Bulgaria," noted Tina Thiart (executive director of the INWF).

Each grew and adapted to the cultural and political context of their own countries, and drew on the knowledge of many existing funds. "We are each different. Semillas has done capacity building and has helped our grantees build their own donor base. Tewa has a strong volunteer base. As we've created our fund, we've drawn from many experiences, including those of the U.S.-based Women's Funding Network and others," Emilienne de León (executive director of Semillas) explained.

As they developed, many of the foundations followed Tewa's lead and successfully pursued strategies to raise money within their own countries, though most still receive significant funding from U.S. and European sources. Both WHEAT Trust (Women's Fund, South Africa) and Semillas raised roughly a quarter of their total budgets from within their own countries in 2007, with WHEAT Trust raising almost $39,000 internally and Semillas just over $250,000.[9]

Semillas developed its fundraising strategy for Mexico, which included efforts to develop relationships with upper-class women, through a feasibility study. "We interviewed ninety-five women in Mexico," Emilienne explained. "We learned they were prepared to give but that they didn't because nobody asked them. But women wanted to belong to a community, so we created a network called Women Investing in Women because it gave them the sense of being part of their own community."

Meanwhile, in Nepal, Tewa continued to find new strategies for strengthening its financial sustainability. "They bought a huge piece of land with big properties that they've rented out to women's organizations to fund their own salaries," Tina Thiart noted.

As part of their fundraising strategies, some funds have also helped bridge the divide separating grantees and donors. In Mexico, to reduce the sense of hierarchy, Semillas has been inventing its own language—using such terms as "investments" instead of "grants," and "project developers and supporters" instead of "grantees and donors." In Nepal, Tewa has encouraged even its poorest grantees to donate a rupee or two back to Tewa to give them the opportunity to act as both donor and grantee.

Changing the Role of Women

Many of the women's funds have contributed to the strengthening of leaders and organizations leading change in the countries within which they work. Enhancing women's rights, democratic practice, and the rule of law, grantees have helped bring women's voices into arenas where they had been excluded.

"In 2006 there were so many women who participated in the democracy movement in Nepal," Rita Thapa noted. "Women participated even more than men." One result women leaders

helped secure was a statute making mandatory "that the constitu-
ent assembly needed to be 33 percent women," which resulted in
191 female parliamentarians out of 575 total in 2008.[10]

"Tewa had an indirect role in that. We've lent greatly to the visibility of women in Nepal," Rita continued. "Many of the women
leaders who became important in the movement had been part
of organizations that received initial grants from Tewa—I think at
least 10 percent," Rita explained. "In 2008, there was a congratu-
latory ceremony with fifty-five parliamentarian women present.
I personally garlanded two of these [who were both former
grantees—Mohamadi Siddiqui and Khinu Limbu].

"Ours is a revolution," Rita reflected of the work Tewa has supported in communities. "But it is quiet, like an undercurrent, and
very deep."

In Mexico, Semillas has also been an important force supporting the women's movement there. Semillas' grantees have focused
on marginalized populations including those living in urban slums
where femicides have become rampant.

Supported by Semillas, Nuestras Hijas de Regreso a Casa, an
organization of mothers of several murder victims in the U.S.-
Mexico border town of Ciudad Juarez, sought justice through
the international legal system. According to Emilienne de León,
almost four hundred women have been murdered in this town
over the last decade.[11] In 2002 and 2005, the Asociacion Nacional
de Abogados Democraticos—legal counsel to Nuestras Hijas de
Regreso a Casa—and others filed three complaints with the
Inter-American Commission on Human Rights of the Organization
of American States (OAS) against the State of Mexico.[12] Emilienne
explained that the complaints "accused the Mexican government
of negligence and not investigating the cases like they should." The
commission admitted these complaints in 2005 and accumulated
them in a single case, which in 2007 it took to the highest legal
body of the OAS—the Inter-American Human Rights Court.[13]

"This has been paradigm shifting," Emilienne noted. Due to
strong media coverage encouraged by Semillas grantees, the case
has become well known within Mexico. Under pressure, the Mexican government has responded to the growing crisis. "Congress-
woman Marcela Lagarde was able to establish a commission to
study femicides within Mexico," Emilienne continued. The final

study recommended a federal law on gender violence, and in February 2007, such a law was passed.[14] "Things have changed as a result of this law. Now rape by a husband has become illegal. It has still been hard to demonstrate, but at least it has become an issue. And a woman now has the right to keep her own documents—her birth certificate and marriage certificate—so she can leave her home with her children if she is abused."

Emilienne noted that Semillas was not involved in the creation of the law. However, grantees helped generate the public concern that encouraged the government to take action.

In some instances, these funds have banded together to create funding collaboratives in support of women's rights and gender issues. "Six women's funds—Semillas (Mexico), the Central American Women's Fund (Nicaragua), Angela Borba (Brazil), Alquimia (Chile), Fondo de Mujeres del Sur (Argentina), Fondo Mujer (Colombia), and Astraea (United States) have come together for the lesbian, gay, bisexual, and transgender movement in Latin America," Emilienne explained. The effort has attracted roughly $1.5 million—largely from international sources. For such an underfunded field, this amount is significant.

The collaborative, an idea that emerged in the global south, has focused on building both the capacity of organizations in the region and stronger relationships between these groups. Its small grants program is called Beyond Invisibility: Latin American Women's Funds Mobilizing for Lesbian, Bisexual and Transgender Communities.

Transforming Philanthropy

The efforts of women's funds around the world to raise money within their own countries has challenged traditional notions of philanthropy. "In Nepal we broke new ground," Rita Thapa reflected. "This kind of philanthropy was very rare and it has become much more common." At the same time, the continued dependency of many funds on international dollars shows how difficult raising funds within the global south can be.

Even when raising money from U.S. and European sources, however, these foundations represent an important step toward the autonomy of the global south. These foundations are building relationships with a more diverse array of funding partners in the United States and Europe, reducing dependency on any one source.

Kavita Ramdas of the Global Fund explained how the act of women donating to funds was often transformational for those who contributed. She recalled, "At the tenth anniversary of Tewa we did a ceremony in Katmandu where we were asked to contribute something." The ceremony was a reenactment of the moment in which Rita Thapa had offered her gold bracelet to create Tewa.

"This widow came up and said that her husband had given her the gold chain she offered, and it was Rita who freed her to realize she had value in this world after her husband's death. People were crying it was so emotional."

Conclusion

In 1987, Anne Firth Murray was inspired to leverage her position as a member of the U.S. grantmaking community to create the Global Fund for Women. By 2006, the Global Fund had "provided $47 million in grants to 2,991 women's groups in 162 countries."[15]

Not content simply to give away money, the Global Fund for Women began to challenge north-south dynamics by working with grantees to establish women's funds in their own countries. In spite of tremendous odds, these funds are finding ways to raise money within their own countries, and have been central to fueling women's movements within their national contexts and beyond.

Summing up the mission of these foundations, Kavita Ramdas (Global Fund) noted, "The question of gender equality and full participation of 51 percent of the world's population has continued to be the big untold story. What the world has done time and time again has been to leave these people out. In early 2008, the Gates Foundation announced a major initiative focused on agriculture that is primarily intended to help women farmers in Africa, but when I looked at the grant recipients, I didn't see one local African women's group on the list. Locally supported women's funds are helping to change that dynamic."

By supporting women directly, these funds have given this constituency greater opportunity to lead within their own countries. "In Cambodia today, for the first time in history, the secretary general of the leading opposition party is a woman, and she received her first grant from the Global Fund years ago when she was organizing against trafficking," Kavita recounted. "Another woman became the minister of foreign affairs in Sierra Leone. These women didn't go to a special leadership training course. They learned to lead by mobilizing women to address needs they saw in their own community."

The women's funds have been part of a small but growing infrastructure for women leaders. In turn, these women, and their organizations, have been leading the way in a struggle to ensure that half the world's population become full participants in their households, communities, and nations, as well as on the global stage.

Lessons Learned

The Global Fund for Women has played an important role empowering women in the global south to assume leadership roles in their own countries and internationally. How can your foundation successfully fund systemic change overseas?

- Give money to a local fund, such as Semillas or Tewa, based in the country you hope to reach. Such a fund will have the country-specific knowledge to be able to effectively identify grantees.
- Provide funding to a public charity based in the United States that is already giving internationally and has the networks and relationships in place to identify effective organizations.
- Develop a network of advisers within your targeted countries.
- If you would like to fuel the growth of international funds, avoid simply telling local women to start funds; instead, give them tools and experiences that may help build their excitement for embarking on such a venture (through fundraising training, site visits, residence-in-training programs, and so on).
- Be particularly sensitive to power differentials in your relationships with partners from the global south. The lack of philanthropic dollars in many countries can exacerbate already common feelings among grantees that they must please you. Within this context, they may interpret your suggestions as demands.

10

Responding to Disaster Recovery and Beyond

The Case of the Gulf Coast Fund for Community Renewal and Ecological Health, a Special Project of Rockefeller Philanthropy Advisors

The Gulf Coast Fund for Community Renewal and Ecological Health has responded to the aftermath of Hurricanes Katrina and Rita by creating an advisory group of people from the Gulf Coast region to serve as the fund's primary decision-making body. Through its structure and funding strategies, the fund aims to counter a legacy of environmental degradation and human rights abuses in Mississippi, Alabama, Louisiana, and coastal Texas.

"I was scared when I heard on the radio that the levees had broken—that's when I realized Katrina was going to be really bad," recalled New York–based Penny Fujiko Willgerodt, a founder of the Gulf Coast Fund for Community Renewal and Ecological Health, then vice president of Rockefeller Philanthropy Advisors and now executive director of the Prospect Hill Foundation. One of the major U.S. disasters of the century, first Hurricane Katrina and then Hurricane Rita pummeled the Gulf Coast of Mississippi, Louisiana, Alabama, and Texas during summer 2005, taking a reported eighteen hundred lives and destroying hundreds of thousands of homes across the Gulf.[1] "As the story unfolded, and

I saw the government's abysmal response, how we literally abandoned our citizens there, the rights violations taking place [particularly to those who were] poor and black, I felt enraged," Penny continued. "I was also keenly aware of how many Superfund sites and petrochemical plants exist along the gulf in the New Orleans area, and that people were going to be exposed to a toxic soup."

Shortly after the first hurricane struck, a group of funders joined together to create the Gulf Coast Fund collaborative, housed at Rockefeller Philanthropy Advisors. In addition to Penny, other core founders included Sarah Hansen (formerly with Environmental Grantmakers Association), Annie Ducmanis (Rockefeller Philanthropy Advisors; formerly Environmental Grantmakers Association), Marni Rosen (Jenifer Altman Foundation), and Michelle DePass (Ford Foundation).

Gulf Coast Fund Snapshot

Type: Funder collaborative

Year founded: 2005

Grant range (2005): $5,000–$37,000

Grant range (2007): $500–$25,000

Total grants awarded since founding: $2.2 million

Collaborative assets (2005 and 2007): The collaborative does not have an endowment

Geographic focus: Gulf Coast region (Alabama, Louisiana, Mississippi, Texas)

Primary funding areas: Just and sustainable redevelopment; right of return; environmental justice and health; youth, children, and education; workers' rights; arts and culture; housing; environmental protection; wetlands restoration; empowerment of women; health care and mental health

Full- and part-time staff (2007): Three

Location: New York City

Note: Snapshot information for each chapter varies depending on data available. Dates refer to either the calendar year or the end of the fiscal cycle. For snapshot sources, refer to the Notes section at the end of the book.[2]

"Everyone knew that what we were facing in the Gulf was bigger than what any foundation could address alone," Penny recalled. "There were so many issues here that donors regularly fund—environment, employment, housing, education. Typically foundations have discrete funding agendas, so if we wanted to address all these issues, we needed to bring a lot of foundations and donors together."

So when Kathy Sessions, coordinator for the Health and Environmental Funders Network (a program of a grantmakers forum called the Consultative Group on Biological Diversity), volunteered to host a funder call to brainstorm how to respond, Penny, Marni, Michelle, Annie, and several other funders cleared their schedules. "We all realized that something extraordinary needed to happen quickly," Kathy recalled. "We were aware that there would be at least initial willingness to help from philanthropy, but that most funders would not have a vehicle for how to do so. There were only a few foundations with grantees and experience in the Gulf. We wanted to create some alternatives to funding the Red Cross and United Way that would empower communities and meet the needs of people being overlooked in the rescue efforts."

This geographic area has received the least amount of philanthropy dollars," Penny elaborated. "Most philanthropy money is based in New York and California, so people tend to concentrate on the coasts. Nonprofit infrastructure is also not as developed in the deep South. Many nonprofits there don't have resources to create a national presence, so funders don't know about them."

FOR COMMUNITIES WITHOUT SUPPORT, SOCIAL JUSTICE NETWORKS FILL THE GAP

Alabama-based community organizer Latosha Brown (Gulf Coast Fund adviser)—transformed her Get Out the Vote networks into service delivery operations after Katrina hit. Members of these networks were finding that many communities—and particularly those that were African American and rural—were not receiving help from rescue operations.

Through her DC connections from her political work, Latosha secured a meeting with a Red Cross Gulf Coast director to coordinate efforts. As she described,

The director told me, "We are telling people on the radio to come to our Red Cross facilities," and I'm saying to her, "There is no electricity, so they can't hear your radio. And there is no public transportation, so they can't get to your site." If she had been an organizer, she'd know that. I told her, "We've set up some sites. That's where the communities are going. Can you bring food to these sites?" But [the director] couldn't do that. So I said to her, "What can you give us?"

And there was a bunch of bananas sitting next to her. And I'm sure she didn't mean for it to come out as bad as it sounded, but she said, "Take these bananas cause they're almost past ripe."

I left the meeting and sat down in the parking lot and I cried. And I prayed. I said to God, "They have everything, and we have nothing."

And the miracle was that from that day forward, we never went without.

Crying, I got on the Internet. I was looking for a black foundation. I found the Twenty-First Century Fund, and I wrote an e-mail to them and a couple other organizing friends. And somehow that e-mail got circulated across the Internet.

It's not that I didn't think we could get funds from other foundations, but I knew there was a dance. You have to submit the proposal. You gotta have the relationships. I knew the Twenty-First Century Foundation would also have their regulations, but my hope was that this black foundation would be creative to meet the need. And I needed someone to move money now. They did—and they were the first foundation to send us $5,000.

The truth in the e-mail moved people. The calls started pouring in. People were driving in food and supplies. Pretty soon we were a network of dozens of organizations [which we named Saving Our Selves]. We had twenty vans going out every day and temporary shelters across Alabama.

"If there are lessons learned with respect to best practices for the funding community, it's the importance of funding community organizing," Latosha reflected. "It creates an infrastructure that can be used in any situation—whether that's a policy issue or a get out the vote drive or a crisis like Katrina and Rita."

Communicating with the few grantees they had in the region, within two weeks the funders began to sketch a game plan. "The most important piece came to the table when Penny said, 'Let's create a pooled fund, and Rockefeller Philanthropy Advisors can provide a home for it,'" Annie Ducmanis recalled. Shortly thereafter, the Environmental Grantmakers Association also offered to donate a percentage of Annie's time to hurricane disasters, including work with the collaborative.

Supporting work in the Gulf following Hurricanes Katrina and Rita was a natural fit for the Rockefeller Philanthropy Advisors, a steward of over $200 million in annual gifts and grants for more than 160 clients.[3] "Whenever there is a major earthquake, mudslide, or other natural disaster, our clients expect us to provide options for who and what to fund," Penny Fujiko Willgerodt explained.

The founders' intent, however, was for the funder collaborative to channel goodwill dollars beyond traditional disaster recovery. "We wanted to address preexisting conditions that exacerbated the disaster, and to be in this for the long haul," Annie recalled.

"This was a manmade disaster—a result of decades of environmental degradation, pollution, and human rights abuses. Solutions needed to be developed within that context," Penny elaborated.

Annie added that the collaborative's foundations wanted to support community leaders in the region rather than large international rescue entities. They saw building leadership and organizational capacity in the Gulf as fundamental to ensuring its long-term sustainable development.

Further, the founders felt that people living in the Gulf should decide who received funding. "The legacy of structural racism is persistent in every corner of the Gulf, so we wanted a funding structure that counterbalanced this by empowering people of color in the region," Annie explained, listing African American, Southeast Asian, Native Americans, and Latinos as important ethnic groups in the Gulf.

"Figuring out a mechanism where philanthropic dollars could be entrusted to community-based leadership wasn't easy," Kathy Sessions added. "People were concerned about conflict of interests, and whether we could actually attract dollars into a fund led by community leaders."

Penny also had to sell the idea to her organization, Rockefeller Philanthropy Advisors. Her strong relationship with her boss, Doug Bauer, senior vice president, was what enabled her to move forward. Doug recalled saying to her, "This is going to take an enormous amount of time and will be fraught with issues." He explained, "I had enormous trust in Penny and gave her my support, but I had to manage people at Rockefeller Philanthropy Advisors who were second-guessing her."

PREEXISTING CONDITIONS IN THE GULF EXACERBATE EFFECTS OF KATRINA AND RITA

The oil and gas industries in the Gulf Coast region exacerbated the effects of Hurricanes Katrina and Rita. Aaron Viles of the New Orleans-based Gulf Restoration Network and adviser to the Gulf Coast Fund explained that "10,000 miles of oil and gas exploration and navigation canals have sliced and diced our wetlands. These wetlands used to act as a buffer between coastal towns and the sea during storms that whipped up the ocean waters." The canals, however, have brought saltwater into the freshwater marshes, killing the plants there.

The result is that, as Ariane Wiltse, a New Orleans–based guest blogger for the *Los Angeles Times,* put it, "the land [in the swamps] is literally falling into open water, and in doing so is allowing the Gulf of Mexico to creep closer and closer to our fragile city."[4] The National Wetlands Research Center estimates that between 1932 and 2000, Louisiana has lost nineteen hundred square miles of land, mostly marshes, an area almost the size of the state of Delaware.[5]

The pollution caused by the oil, gas, and waste disposal companies in the area also contributed to the disaster. "Even before Katrina, Superfund sites were leaching toxic chemicals into the water system," explained Anita Nager, executive director of the Beldon Fund (which committed early funding to the Gulf Coast Fund). The often inadequately stored toxic waste from the many Superfund sites in the Gulf region mixed with flood waters, spreading chemicals across African American, Native American, and other communities situated near the sites.

(Continued)

"Texas and Louisiana are the heart of chemical and oil refinery industries in the United States," explained Gary Cohen (Healthcare Without Harm). "They are the national sacrifice zone around the country's addiction to oil and chemicals."

Throughout the 1900s, oil, gas, and petrochemical industries mushroomed in the Gulf, encouraged by lenient tax policies that still exist today. As they grew, "these industries created a political culture that was totally supportive of polluting industries," Gary elaborated.

Nor did federal laws help counterbalance the lenient state laws, according to Anita. "There is no federal law stating that chemicals need to be tested before they are manufactured," she said.

Raising the Profile of the Gulf Coast Fund

With the basic structure in place, the funders moved quickly to raise the profile of the Gulf Coast Fund within the broader philanthropic community. To do this, they took advantage of the Environmental Grantmakers Association (EGA) fall conference, held in September 2005.

At first New Orleans–based lawyer Monique Harden (Advocates for Environmental Human Rights), whom founders asked to speak about the fund at the conference, was skeptical. "Unless you can raise a million dollars, don't even bother [starting a fund], cause it's not worth our time," she said. Anything less could not justify asking traumatized and overburdened community leaders in the Gulf to support its development. Only after the founders assured her that the fund would be community driven and of a significant size did she agree to be the featured lunch speaker at the conference.

Explaining Monique's reaction, Annie said, "the whole country was coming down on the heads of people in the Gulf, and often for the worse."

At the EGA conference, Penny, Annie, Michelle, and a few others met before the plenary to develop a plan of action. "I started writing [a document to give to people asking them to contribute to the fund], but Monique kept scratching out what I was writing," Penny remembered. "Finally I said, "Monique, you draft the thing!' My original draft was in 'philanthropese.' She wanted to use much stronger language. She wanted the words 'pernicious racism' in the first line of the document."

At another point in history, the funder audience might have been turned off by the strong language. "But funders were seeing images of people stranded on roofs in New Orleans, mostly black, and no one coming to rescue them. So people were in that frame of mind," Penny explained. "It set a tone that this was not going to be watered down to the lowest common denominator."

"Of course we were not saying we were the only game in town," Penny added. The Twenty-First Century Foundation, the founders of Move On (who set up a client-advised fund at the Tides Foundation), and many others were also developing initiatives. In 2005, the Louisiana Disaster Recovery Foundation was also formed.

Many of the hundred or so grantmakers at Monique's lunch presentation expressed interest, and over the next few months the fund had raised a large percentage of its million-dollar goal. The initiative provided an attractive proposition for the funding community, many of whom—as predicted by the Gulf Coast Fund founders—were struggling to find ways to respond.

Anita Nager (Beldon Fund) explained why the collaborative attracted dollars from her foundation. "We didn't know the region. We have a small staff and weren't able to get to New Orleans to do in-depth research. We knew how hard it was to create change in the region because of the collusion between industry, the government, and the courts to keep things the same. The Gulf Coast Fund was much better placed to invest our dollars effectively."

Strengthening Contacts in the Gulf

The fund founders, working with their few contacts in the region, decided to create an advisory group of people from the Gulf that would "essentially be the board," Annie Ducmanis recounted.

Advisory members would play several critical roles. "They would make the decisions regarding who to support and what activities the fund should organize," Penny explained. "They would identify funding priorities and disseminate information on the fund to potential applicants."

"We knew their role would be essential," Penny continued. "It was the people in the region that knew what the needs really were and who was doing the most effective work on the ground."

Penny, both together with cofounder Marni and on her own, visited the Gulf to identify possible candidates. The other founders wanted to avoid overwhelming the leaders in the Gulf; for this reason, most relied on Penny and Marni's information-gathering site visits and did not visit the Gulf themselves.

"People were cautious because they didn't know me, but optimistic," Penny recalled. "They saw this as an opportunity to build a people's movement all along the Gulf Coast, which hadn't really happened since the civil rights movement." In 2005, most community leaders in the Gulf were focused exclusively at the local or state level.

The work was welcomed, mentioned Kathy Sessions (Health and Environmental Funders Network), because "Penny, Marni, Annie, and Michelle had such an attitude of service." Penny also noted that, to build trust, she traveled with Gulf Coast community leaders.

The founders also made an effort to meet with Gulf Coast residents visiting New York. In addition to educating the funders, the visits often inspired Gulf residents caught in the despair enveloping their region.

One such visitor was Pam Dashiell, an African American community leader from New Orleans and Fund adviser. She recalled,

> Going to the Rockefeller building [in November 2005] was something. The building itself was imposing—big and granite. There were all these security things. But I felt I was in a place that would help. I was excited because it was Rockefeller. It felt real and that help would come.

> When I came in, there was a room full of funders. That was the first time I had expressed in a formal setting what had happened and what the reality was. They were so compassionate and wanting to do something. It was incredible. I cried, and so did some of them.

Creating the Advisory Group

By January 2006, Penny had chosen the twenty-one-person advisory group, which included lawyers, nonprofit leaders, workers, community organizers, and academics, among others. "I presented different slates to both funders and organizers and said, 'What do you think of this combination?' We were looking for diversity—age, gender, issue area, geography, race, culture, profession, political orientation. We wanted a reflection of the Gulf Coast region from a perspective of historical disenfranchisement."

In choosing whom to invite, advisory group member Pam Dashiell said, "[Founders] weren't looking for people with titles. They were looking for people who had credibility on the ground because they were doing the work." Pam also emphasized that they looked for individuals throughout the region, which was particularly important given that the federal government and funding agencies focused much of their attention on New Orleans, while other devastated areas were receiving minimal support.

CURRENT AND FORMER ADVISORY GROUP MEMBERS, GULF COAST FUND FOR COMMUNITY RENEWAL AND ECOLOGICAL HEALTH

Sharon Alexis	Shana Griffin
Dr. Regina Benjamin	Monique Harden
Bishop James Black	Jaribu Hill
Elodia Blanco	Derrick Johnson
Stephen Bradberry	Rose Johnson
Latosha Brown	Genaro Rendon Lopez
Hui Bui	Brenda Robichaux
Ruby Campbell	Wilma Subra
Victoria Cintra	Aaron Viles
Pam Dashiell	Thao Vu
Scott Douglas	Angela Winfrey-Bowman
Derrick Evans	Beverly Wright
Joe Forte	

For the organizational affiliations and locations of these individuals, go to http://rockpa.org.

Conflict of Interest Buffers

Gulf Coast Fund founders also knew that because the affected communities were small and interconnected, it was essential to address conflict-of-interest concerns. They did not want to rule out the possibility of advisers' organizations applying for funding.

"Everybody had to sign a conflict-of-interest policy," Annie explained. "They declared all their affiliations and committed to recusing themselves from any decision that involved financial gain for any organization in which they, or their immediate family, were involved."

"Every adviser got $10,000 discretionary funding that they could direct to an organization of their choosing, including their own," Annie continued. "This helped take the issue of whether their organization would receive funding off the table. To many of these groups, $10,000 was a big deal, especially at that moment when nonprofits were still reeling from the impact of the storms."

Annie continued, "And we created panels of advisers, each responsible for reviewing twelve to fifteen proposals during a grant cycle. If an adviser was affiliated with an applicant organization, we would make sure that person sat on a different panel."

Given the delicacy of the issue, the founders and other individuals who had helped them think about whom to invite had also stressed the importance of choosing advisers with strong moral integrity. "People needed to be a cut above, ethically," Derrick Evans (Gulf Coast Fund adviser) emphasized.

Anita Nager noted that her foundation felt so strongly about building conflict-of-interest safeguards into the advisory group structure that the Beldon Fund wrote a conflict-of-interest conditionality into their initial grant of $50,000, one of the first investments that the fund received. "You can get yourself into a lot of trouble," she noted. "People lose credibility if they self-deal [and give money in ways that directly benefit organizations with which they are affiliated]. It's a violation of the public trust."

First Advisory Group Meeting

In planning the first advisory group meeting, held in March 2006, the founders knew that every decision—from the choice of location and facilitator to the documents they prepared—would send a signal. Annie Ducmanis explained, "We held the meeting at the Ashé Cultural Arts Center—a pillar of the African American community in New Orleans—and chose an African American facilitator. The venue sent the message, 'This is your space. We are coming to you.' This was not going to be a funder interaction where everything says the funder is setting the agenda. People got that right away."

Of the meeting day, Annie recalled, "It was several months out from Katrina and Rita, but people were still living out of their suitcases. Simply going around the room and saying 'How are you?' took a long time. There were a lot of tears."

"I'll never forget that first meeting," fund adviser Pam Dashiell recounted. "To hear people from Mississippi talking about the same issues we were dealing with in New Orleans was really eye opening. It allowed me to put together the big picture. There was a pattern of the poorer communities and the blacker communities getting less support across the states. The aid was absolutely selective."

"Listening to Bishop Black speak, I learned that painting what was happening in stark racial and class terms civilly was really helping him get the Mississippi state government to respond. In the lower ninth ward [in New Orleans], we'd been being more confrontational in our tone, but for Bishop Black the confrontation was implicit in his message [but wasn't in his tone]. It opened up a whole new way of doing things for me."

Although most advisory group members found the meeting cathartic, New Orleans–based Aaron Viles had a different experience. "A lot of this was collective storytelling—people crying and telling their stories. I was less and less comfortable as we went around the room. Almost everyone else were people of color, and that's not my background at all. I am quite white, of Scandinavian descent, so I kind of stood out. My experience of Katrina was very different. My house was on elevated land and wasn't affected."

Aaron noted that because his personal life had been less touched by the hurricanes, he had greater luxury to think about Katrina within the larger frame of global warming. "The night before the meeting, I'd heard Al Gore speak. He'd given his PowerPoint presentation, and I was thinking about how to use Katrina as this big-picture moment of the effects of climate change. How the world would [likely] be experiencing more and more weather-related disasters because of climate change and how to ratchet down carbon emissions to make sure it didn't happen again. I'd felt comfortable in the National Wildlife Federation room the night before, and then I walk into this room of people whose lives were still devastated. It made my head spin."

"But the amazing thing is that the goals of this fund are goals that I still stand by to this day," Aaron continued. "We crafted our mission statement, and people were able to transition between the immediate needs [of devastated communities for basic services] to big-picture thinking. When I saw the document that came out of it, I knew the tough moments had been worthwhile."

Fund Priorities

The advisory group outlined two primary objectives for the fund: (1) to meet the immediate needs of hurricane survivors in the region, particularly those in low-income and people of color communities who were often ignored both by government agencies and by traditional disaster relief nonprofits; and (2) to build a movement capable of supporting long-term structural change in the Gulf.

Working in the context of these goals, the fund would focus on a host of issue areas. "We couldn't boil it down to one or two things," Monique Harden (Advocates for Environmental Human Rights) said. "There was too much need because everything was unraveling."

Foci included the restoration and support of coastal wetlands and healthy coastal communities; encouraging green and healthy buildings; and reducing fossil fuel use and production in the Gulf Coast. In addition, the fund would support protection of right-to-know laws and rights to housing, education, health care, a living wage, and cultural preservation.

The focus on disaster recovery came in part from advisers' concern that local, state, and federal governments had failed to meet the needs of many communities. "FEMA trailers were infected with formaldehyde. Residents were being blocked from returning home. Hospitals, schools, and day-care centers were not up and running. Teachers were being cut from their jobs overnight," Monique recounted.

The fund's long-term goal, however, was to build a social change movement in the South. Nurturing leaders, building organizational capacity, and helping build bridges across political groups—the fund's intent, Penny explained, was to build a movement strong enough to address the underlying causes that contributed to the severity of the disasters.

The meetings of fund members helped contribute to this larger goal. The fund provided an opportunity for activists to sit together and make decisions together," Peter Teague of the Nathan Cummings Foundation (which provided early support to the fund) reflected.

Choosing Grantees

"Between May and December of 2006, the Gulf Coast Fund held three full grant cycles," Annie recalled. "For each round, Penny and I would read all the applications."

Next Annie and Penny would provide recommendations for each panel—topic areas, money to distribute, and advisers to sit on each one. "People occasionally asked for changes. Maybe they wanted to sit on a different panel that focused on a particular issue area. If there was no conflict of interest, we tried to honor that," Annie recounted.

The insider knowledge that the advisory team members brought to the decision-making process strengthened the selection process, which was usually carried out by phone. "[For example,] we'd get on the call and someone would say, 'That community group you put in the "no" pile—that group is going to do great things. And that group in the "yes" pile—they have no credibility and know how to write a good proposal,'" Penny recalled.

Adviser Derrick Evans explained how panel members handled one difficult situation. "During a call, a panel member said, 'Wait a minute, I have a serious question about this application. There are accusations that the organizational head acted as an interpreter for a company that was caught abusing immigrant workers right after Katrina.' Another person responded that they knew the person personally but had never heard this claim."

To address the situation, the panel member with the personal relationship put his phone on mute so as not to participate in the subsequent discussion. Derrick noted that the group did not feel it was necessary for the individual to hang up because they felt confident that this person would respect the group's process and keep the conversation confidential.

"The rest of us decided to discuss the proposal's merits as if the charge hadn't come up. How much funding would we recommend? Then, rather than award that, we decided we would have an adviser not working in the applicant's field—someone who could be more impartial—investigate the claim. That person looked into it, and it turned out that the incident did happen and that it was a very bad lapse of judgment. Our group felt it was serious enough that we couldn't go forward with the grant. It would have hurt the integrity of the fund. The panel member who had sat out and listened completely agreed and commended our process."

Derrick noted that even more important than the conflict-of-interest rules was the integrity of the people involved. "Something might be in my best interest or your best interest, but it's the higher ideals that brought us all here that have to be protected."

"Being an adviser can cause tension in the region," Annie reflected, "particularly when they have to turn people down. But there's something to be said for the safety in crowds. People outside the fund don't know who voted for what."

Penny also emphasized the importance of having an outside facilitator for every call. "We were always really careful about who did this. We haven't had a lot of conflicts because we clarified everything at the beginning of every call, including repeating the ground rules. I'd say, 'I know everyone knows this, but everything we say here is completely confidential. Can everybody verbally say that you agree with that?'"

"[A major reason] the advisory committee works is because people trust that things will be kept confidential," Penny added. "That's the primary reason why these vehicles sometimes break down."

Time Commitment Takes a Toll

In fall 2007, the bootstrapping nature of the collaborative began to take its toll. "I was burning the candle at both ends and eventually got sick," Annie recalled. "There were delays in the grant cycles. We realized we had to give ourselves more time between grant deadlines."

Peter Teague of the Nathan Cummings Foundation noted, "When the fund started, Rockefeller Philanthropy Advisors said they would [reduce] their fee, but it meant that the collaborative was always understaffed. As nice as it was to say that they weren't charging [their regular] overhead, it would have been better to start it off right."

Another funder noted, however, that "even with a staff of ten it would have been a struggle. The workload was immense." This individual also expressed concern that a regular fee would have discouraged other funders from contributing.

"Penny put in hundreds of hours on this project—far more than even the standard fee would have covered," added Doug Bauer, senior vice president at Rockefeller Philanthropy Advisors. "Startups take time. It was time-consuming to empower the communities to have input into the process. It was very intense what had happened to people, so there was a lot of time in terms of being understanding and supportive. There was fierce paddling going on. I told Penny she needed to be careful of the time she was investing." Penny noted that she began to spend more time after hours on the Gulf Coast Fund work in order to meet other Rockefeller Philanthropy Advisor client obligations.

In 2008, the collaborative was able to increase its staff size and hire two additional part-time individuals. To make this happen, the Gulf Coast Fund had to invest more in oversight and administration, and Rockefeller Philanthropy Advisors was able to maintain some donated staff time and its reduced fee. At the same time, some of the demands of the startup began to ebb.

"We now have a smooth operation, and it takes less time to manage," Doug reflected.

Building a Green Economy

Grantees and partners of the Gulf Coast Fund have been building stronger alliances between community-based organizations, local environmental organizations, and larger national groups.

They are also leveraging neighborhood voices into state and national dialogues.

One such effort has been led by the Holy Cross Neighborhood Association and its project, the Lower Ninth Ward Center for Sustainable Engagement and Development. The association is a membership organization for residents of the Holy Cross community in the lower ninth ward of New Orleans.

The Center is working to rebuild the neighborhood as the first carbon-neutral community in the United States, Pam explained. Such a neighborhood would not add greenhouse gases, such as carbon dioxide, to the environment.

To achieve this goal, the Center has focused efforts on reducing energy use in neighborhood buildings and homes. Construction and maintenance of buildings represent almost half of U.S. energy use.[6]

"[Residents] felt that they would never attract the support they needed to rebuild their community unless they were organized and could present to the world that they were going to become a model of sustainability," explained Elizabeth Galante, director of the New Orleans Resource Office and Center for Global Green.

The endeavor has been complicated by the fact that less than a quarter of residents have returned to the lower ninth ward, which had a population of sixty-eight hundred in 2000.[7] Destroyed houses and fear of continued flooding have discouraged people from returning.

The Center, in part strengthened by Gulf Coast Fund dollars, forged a partnership with Global Green USA (founded by Mikhail Gorbachev). Together with movie star Brad Pitt, the organizations sponsored an international competition for architects to design green buildings for the Holy Cross neighborhood. "We had this half block in the lower ninth ward—eighteen apartments, six single-family homes, and a community center—that they needed to design," Elizabeth elaborated. The Sierra Club also donated funds for a revolving fund to purchase materials in bulk.

The combination of Brad Pitt's star power and existing national media attention on the disaster proved to be a potent one. In 2006, the competition attracted more than 125 entries, and the event was covered by major media networks and newspapers—including two segments on NBC's *Today*, Elizabeth noted.[8]

"Every design firm in the city entered," Elizabeth elaborated. "There was an incredible awakening citywide to green building and sustainability and climate change. Everyone was talking about it, from architects to plumbers to electricians to the sheet rock guys."

"The intent is to change public consciousness not only in the ninth ward and New Orleans but nationally," Pam explained of the importance of the media coverage.

"This is the wave of the future," Brad Pitt stated on NBC's *Today*, which filmed his interview in New Orleans in a neighborhood still decimated by the hurricanes. "We need to regroup and adopt a new paradigm [that includes green building]."[9] Choosing New Orleans—an international symbol of the perils of global warming—as the focus of the competition helped create a story meme (a story that propagates itself) within the U.S. cultural dialogue that a world free of addiction to oil was possible.

As construction for the site has moved forward (financed in large part by the Home Depot Foundation), the two organizations have also been working with residents to retrofit existing homes. Some of the technologies they are employing include radiant barrier, which reflects the sun off of houses to reduce heating and cooling bills, fluorescent light bulbs, and solar paneling.

Whereas in 2008, only about seventy homes had radiant barrier, Elizabeth (Global Green) explained, "They represent the first wave and—because they are the first—the most difficult wave of safe and sustainable homes."

The competition and the model housing in turn helped create a policy environment more conducive to the promotion of solar energy, according to Darryl Malek-Wiley of the New Orleans Sierra Club chapter. "The solar paneling installed in the Holy Cross neighborhood houses helped drive the passage of a New Orleans net metering law, which hooked these solar panels to the city grid. So if a house generates more energy than it uses, the energy goes back onto the grid, and the power company gives that household a credit." In addition, the recently passed Louisiana Wind Energy System or Solar Energy System Tax Credit gives homeowners a 50 percent tax credit for the cost of buying a wind or solar energy system, up to a total rebate of $12,500 for each system.[10]

The model homes and the emerging policies are encouraging New Orleans and the State of Louisiana to join a growing global movement to create an energy economy that is green, clean, and decentralized. The cornerstone of such an economy is "buildings that produce, rather than just consume, energy. Instead of sucking energy from a centralized plant, these homes and office buildings convert wind, solar and biomass into electricity, which they [both use and] 'upload' onto the grid."[11]

To supplement the work, partners have been working together with the Center to train residents for jobs in a green economy. According to Darryl, a grant of just under a million dollars from the Louisiana Department of Labor has been funding training, including for ninth ward residents, on how to weatherize houses.

As part of the neighborhood revitalization effort, the community and its partners are also trying to revive the neighborhood commercial district, though up to this point with little success. "We haven't been able to get people to come back, due to lack of resources. Their insurance often didn't pay them, there aren't state programs to help with this, and there aren't enough customers," Darryl acknowledged.

Restoring Gulf Wetlands and Beyond

As part of a separate initiative, several local grantees—including the Holy Cross Neighborhood Association and the Gulf Restoration Network—have leveraged Gulf Coast Fund dollars and built alliances with national organizations to restore the Gulf wetlands. These include the Sierra Club, American Rivers, and the Environmental Defense Fund.

Such efforts have included a successful campaign to close the Mississippi Gulf Outlet (called Mr. GO). This canal, which serves as a shortcut from the Gulf of Mexico to New Orleans, was constructed in part as a hub for international shipping.[12]

Mr. GO played a particularly devastating role in the levee failures in New Orleans, Aaron Viles explained. "Before Katrina, many people in the area saw Mr. GO as a catastrophe ready to happen. We call it hurricane highway because—with more water volume than the Panama Canal—it allowed the hurricane waters to build speed." These waters then hit the New Orleans levees with a vengeance, helping break them.

The Gulf Coast Fund dollars helped build the capacity of local organizations, which played a central role in the campaign. Educating legislators and the public about the perils of Mr. GO, Aaron emphasized that the presence of groups based in the region was critical in giving the campaign national credibility.

The Gulf Restoration Network generated forty thousand e-mails to Congress, which Darryl (Sierra Club) noted "really helped get the word out. Closing Mr. GO would not have been in the national dialogue without us."

"Of course the dam to close Mr. GO is not built yet," Darryl warned.[13] "And a dam will help stop salt water intrusion, but it won't restore the wetlands. There's still a lot of work to do. The scope of what we are talking about in terms of coastal restoration is huge—the area is bigger than the Everglades."

Aaron Viles (fund adviser) explained that Gulf Coast Fund grantees are moving beyond their local concerns to create a larger movement in the region. On April 14, 2007, the Gulf Restoration Network and partners organized a rally in New Orleans, one of hundreds held across the country on that day.[14] Organized by a national campaign called Step It Up, the rallies aimed to send a signal to Congress to cut carbon emissions by 80 percent by 2050.[15] "It coincided with a Gulf Coast Fund event, so all the grantees were there," Aaron recounted.

"New Orleans was such an iconic location; we considered our partners in that region particularly powerful," explained May Boeve, co-coordinator of the Step It Up campaign. She also pointed out that by 2008, relevant legislative bills had been introduced, including the Lieberman-Warner Climate Security Act, which aimed to cut U.S. carbon emissions by amounts similar to those targeted by the campaign.[16]

"The great thing about the Gulf Coast Fund is that it keeps providing opportunities to bring groups together around a larger message," Aaron emphasized. "A lot of fund grantees are understandably focused on the really bad sewage treatment plant in their neighborhood, or the fact that their houses have been built on a dump—but the fact that they can get together and say that everyone needs sustainable communities—that is huge payoff."

"The Gulf Coast Fund is providing a regional framework with diverse stakeholders. It's that combination that will position it to offer up some alternatives that are much bigger in scale down the road," Penny Fujiko Willgerodt explained of the long-term implications of these initiatives.

Conclusion

When first Katrina and then Rita devastated communities along the Gulf Coast, a group of funders came together to find a way to help. Their goal was to address not only the immediate needs of people in the Gulf but also the history of environmental degradation and human rights violations that had exacerbated the disaster.

The funders quickly realized that the most effective strategy would be one that challenged traditional funder-grantee power relations. Drawing on the experience of other foundations that have shared power with community leaders, they decided to create an advisory board of people from the Gulf who would make decisions regarding whom to fund and what activities to organize.

The decision helped them attract many of the most sought after Gulf Coast grassroots leaders. "Following Katrina, there were all sorts of funders and policy groups struggling to identify and assemble such an impressive cohort of community stewards from across the region. But what we made time for was the Gulf Coast Fund," Derrick Evans (fund adviser) emphasized. "Each of us is a custodian of invaluable community wisdom and relationships. The Gulf Coast Fund founders respected this from the beginning and wisely asked us to envision and build rather than just approve and promote an idea. They deeply respected the fact that *relationships* are what make stuff happen—particularly in the Deep South."

Given the newness of the funder collaborative, the effort is still an experimental one, with results still emerging. However, the fund's grantmaking has already helped to attract new funding to the region, bolster the voices of Gulf Coast communities as they seek to promote a positive vision for the Gulf—one that includes sustainable and carbon-free communities as well as green, decentralized energy sources—and shape the national and regional cultural dialogue on global warming.

The Gulf Coast Fund has also provided a catalyst for leaders and organizations throughout the region to begin to work

together in new and creative ways. "Not since the civil rights movement has there been such a coming together across four states,
across racial lines, across cities and rural areas. It's a remarkable
convergence—cross-issue, cross-region, cross-community, and
cross-generation," Penny emphasized. Many within the collaborative see these growing regional ties as critical to building economic, social, and political power in the Gulf that will, over the
long term, be able to bring forward a more just and sustainable
reality for the region.

Lessons Learned

The Gulf Coast Fund responded to hurricanes Katrina and Rita by
recognizing Gulf residents' immediate needs and helping them
address the preexisting conditions that exacerbated the crisis.
How might your foundation respond to such a crisis?

- Plan to stay engaged for at least twelve years, as disaster recovery is a long-term process. Progress can be slow, but strengthening networks of affected communities will have long-term
  benefits.
- Embrace a holistic approach to crisis response that also
  addresses the underlying causes of the disaster. Focus on cross-
  cutting and multi-issue approaches, especially where the need
  to address many problems at once can lead to the establish-
  ment of false and sometimes harmful choices (focusing on
  affordable housing to the detriment of environment, health,
  or community continuity, for example).
- Fund disaster responses that focus on government accountability and ensuring that the public sector responds appropriately, but also support the nonprofit community, which plays
  a vital role in providing services that government is unable or
  unwilling to provide.
- Seek out trusted community leaders and create space for them
  to determine how best to use philanthropic resources, as there
  is no substitute for local knowledge after a disaster. Funding
  responses made without understanding and deference to local
  nuances and cultural realities can do more harm than good.

- If you create a participatory decision-making structure with people in the affected region, strive to prevent real or perceived conflicts of interest by working with community leaders with integrity and the trust of their constituencies. Establish strong structural mechanisms and transparent decision-making processes to avoid any opportunities for conflicts of interest to arise. Also be aware that such initiatives will take considerable time, even as they will provide enormous benefit.

PART
SIX

Gleaning Lessons for Change

Lessons for the Road

As the stories in this book highlight, every type of foundation can effectively leverage its dollars to help grantees create a fairer world. Whether small or large, private or public, local, national, or international, foundations have the capacity to support successful efforts to level the playing field—economically, socially, and culturally.

Such philanthropic strategies are possible, and foundations that are considering giving in support of equity and justice can draw on many resources. This book is one. GrantCraft, a project of the Ford Foundation, also offers videos and publications that are based on grantmakers' real stories. Another resource is the National Committee for Responsive Philanthropy.

Building a Strategy for Change

Systems change is a massive goal. Whether grantees are shifting cultures, influencing policy, or building new economic structures, such work entails leveraging scarce foundation dollars for broader societal transformation. Grantees, working with support from foundations, may not reach ambitious goals for decades.

Thus, to be successful, foundations must be particularly strategic in how they deploy their multiple resources. Such efforts rely on a foundation's analyzing a problem effectively, choosing its partners and path wisely, and then continually evaluating benchmarks along the road to see if progress has been made.

As shown by the stories in this book, a successful strategy typically includes the following steps:

1. Analyze the problem.
2. Find a niche.
3. Identify powerful levers.
4. Choose strong grantees.
5. Give organizations what they need to succeed.
6. Evaluate progress.

Step 1: Analyze the Problem

Several foundations began with an issue area of concern, such as lack of funding for public education or poverty, and analyzed, often as an iterative process, this problem from a perspective of root causes. Asking questions regarding the "Why?" behind the issue led them to a social justice approach to their grantmaking.

After the passage of welfare reform, the Open Society Institute initially considered reacting with only a service approach to the problem. Founder George Soros wanted to provide money to support legal residents in naturalizing. The hope was that citizenship would protect new Americans from the harshest aspects of welfare reform.

However, some OSI staff went further: they asked why democracy in the United States was not working for U.S. residents. As a result, the foundation also supported organizations (often made up of immigrants themselves) that were holding public institutions accountable to their needs.

The Polk Bros. Foundation (discussed in Chapter Six) also asked the question "Why?" when, following the passage of welfare reform laws, grantees were besieged with requests for legal support. At this time, many people, and particularly immigrants, were being taken off welfare when they should not have been. Instead of simply providing additional funds to legal support centers, the foundation also looked further upstream. Why were many people—and particularly immigrants—in need of such assistance? In response, the foundation decided to include a new focus on advocacy, supporting grantees efforts to challenge existing policies.

Step 2: Find a Niche

The foundations described in this book demonstrate that focusing resources is critical to achieving large-scale change. Transforming institutions, cultures, policies, and structures is difficult. Foundations without clear direction risk pouring their resources into a vast sea and watching them disappear—like a bucket of water—having made minimal impact. Of course, not all grants succeed, but taking calculated risks within the context of a well thought out strategic frame can lead to large payoffs.

Highlighted foundations find a niche—a particular point of focus that matches the size of their resources. In doing so, many highlighted foundations begin by supporting grantees achieving small-scale wins. These efforts then build momentum for larger victories.

The foundations are finding the niche where they can have the most impact by dovetailing two or more of the following:

- Issue area (such as education, living wages, urban renewal, sustainable business)
- Identity group (for example, women, immigrants)
- Process (such as revitalizing democracy, building leadership capacity)
- Type of organization supported (for example, legal institutions, community-based organizations)
- Geographic location (for example, state, city, neighborhood)

Highlighted foundations take diverse paths and are pulled by different interests as they determine which of these areas they should use to guide them. Some follow their passion. Others seek areas where people are already in motion in order to capitalize on existing energy and momentum. All continue to monitor whether their grantmaking is having impact and, through hard analysis, at times shift their perspective and change direction.

Among the highlighted foundations, choosing a niche by **issue area or identity group** is the most popular means for determining a strategic focus. Often they define goals and measure progress by focusing efforts around an issue-based policy objective, such as increasing funding for education.

Some foundations find the most effective way to help grantees achieve results is through **strengthening processes and types of organizations.** The Mott Foundation, the Liberty Hill Foundation, the Gulf Coast Fund, and the Needmor Fund, for example, are working to revitalize democracy. To do this, they are strengthening grassroots membership organizations that in turn are providing a platform for citizens to engage in democratic life. By targeting a type of organization, they are empowering grantees to define their own priorities—rather than driving their agendas for them.

For the Mott Foundation and the Needmor Fund, focusing on community engagement and organizing helps them bridge political divides among trustees. Whereas board members sometimes have differing views on such issues as the government's role in health care, all board members agree that active and engaged citizens are a vital part of a healthy democracy.

Many foundations also find their niche by focusing on a **geographic area.** Instead of supporting a national agenda, the Schott Foundation, for example, focuses its education work primarily in two states—Massachusetts and New York—though it is currently aiding grantees federally who are capitalizing on state wins. The Discount Foundation is selecting grantees achieving living wages in cities across the United States. Early wins at the city level helped create a snowball of momentum that is shifting policy nationally, including increasing the national minimum wage in 2007.

Focusing on a small geographic area allows the Jacobs foundations to branch out and support many issue areas simultaneously. They are targeting economic revitalization efforts in only a few neighborhoods in San Diego. The small area of focus allows them to take a holistic approach, supporting communities as they not only stimulate business in their area but also engage youth, reduce gang violence, and address racial conflicts.

Step 3: Identify Powerful Levers

The highlighted foundations are supporting partners as they build powerful levers for change. By finding entry points, these grantees are moving systems much larger than themselves.

The Discount Foundation, for example, identified three powerful constituencies that embody many of the foundation's own values and are helping shape the U.S. landscape. These are faith, labor, and community-based organizations. When working together, these three groups represent a much more powerful force for change than when they work alone. The trustees and staff are defining a niche area—living-wage campaigns—in which powerful alliances among these three constituencies already exist.

For the Jacobs Center for Neighborhood Innovation, one entry point to ensure that businesses support social aims is to own—together with the community—an entire commercial block. It can then guarantee companies that they will not provide licenses to competitors. With this assurance, national businesses have been much more willing to negotiate social benefits, such as providing living wages and hiring locally.

Foundations often support grantees' communications campaigns, including research connected to such efforts, in order to help activists amplify their voices. Money for engaging the media, including training on how to speak to reporters, is often critical. Reframing language can also be key—as shown in the momentum built when organizers started speaking about a "living wage" instead of a "minimum wage," first in Baltimore and then across the country (see Chapter One).

Research provides grantees talking points and can reduce opposition to initiatives. For example, the Discount Foundation helped fund a research paper that provided key statistics on how living-wage laws were not significantly increasing costs for employers. The paper helped diffuse the primary public concern regarding such efforts.

Step 4: Choose Strong Grantees

Having determined their strategic direction, the foundations seek grantees with significant potential. These are often groups that are growing their membership base and building high-impact partnerships. Rather than choosing to support individuals on the basis of the titles they hold, the foundations look for what they have accomplished. Leaders of such organizations often have strong integrity, vision, and a track record.

In choosing grantees, these grantmakers often have similar habits. They have in-depth knowledge of applicants. They take risks by supporting some new and emerging organizations. They are aware of grantee management needs and limitations. They also fund high-performance grantees for twelve years or more, helping them solidify successes.

Highlighted foundations typically invest time learning about potential grantees. Proposals are only supplementary material, as they are often more a test of good writing skills than an indication of an organization's capacity to lead change initiatives successfully. Direct contact and insider knowledge are what most often shines light on an applicant's potential. Site visits are thus vital. Seeking advice from trusted advisers—including activists and other funders—familiar with applicants is also common. To deepen relationships with players in the field, some—such as the Schott Foundation and the Jacobs foundations—are locating their offices in the geographic region in which they work.

One factor that helps foundation staff choose grantees effectively is prior community organizing experience. Particularly when foundation officers are focused on building grassroots strength, such experience—and connections to broad networks—helps community organizers identify high-potential people and organizations.

Most highlighted foundations also embrace risk as they choose which grantees to support, so that they can create space for new and emerging players, not only well-established organizations. When foundations gamble on organizations with little track record but with the potential for high returns, funding sometimes helps new players grow into large and powerful organizations. "If you are not taking risk, you're not doing your job," noted Marjorie Fine, former head of the Unitarian Universalist Veatch Program at Shelter Rock and currently director of The Linchpin Campaign (a project of the Center for Community Change).

When providing opportunities for new players, foundations have found smaller grants can reduce risk, particularly when funding new organizations or those with weak management structures. The Global Fund for Women and the Liberty Hill Foundation, for example, give small grants to multiple emerging organizations and then see which ones mature and develop a track record before deciding which should receive additional grant dollars.

In some instances, foundations and collaboratives (Liberty Hill Foundation, Gulf Coast Fund) are harnessing the wisdom of movement leaders through community funding boards. Responsible for grantmaking decisions, these boards include activists whose inside knowledge is vital in separating high-potential proposals from ones that will not get off the ground.

WHEN ACTIVISTS MAKE GRANTMAKING DECISIONS

The Gulf Coast Fund and the Liberty Hill Foundation stress three factors that contribute to the success of their funding boards. Important for any foundation board, these are

1. Strong conflict-of-interest rules
2. Activist integrity
3. Diversity

Conflict-of-interest rules are critical, particularly because board members are often also part of organizations looking for funding. Such rules ensure that activists are choosing grantees based on merit rather than on personal interest.

In both cases, activists themselves hold to such high standards of integrity that they often self-monitor, recusing themselves from any potentially conflictual situations. Such behavior helps ensure that foundation staff don't find themselves in the awkward position of "policing" activists.

Board diversity brings rich perspective and experience, and reinforces conflict-of-interest rules. When members are part of broad networks, they bring different perspectives and are less likely to choose proposals based on friendships. Diversity also helps ensure that the board includes those with community ties, who can often best identify high-potential grassroots organizations, and individuals who can tie local concerns to state, national, and global movements (of course, some individuals work at all these levels).

For both the Liberty Hill Foundation and the Gulf Coast Fund, participation in the grantmaking process has transformed individuals involved. Lasting relationships are forming between leaders

(Continued)

of different movements. New alliances are developing. Activists are exposed to different strategies for achieving social justice, and leaders are incorporating these into their organizations.

Other foundations (the Needmor Fund and Global Fund for Women are examples) are bringing activists of many backgrounds onto their more traditional boards. This diversity is helping them capture some of the benefits of community funding board models.

Step 5: Give Organizations What They Need to Succeed

Funders highlighted tend to invest heavily in choosing the right grantees, then give them significant freedom in how they use funds. This approach allows organizations the flexibility to respond to unfolding events and opportunities as they emerge.

In line with this philosophy, funders often provide grantees with general operating support rather than tying funding to specific initiatives. Such support allows organizations, with their close-up view of events on the ground, the flexibility to use their wisdom and insight to determine how best to invest limited funds.

General operating support also sends a signal to grantees— that funders trust them to make sound decisions. Such funding can help establish open channels of communication.

A few foundations point to trust as a fundamental aspect of their relationships with organizations, particularly when engaged in social justice work. Catalyzing systems change can be controversial, and foundations need grantees to tell them when things go wrong. Without trust, they are more likely to hide bumps in the road.

Finally, foundations often use their influence and reputation to help build additional support for grantees. Organizing site visits, bringing them to conferences, and establishing affinity groups are a few of the tools funders use to raise interest in initiatives.

Step 6: Evaluate Progress

In ensuring a strategy's efficacy, several highlighted foundations stress the importance of reflecting carefully on their work over time. Only with an eye to results can funders ensure success.

However, grantmakers face challenges in learning how to evaluate efforts. Common questions include, How do we measure progress when a goal might not be achieved for ten or fifteen years? and When systems shift, how can we be sure that grantees played an important role in catalyzing that change?

The foundations highlighted in this book typically find social justice work harder to evaluate than direct services support. When funding a service delivery program, funders can more easily identify a program's beneficiaries and results (patients seen and cured by a clinic, children in tutorial programs who passed standardized testing programs). Systems change, in contrast, often needs more complex measures of success.

Several foundations are finding benchmarks to measure progress, even when the final outcome will take decades to achieve. This can mean finding proxies to measure success, such as the number of (1) legislators that support an issue, (2) emerging new leaders, and (3) stories in the media.

Several foundations caution, however, that evaluations need to be done judiciously so as to avoid stifling innovation. "I think we need to be extremely careful how we think about measurement," warns Luis Ubiñas, current president of the Ford Foundation. "When you move to narrow quantitative measures, you run the risk of moving to narrow quantitatively driven activities. Many of the issues the Ford Foundation works on, important social issues, are long developing, long simmering, long brewing. So we need to bring a very, very sophisticated view to measuring and understanding impact [because] measurement can drive behavior."[1]

To avoid evaluation pitfalls, several foundations are learning to measure processes, rather than expecting immediate and significant issue-area victories. The Liberty Hill Foundation and the Needmor Fund, both focused on supporting the growth of social justice organizations, are finding ways to measure how strong an organization is becoming. Questions they ask to evaluate grantees include the following:

Is the grantee growing its membership?

Are there an increasing number of people going to meetings?

Are grantees building relationships with key allies in government, business, or labor?

Are there new leaders emerging?

Are there other benchmarks along the way that are being met?

To evaluate such processes, some foundations rely heavily on stories. "One leader talked about how when she came to New Mexico she was in total fear and lived like a prisoner in her own house," Frank Sanchez (Needmor Fund) recalls. "Now she is president of her organization and can hold her own with government officials. We look for stories like this where a person was completely transformed through their participation in an organization."

By finding appropriate benchmarks, foundations can then determine whether their analysis and approach are bringing about the anticipated effects. In some cases, such as that of the Discount Foundation, foundations are brave enough to change direction if they are not seeing the kinds of results anticipated.

When a foundation focuses on systems change, there is rarely one factor that causes a change to occur. "There's never a need to put a grantee in the position of saying, 'We did it and no one else did; or we are the best.' It's usually a cluster of groups that created change," notes Marjorie Fine (formerly with the Veatch Program).

However, there are ways to determine which organizations are playing particularly important roles in catalyzing change. Site visits and participation in events sponsored by grantees and others are critical.

"We try to interview all the people involved [in campaigns], including the elected officials. They'll tell you who brought information to them," Frank Sanchez of the Needmor Fund adds.

For Seth Borgos (formerly with the Veatch Program; currently with CCC) peers were "the most reliable source." He recalls, "I found the best index was when peers gave unsolicited credit. I'd also ask people, 'Who are you learning from?' I'd often get real insight into who peers respected and why."

The following are a few questions funders might consider trying to answer:

Which organizations are convening significant numbers of people, including influential decision-makers at events?

Who gets their phone calls returned? In a room, who is the focus
of decision makers' attention?

To which organizations do people working on an issue turn in a
crisis?

"You want to look for an amalgam of issues that point to who
critical players were," Marjorie added.

"[When doing an evaluation,] it's also critical to have the buy-
in of the organization itself," Frank noted. "The result should be
useful to them. And it's important to understand how these groups
are evaluating themselves."

Building Commitment for Social Justice

Several founders created their foundations to support systems
change for equity and justice. Liberty Hill and Discount fall into
this category.

Some, however, originally focused some or all their resources
on direct services (either as an overall institutional strategy or
within individual programs). In these cases, the foundations turn
to social justice strategies when key individuals—often inside the
foundation—agitate for change.

The following are ways to build support for increasing focus
on social justice, including community organizing, within your
foundation:

- Build momentum during times of transition within the
  foundation. These are moments when both leaders and staff
  are questioning traditional practices and are more open to
  new ideas.
- Use unfolding world and other events to transform processes
  within your institutions. You can help frame disasters and
  recently passed legislation that colleagues know about by
  helping them analyze the issue through a social justice lens.
- Find ways for colleagues, including board members and senior
  staff, to meet activists who are succeeding in achieving systems
  change. Face-to-face contact, particularly through site visits, is
  vital to educating people and building their interest.

- Look beyond the activities funded by the foundation to its deeper values. Help board members, senior staff, and other colleagues in your foundation see how supporting systems change connects to their values.
- See if colleagues already have a few grantees working through a social justice lens, and show them how their grantees are part of the larger discipline.
- Share information about your grantees, including organizing events within your foundation for colleagues to meet them.
- Understand what has caused change in the past within your foundation and draw on these lessons.

Affinity groups and collaboratives are also vehicles for encouraging foundations to join exciting initiatives. Many highlighted foundations leveraged these networks.

Affinity groups—often defined as a loose affiliation of foundations around a particular topic of interest—can be a powerful learning tool for funders. They can help build interest within the philanthropic community in a particular issue area, encourage new funders to join an effort, and offer group protection, which funders sometimes need in order to speak difficult truths to their colleagues.

Collaboratives often go one step further, pooling philanthropic dollars from many institutions to develop common strategies for change. Through them funders can coordinate strategies more closely. They can avoid duplication of effort by organizing joint activities—such as grantee evaluations (Four Freedoms Fund took this approach). Further, foundations can support larger-scale change efforts by combining assets, and can introduce one another to grantees.

TRADE-OFFS OF COLLABORATIVES AND AFFINITY GROUPS

Collaboratives and affinity groups sometimes provide opportunities to the field at a cost.

Three former funders note that collaboratives can constrict organizations' access to funding. For many fields of practice, there are only a handful of funders. When these funders form a collaborative, grantees can easily fall out of favor with the collective and find that they do not have alternative sources of funding. In addition, collaboratives are sometimes more likely to support friends rather than the grantees with the highest potential. One former funder notes that meeting grantmakers that are part of a collaborative can be hard, a serious concern given that receipt of money is often based on relationships.

Developing strategies to avoid the pitfalls of collaboratives can be critical. One grantmaker recommends earmarking some funding for new actors. Another suggests inviting organizations to help shape collaborative structures, which she felt helps ensure that the collaboration includes "the best thinking in the field." She emphasizes, "these conversations need to happen before people start putting money on the table."

Another, however, notes that asking organizations to help think about how to form a collaborative can also have drawbacks. "If you ask one group and not another you can create bad feelings."

Affinity groups have grown at a significant pace in the last decade. In the 1990s, they increased at twice the pace of the 1980s, and growth has continued to accelerate in the 2000s.[2]

Whether overall these groups have strengthened the field is still in question. Some believe that affinity groups can distract funders from building relationships with nonprofit actors, instead encouraging them to spend their time forging partnerships with other funders. This dynamic can keep foundation staff from taking the time to learn about new high-potential actors in the field. Such groups can also be expensive, with funders using scarce resources for travel and operating costs—resources that could have gone to grantees themselves.

The following are a few questions funders can ask themselves to determine if an affinity group should continue:

Are our members still learning from each other?
Is the reason we formed still relevant today?
Are we accomplishing something significant through our collaboration?
Is what we are achieving adding enough value to justify the cost?

(Continued)

If some of the answers are no, then members might want to consider disbanding to free resources for grantees and other initiatives.

The Discount Foundation, for example, helped form the Working Group on Labor and Community, an affinity group that continues to have significant impact on how foundations view unions. Organizing site visits and sponsoring speakers at conferences, this affinity group introduces many foundations to positive changes occurring within the labor movement. The work also is helping foundations see the power of coalitions between community organizations, faith organizations, and labor to achieve large-scale change.

The Open Society Institute (OSI) funneled its money through local funding collaboratives, such as the Fund for Immigrants and Refugees in Illinois. The strategy helped deepen funder support of immigrant concerns, and often of social justice more generally. Nikki Stein of the Polk Bros. Foundation, for example, noted that participation in the fund ultimately gave her the courage to work with her board to include social justice strategies in their giving. Antonio Maciel believed that if OSI had sustained its support for collaboratives across the country for a longer period of time, it would have played an even larger role in building new funder commitment to both immigrants and systems change approaches to giving.

Conclusion

Each foundation and collaborative highlighted in this book is increasing its impact and creating a world that is more fair, just, and inclusive. For some their journey has taken them from funding service programs for a few individuals to supporting movements building large-scale change for many. Other foundations, focused on systems change since their inception, are learning over time how to fund this work more effectively.

In every case, the highlighted foundations and the grantees they support are showing tremendous courage—challenging themselves to transform their grantmaking and financial strategies to strengthen their impact. In doing so, they are leveraging their dollars to reinvigorate democratic practices both in the United States and abroad, helping catalyze the emergence of new fields of practice and strengthening social movements.

The journeys of these foundations offer rich insights into how trustees, managers, and program staff, as well as grantees, can ensure that philanthropy is a powerful force in addressing the major challenges of our times. By sharing not only their successes but also their failures, each is illuminating possible paths for foundations—new and old—as the philanthropic field seeks ways to face both the crises and the opportunities of the twenty-first century.

Afterword

Race and Social Justice

It is not enough to humanize the social world. It is neces-sary to change it.
PROFESSOR ROBERTO UNGAR,
HARVARD SCHOOL OF LAW[1]

Social and racial justice are inextricably intertwined. We can identify most of our communities by race, and once we do, we can usually guess rightly how they are doing. We can imagine how their schools look, how much crime they have, whether they have jobs, grocery stores, and parks. Racial disparities are legion. So how do we understand them, and what do they mean for the nation?

In 2000, more than two-thirds of people living in concen-trated urban poverty were black or Latino; 34 percent of poor blacks and 22 percent of Latinos lived in neighborhoods with at least a 25 percent poverty rate, compared to only 6 percent of poor whites.[2]

Today's problems are hardly isolated, yet they are highly racial-ized and gendered. Certainly we are challenged to imagine how, in a world that is predominantly nonwhite and in a nation in which the majority of people will be of color by 2050, we can solve global warming and fossil fuel dependency or any other large social prob-lems without supported leadership and institutions in communities of color that can build bridges across communities and participate in social innovations. How can we secure our national or global well-being without regard to the majority of us?

For some, universal strategies are seen as the best way to solve the complex web of racism, patriarchy, and poverty together. If we see ourselves in the same boat, can't we convince people to row together? The problem is, we are not all in the same boat even while all boats are leaky. Some are taking in water faster and will sink first, never making it to a shore of opportunity. Living-wage ordinances and other job creation strategies that help many people of color in public service jobs do not necessarily address the needs of immigrants in the country legally on work visas whose jobs are threatened if they complain about unsafe or harsh working conditions or not being paid for hours worked.

Race is also used, explicitly and implicitly, in our debates about what kinds of policies we need. As just one example, increasingly images of or references to Central American immigrants are coupled with challenges to calls for health reform and other social programs because these immigrants might benefit.

Social justice work requires attention to traditionally marginalized communities to ensure that they benefit from our structural arrangements. Such work also means working to prevent race from being used as a wedge to undermine programs we all need.

Structural transformation is not a task with an end point. No matter how societies are structured, they will always need to address new challenges. But social, political, and economic institutions can transform themselves and their relationships with one another in ways that help us solve existing inequities and prevent new problems. Such work inevitably demands that our institutions and systems be democratic—designed and influenced by citizens participating actively within them—so that we as a society can innovate collectively to meet future challenges as they arise.

Structural transformation that accounts for race, gender, and class disparities is a huge undertaking. Many fear that the project is too big, too amorphous, and too demanding to be meaningful. But as the chapters of this book make clear, it is possible to engage in transactions and steps that begin to create fissures in existing structures, helping us reconstruct them and construct new ones.

As shown in the cases highlighted, foundations can play an important role in change processes that lead to more racially just societal systems. To participate effectively, they must remain open to innovation and stay committed for the long haul. Further, as demonstrated by many of the examples highlighted, they must be

willing to reinvent themselves, their strategies, and their relationships over time.

We live in tumultuous and challenging times; we stand on
the edge of a precipice. We can fall headlong into an abyss of
unprecedented poverty, shrinking opportunities, environmental
devastation, and increased social turmoil. Or we can embrace our
current set of crises as an opportunity. As we are forced to cope
with food shortages, high fuel costs, a shrinking middle class,
growing wealth divides, global migrations, and cataclysmic environmental events, so too must we face changing the social world
because we cannot afford merely to tinker with the consequences
of these problems. We must move more deeply into the roots of
these challenges in order to solve them.

The experiences of the grantmakers in this book, and many
others not recounted here, show us that there is not one field
or one crop. Nor is the goal to fill up on one meal. We must be
able to produce what nourishes all of us—black, white, Latino,
and races of all types—over and over again. Our goal is a global
banquet at a table we all helped set, with nourishment we were all
able to enhance with our own spices, secret ingredients, and cooking styles. This book invites us to the kitchen. As my grandmother
would say, let's get to cooking.

June 2009   MAYA WILEY
                                                      Executive Director
                                                      Center for Social Inclusion

APPENDIXES

APPENDIX A

Words You Need to Know to Read This Book

Advocacy

A category of activities whose primary purpose is to influence people's opinions or actions on matters of public policy or concern.[1] Advocacy can be directed at governments, corporations, nonprofits, the media, and the broader public.[2]

Charity

In recent years, charity has come to mean almsgiving or relief for the sick and afflicted. However, originally the word had much more of a connotation of people taking care of each other. Legally, "charity" is often used as a shorthand for "public charity" (see *public charity*).[3]

Community-based or grassroots organization

An organization that has a membership base that is tied to a neighborhood or particular constituency.

Community organizing

The process of building an increasingly broad-based, democratic organization, typically rooted in disenfranchised communities, and bringing that power and collective voice to bear on the issues that affect those communities by engaging with relevant decision makers. Commonly, the goal is to build a large, well-disciplined organization with membership, leadership, knowledge, vision, power, and capacity to make increasingly significant gains on vital issues. This requires a continuing process of actively reaching out, involving larger numbers of people, bringing leaders to the fore (including giving them training and increasing authority), and helping members move into effective action on the issues that most concern them. Usually this is done by organizers on staff. Community organizing can be one part of an overall advocacy or public policy campaign strategy, but it is distinguished by the fact that affected constituencies—rather than paid advocates who attempt to represent the interests of such constituencies—are the agents of change.[4]

501(c)(3) organization

An organization that qualifies for exemption from federal income tax because it engages exclusively in charitable or educational activities and meets other legal requirements. Donors to 501(c)(3)s may be eligible to take a deduction from their personal income taxes, and most foundations will give grants only to 501(c)(3) organizations. In general, 501(c)(3)s are highly regulated—for example, they can't support or oppose candidates for office and can do only a limited amount of lobbying.[5]

501(c)(4) organization

An organization that is exempt from federal income tax because it primarily engages in activities to benefit society in general ("social welfare" activities), but which may also engage in other activities to a lesser degree. Donors generally may not take tax deductions for contributions to 501(c)(4)s, and foundations rarely give to these organizations. Generally, 501(c)(4)s have more latitude than 501(c)(3)s: 501(c)(4)s can engage in an unlimited amount of lobbying and usually can even support or oppose candidates for public office, subject to the restrictions that may apply under federal, state, or local election law.[6]

Family foundation

A foundation (typically a private foundation) generally understood to be created and usually managed, at least in part, by members of a single family.[7]

Funder collaborative

Most commonly used to describe an entity created by a group of funders who want to pool their financial resources in support of a common mission (though sometimes collaboratives are more informal). The collaborative receives the grants and then regrants the funds.

Funder network or affinity group

Groups of grantmakers that act collectively to support a particular population, region, interest, or other identifying characteristic.[8]

(General) operating support or general support grant

A contribution that the recipient organization can use for any of its expenses. Monies might cover ongoing expenses, such as salaries and office space, as well as generally some lobbying, unless prohibited from doing so by the terms of the grant or other restrictions.[9]

Lobbying

In general, any attempt to influence a legislative proposal through direct or grassroots contact with public officials or members of their staff. Legally, specific definitions (and exceptions to those definitions) vary. However, most of the time, asking a legislative body to take a specific action to address a problem is considered lobbying, but simply describing a problem without supporting a particular solution is not. For example, it is typically not lobbying to meet with legislators to educate them about the general problem of air pollution. It probably is lobbying to urge Congress to require automobile manufacturers to cut car emissions.[10]

Matching or challenge grant

A grant or gift made with the specification that the amount donated must be matched on a dollar-for-dollar basis or according to some other prescribed formula.[11]

Mission-related (or program-related) investing

Using a foundation's financial portfolio to further the foundation's mission as well as protect the principal invested or earn financial returns.[12] For example, a foundation might provide a low-interest loan for the development of a commercial property to help revitalize a low-income neighborhood.

On the ground

Activity that is happening in communities and neighborhoods, in contrast to actions taken by Wall Street, Capitol Hill, or other traditional power arenas.

Payout requirement

The minimum amount that a private foundation is required by the IRS to expend for charitable purposes (including grants and necessary and reasonable administrative expenses). In general, a private foundation must annually pay out approximately 5 percent of the average market value of its assets.[13]

Power analysis

An examination of the external forces surrounding a government, corporate entity, individuals, or others you are trying to influence. Such an analysis uses a systematic approach to look at where you are positioned in relationship to decision makers, including who will support and who will oppose an initiative, how important their point of view is to an effort, and how to build allies to move key decision makers.[14] This analysis helps in planning strategy.

Private foundation

Under federal tax law, a 501(c)(3) that does not qualify as a "public charity." A private foundation is a nongovernmental, nonprofit organization with funds usually from a single source (such as an individual, family, or corporation) and a program managed by its own trustees or directors, established to maintain or aid social, educational, religious, or other charitable activities serving the common welfare, usually through grantmaking.[15] Private foundations face more legal restrictions than public charities. They are prohibited from engaging in lobbying or making grants designated for lobbying ("earmarking" grants for lobbying), though most of the time they may provide general support grants to organizations that then use the funds for lobbying. Such foundations must meet an annual payout requirement (see *payout requirement*).[16] The Ford Foundation is an example of a private foundation.

(Private) operating foundation

In general, a private foundation that uses the bulk of its income to provide services or to run programs of its own. Often, though not always, operating foundations make few, if any, grants to outside organizations. For a foundation to qualify as an operating foundation, it must follow specific rules.[17]

Public charity

A 501(c)(3) that receives its financial support from a diverse array of funders ("public support"), rather than a small number of wealthy individuals or corporations, or that qualifies as a public charity in one of the other ways defined by federal tax law. In contrast to 501(c)(3) private foundations, public charities are generally subject to less stringent regulatory and reporting requirements, particularly with respect to lobbying.[18] The Liberty Hill Foundation is an example of a public charity.

Public foundation

Not a technical legal term, but one often used to refer to a grant-making entity that qualifies as a 501(c)(3) public charity (see *public charity*).

Relationship building

An organizing technique that focuses on getting to know people and discovering how to work together, before discussing a project or policy outcome. One tool used for relationship building is a "one-on-one," through which an organizer meets with one person, such as a member or a decision maker, to uncover his or her needs and concerns, identify themes, and then determine issues of focus.

Site visit

A fact-finding visit that staff and board from one or more foundations make to a grant applicant's or grantee's office location or area of operation (or to participate in its events) to see the grantee and its partners in action. This may involve meeting with the non-profit's staff, its directors, and the recipients of its services. Site visits are normally conducted before a grant is approved, during project implementation, or during project evaluation (or some combination of these).[19]

Social justice philanthropy

Leveraging grantmaking dollars, as well as other foundation resources such as endowments and staff time, in order to support structural change that enhances opportunities for those who are the least well off politically, economically, and socially.[20]

(Social) movement

A social movement is characterized by groups of people organized and coordinated to achieve some task or a collection of goals. Although movements often include spontaneous action by grassroots people who have an interest in bringing about social change, they often also have strong organizational structures that help catalyze and support grassroots action.[21]

Strategic giving

Giving and investing philanthropic dollars in a way that leads to large-scale systems change. Such giving clusters grants together to form a cohesive grantmaking strategy.

Technical assistance

A type of support given to an organization to build its capacity, usually through training or coaching. Such support might be focused on, for example, fundraising, leadership skills, speaking with the media, database management, organization development, or accounting.

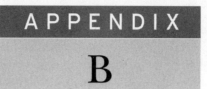

APPENDIX B

Lobbying

The description that follows is only a general summary of the laws governing lobbying and tax-exempt organizations as of 2008 and should not be taken as legal advice. It is intended to help foundations and their grantees understand the basic outlines of these laws, but there are too many details to cover fully here. There are specific rules that vary depending on the legal status of the funder and the grantee. Furthermore, laws can change. Foundations and other nonprofits should consult with a knowledgeable lawyer and should not rely on this book nor on resources listed in this book to answer their legal questions.

Within the context of federal tax laws limiting lobbying by charities and foundations, there are generally many ways for organizations receiving foundation dollars to lobby legally.

Within limits, most 501(c)(3) public charities (including so-called public foundations) may lobby. Generally, those limits may be set as a percentage of the organization's expenditures under the so-called 501(h) expenditure test (named under the section of the tax law that created it) or simply left vague, with the charity promising to do no "substantial" amount of lobbying. (In most cases, the charity can choose which of these two tests to use.)

Typically, organizations that are exempt from tax under section 501(c)(3) may engage in an unlimited amount of nonlobbying advocacy, such as preparing a substantive analysis of a public policy issue.

As for 501(c)(3)s that are private foundations, the rules for lobbying are more strict, but these foundations still may play important roles in public policy efforts.

Private foundations are not allowed to directly engage in lobbying or designate grants specifically for lobbying (they cannot "earmark" grants for lobbying). However, private foundations, like charities, may engage in nonlobbying activities, and most foundations may also provide support to charity grantees that lobby.

Generally, there are two ways for private foundations to provide funds that grantees may use for lobbying. First, foundations may make general support grants to public charities without violating the ban on grants earmarked for lobbying—even if the grantee ends up using the grant to lobby. A foundation may also make a grant to support a particular project of a charity that includes lobbying, provided that the amount the foundation gives is less than the total nonlobbying budget for the project.

Legally, most foundations do not have to restrict grantees from using grants for lobbying activities, although such language is common. There is usually no legal requirement that a foundation include such a "no lobbying" provision in grants to public charities.

John Pomeranz
Harmon, Curran, Spielberg & Eisenberg
Attorney for the Center for Community Change

Ten Questions to Consider Asking Inside Your Foundation

1. If there were a sequel to this book highlighting your foundation, what would you want it to say about your foundation's legacy?
2. What is social justice? How might social justice relate to your foundation?
3. What analyses and events led the showcased foundations and their founders to choose a social justice approach to philanthropy? What kind of analysis or actions might help your foundation embrace such an approach?
4. What strategies did foundations use to secure results? What kinds of levers did they support to influence large-scale systems?
5. What role did power play in the success of the initiatives highlighted? What were some of the strategies foundations used to support their grantees in building their ability to create change?
6. How were power relations between grantees and funders addressed by foundations highlighted in the book? What questions did such efforts raise for you?

7. What role did champions of the change process play within each foundation highlighted? Who could be a champion for a new set of ideas, and in particular a social justice approach, within your foundation?

8. What were some of the internal emotional and political challenges faced by agents of change within each foundation? How might resistance to a change process be addressed in your foundation? What would others in your foundation (staff, trustees, and so on) need to know to support such an initiative?

9. What were some of the external challenges faced by these foundations? How might your foundation proactively address similar challenges when working on large-scale change initiatives in support of equity and justice?

10. Was there someone in the book with whom you particularly identified or whose story you feel will influence your work in your foundation? What were the book's biggest takeaways with respect to effective grantmaking in support of equity and justice?

APPENDIX
D

Where to Turn for Next Steps

Alliance for Justice

Alliance for Justice (www.allianceforjustice.org) is a national association of environmental, civil rights, mental health, women's, children's, and consumer advocacy organizations. As a service to the nonprofit and philanthropic community, the Alliance provides periodic updates on advocacy and lobbying laws relevant to the sector.[1]

The Foundation Center

The Foundation Center (www.foundationcenter.org) is a resource that provides information on grantmaking foundations to would-be grantees and other interested people. It offers training and maintains a searchable database of foundations and other online resources, and offices in several cities across the country.

GrantCraft

A project of the Ford Foundation, GrantCraft (www.grantcraft.org) is a source of practical wisdom from grantmakers on the tools and techniques of effective grantmaking. GrantCraft offers videos and guides based on grantmakers' stories about tools and skills they use to be effective in their work.

National Committee for Responsive Philanthropy (NCRP)

NCRP (www.ncrp.org) is a nonprofit membership organization that includes individuals, nonprofits, and foundations. NCRP promotes philanthropy that serves the public good, is responsive to people and communities with the least wealth and opportunity, and is held accountable to the highest standards of integrity and openness.[2]

Regional associations of grantmakers

Regional associations are membership organizations for funders in a particular region that aim to strengthen the field of philanthropy in their areas. Many such associations include work on social justice.

Other resources include

- BoardSource (www.boardsource.org)
- Center for Lobbying in the Public Interest (www.clpi.org)
- Council on Foundations (www.cof.org); see its list of council-affiliated affinity groups
- Independent Sector (www.independentsector.org)
- The Linchpin Campaign (www.communitychange.org/our-projects/linchpin)
- Neighborhood Funders Group (www.nfg.org)

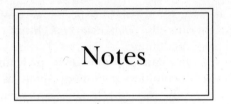

Notes

Introduction

1. Steven Lawrence and Reina Mukai, *Foundation Growth and Giving Estimates: 2008 Edition* (New York: Foundation Center, 2008), http://foundationcenter.org/gainknowledge/research/pdf/fgge08 .pdf. Total includes giving for independent, community, and operating foundations and for corporate foundations. The amount is based on a Foundation Center survey, and may not include all foundations. For full details on survey methodology, see report.
2. Debasis Chaudhuri, *Government Receipts and Expenditures: Fourth Quarter of 2007* (Washington, DC: Bureau of Economic Analysis, U.S. Department of Commerce, Apr. 2008), 7–8, http://www.bea.gov/ scb/pdf/2008/04%20April/0408_gre.pdf.
3. Lawrence and Mukai, "Foundation Growth," 2; "Fortune 500," CNN Money.com, 2008, http://money.cnn.com/magazines/fortune/ fortune500/2008/full_list/.
4. The Foundation Center's Statistical Information Service, "Number of Grantmaking Foundations, Assets, Total Giving, and Gifts Received, 1975 to 2006," http://foundationcenter.org/findfunders/statistics/ pdf/02_found_growth/2006/04_06.pdf.
5. Lawrence and Mukai, "Foundation Growth," 2.
6. Steven Lawrence, ed., *Social Justice Grantmaking II: An Update on Foundation Trends* (New York: Foundation Center, 2009). The sample is based on the Foundation Center's grants sample database. The sample includes all the grants of $10,000 or more reported by a sample of over a thousand of the largest U.S. private and community foundations for 2006.

Chapter One

1. Discount Foundation, "About Us," http://www.discountfoundation .org/about_us.htm.
2. Redlining is a term used to describe "a discriminatory practice by which banks, insurance companies, etc., refuse or limit loans,

mortgages, insurance, etc., within specific geographic areas, esp. inner-city neighborhoods." Dictionary.com, http://dictionary.refer ence.com/browse/redlining.

3. Foundation snapshot data are from Discount Foundation, "About Us," http://www.discountfoundation.org/about_us.htm, and from Henry Allen (executive director, Discount Foundation), e-mail message to author, August 2, 2008, and November 5, 2008.

4. Laureen Lazarovici, "Transforming Low Pay into a Living Wage," America@work, http://www.aflcio.org/aboutus/thisistheaflcio/pub lications/ magazine/corp_transforming.cfm.

5. Christopher Neidt, Greg Ruiters, Dana Wise, and Erica Schoenberger, "The Effects of the Living Wage in Baltimore: Working Paper No. 119" (unpublished report, Economic Policy Institute, Washington, DC, February 1999), 5.

6. Living Wage Resource Center, http://www.livingwagecampaign .org/index.php?id=1958.

7. Louis Uchitelle, "Some Cities Flexing Fiscal Muscle to Make Employers Raise Wages," *New York Times*, Apr. 9, 1996, A1, http:// query.nytimes.com/gst/fullpage.html?res=9900EFDD1039F93A A35757C0A960958260.

8. Susan Chinn, "Discount's Economic Grant Program: Supporting Jobs and Living Wages for the Poor" (unpublished internal document, Discount Foundation, Apr. 1997), 7.

9. John Pomeranz, personal communication with author, January 2009.

10. Chinn, "Discount's Economic Grant Program," 1.

11. Neidt and others, "The Effects of the Living Wage in Baltimore."

12. Susan Chinn, e-mail message to author, October 31, 2007.

13. U.S. Department of Labor, Bureau of Labor Statistics, "Economic News Release," http://www.bls.gov/news.release/union2.t02.htm. Excluded are all self-employed workers, regardless of whether or not their businesses are incorporated.

14. J. Lynn Lunsford, "Staples Center Plan Required to Provide Community Services," *Wall Street Journal*, June 1, 2002, http://www .saje.net/site/c.hkLQJcMUKrH/b.2315847/k.A39D/Staples_Center_ Plan_Required_to_Provide_Community_Services.htm; Lee Romney, "Staples Plan Spotlights Invisible Communities," *Los Angeles Times*, June 2, 2001, http://www.saje.net/site/c.hkLQJcMUKrH/b.2315845/ k.53D3/Staples_Plan_Spotlights_Invisible_Communities.htm.

15. Los Angeles Alliance for a New Economy, "A Track Record of Success," http://laanenetwork.laane.org/laane/victories.html.

16. Living Wage Resource Center, http://www.livingwagecampaign .org/index.php?id=1958.

17. Tom Gallagher, "America Gets a Raise—One State at a Time: A Report on State Minimum Wage Campaigns Prepared for the Discount Foundation" (unpublished report, Discount Foundation, 2007), 6.
18. Ibid.
19. U.S. Department of Labor, Employment Standards Administration, "History of Federal Minimum Wage Rates Under the Fair Labor Standards Act, 1938–2007," http://www.dol.gov/esa/minwage/chart.htm.

Chapter Two

1. The Caroline and Sigmund Schott Foundation (a private foundation, which later became called the Caroline and Sigmund Schott Fund) received its tax exempt status in 1987, but didn't officially launch as a foundation until 1991. In 1999, the Schott Center for Public and Early Education was created (a public charity, which later became called the Schott Foundation for Public Education). The public charity is referred to only as the Schott Foundation for Public Education throughout the book, and the private foundation is referred to only as the Caroline and Sigmund Schott Fund.
2. Snapshot data are from Vahe Karlozian (vice president of finance and administration, the Schott Foundation), e-mail message to author, January 28, 2009.
3. Foundation snapshot data are from Vahe Karlozian, e-mail message to author, January 28, 2009, and from the Schott Foundation, *Annual Report, 2007: A Positive Impact*, 2008.
4. IRS 501(c) Determination Letter, Schott Foundation, June 11, 1999.
5. From Annie Casey and W. K. Kellogg foundations, "Using Logic Models to Bring Together Planning, Evaluation, and Action: Logic Model Development Guide" (Battle Creek, Mich.: W. K. Kellogg Foundation, January 2004), 3, http://www.wkkf.org/Pubs/Tools/Evaluation/Pub3669.pdf.
6. Schott Foundation internal grants database. Grant was for August 1999–August 2000.
7. David Croteau, William Hoynes, and Charlotte Ryan, *Rhyming Hope and History: Activists, Academics and Social Movement Scholarship* (Minneapolis: University of Minnesota Press, 2005), 163.
8. Ibid.
9. Campaign for Fiscal Equity, "CFE v. State of New York," http://www.cfequity.org/remorder.html.

10. Croteau and others, *Rhyming Hope and History*, 170.
11. Norm Fruchter, "Reclaiming Urban Education," *Dissent* 48, no. 4, 2001, 5, 48.
12. D. McKay Wilson, "Education-Aid Reformers Begin Walk to Albany," *Journal News*, May 2, 2003, http://www.cfequity.org/Clippings/05 -02-03journalnews.htm.
13. Croteau and others, *Rhyming Hope and History*, 164–165.
14. Ibid., 166–167.
15. New York State City Council, "Council Members," http://council .nyc.gov/d7/html/members/home.shtml.
16. New York State Alliance for Quality Education, "Files," http:// www.aqeny.org/cms_files/File/pdf/AQE%20History%20&% 20Timeline.pdf.
17. Jay Chambers and others, *The New York Adequacy Study: Determining the Cost of Providing All Children in New York an Adequate Education*, American Institute for Research and Management Analysis and Planning, March 2004, http://eric.ed .gov:80/ERICDocs/data/ericdocs2sql/content_storage_01/ 0000019b/80/29/00/25.pdf.
18. David M. Herszenhorn, "In the Race for Governor, a Big Divide on School Aid," *New York Times*, Nov. 2, 2006, http://www.nytimes .com/2006/11/02/nyregion/02schools.html?partner=rssnyt&emc=rss.
19. Campaign for Fiscal Equity, "CFE Chronology," http://cfequity.org/ CFEchronology.htm.
20. Bill Porter (director of education finance, New York State Education Department), interview with author, August 2, 1007.

Chapter Three

1. Needmor Fund, "Elders," in *The Needmor Fund: 50 Years, 50 Stories* (Toledo, Ohio: Needmor Fund, 2007), 5.
2. Needmor Fund, "Growing Up Needmor," in *The Needmor Fund*, 8.
3. Foundation snapshot data derived from the Needmor Fund annual report for 1968 and from IRS Form 990 (Return of Organization Exempt from Income Tax: 2007), provided by David Beckwith (executive director, Needmor Fund), e-mail message to author, November 10, 2008.
4. Needmor Fund, "Elders," in *The Needmor Fund*, 5.
5. Marshall University, "The Sullivan Principles," http://www.revleon sullivan.org/principled/principles.htm.
6. *Tenth Report on the Signatory Companies to the Sullivan Principles* (Cambridge, Mass.: Arthur D. Little, December 1986), 33, 39.

7. Definitions are adapted from Sarah Cooch and Mark Kramer, *Compounding Impact: Mission Investing by US Foundations* (Boston: FSG Social Impact Advisors and David & Lucile Packard Foundation, 2007), http://www.cof.org/files/images/ExecEd/FSGCmpndImpctReport.pdf. Definitions adapted by Tim Smith, director of socially responsible investing at Walden Asset Management, and Steve Viederman, former president of the Jessie Smith Noyes Foundation.

8. Kerr-McGee was a petroleum, nuclear, and chemicals manufacturer accused of sloppy safety standards that put the health of its employees at risk. "The Silkwood Mystery," *Time*, January 20, 1975, http://www.time.com/time/magazine/article/0,9171,912701-1,00.html.

9. Needmor Fund, "Mission Related Investing," in *The Needmor Fund*, 31.

10. Ibid.

11. Robin Sweberg (portfolio administrator, Neuberger Berman), e-mail message to Tracy Hart, October 12, 2007. Figure includes both separate accounts as well as the socially responsive mutual fund, consisting of the investor and trust classes.

12. Needmor Fund, "Mission Related Investing," in *The Needmor Fund*, 31.

13. Working Assets, "About Working Assets," http://www.workingassets.com/About.aspx.

14. Laura Scher (CEO, Working Assets Funding Service, Inc.), interview with author, September 27, 2007.

15. Amy Domini (founder and CEO, Domini Social Investments), e-mail message to author, May 15, 2008.

16. Trillium Asset Management, "Resolution at YUM Brands Captures 35.2% of Shareholder Votes(A)," http://trilliuminvest.com/news-articles-category/hot-news-articles/resolution-at-yum-brands-captures-352-of-shareholder-votesa/.

17. Andrew Stelzer, "Taco Bell Agrees to Meet All Immokalee Worker Demands," *New Standard*, March 2008, http://newstandardnews.net/content/index.cfm/items/1523.

18. Coalition of Immokalee Workers, "Victory at Taco Bell," http://www.ciw-online.org/agreementanalysis.html.

19. Coalition of Immokalee Workers, "What They're Saying About the Taco Bell Victory," http://www.ciw-online.org/2004-05news.html.

20. Coalition of Immokalee Workers, "Campaign Analysis—CIW Campaign for Fair Food," http://www.ciw-online.org/images/BK_Campaign_Analysis.pdf.

21. The term *shareowner* is used to emphasize that shareholders have ownership and responsibilities within a company.

22. Ceres, Investor Network on Climate Risk, and Environmental Grantmakers Association, *A Toolkit for Foundations and Individual Investors: Harnessing Your Investments to Help Solve the Climate Crisis*, 2008, 2, http://www.ceres.org/Document.Doc?id=383.

Chapter Four

1. Joseph Jacobs, *The Anatomy of an Entrepreneur: Family, Culture and Ethics* (San Francisco: Institute for Contemporary Studies Press, 1991), 167.
2. Foundation snapshot data are from Jennifer Vanica (president and CEO, Jacobs Center for Neighborhood Innovation), e-mail message to author, November 25, 2008; Tracey Bryan (communications team member, Jacobs Center for Neighborhood Innovation), e-mail message to author, February 10, 2009; Jacobs Family Foundation, "What We Do," www.jacobsfamilyfoundation.org/what.htm; and Jacobs Family Foundation and Jacobs Center for Neighborhood Innovation, *The Jacobs Foundations: History 1988–2001* (San Diego: Jacobs Family Foundation and Jacobs Center for Neighborhood Innovation, April 2002), 1.
3. "Information Document: The Village at Market Creek" (unpublished document, Jacobs Center for Neighborhood Innovation, 2008), 1. Data taken from 2000 U. S. Census of Population.
4. Jacobs Center for Neighborhood Innovation, *1997 to 2005: The Journey to Market Creek Plaza* (San Diego: Jacobs Center for Neighborhood Innovation, September 2005), 8.
5. Jacobs Center for Neighborhood Innovation, *Innovation. Investment. Impact. Program of Events for New Markets Tax Credit Loan, 2004*, brochure, June 29, 2004, 2.
6. Jacobs Center for Neighborhood Innovation, *Social and Economic Impact Report, Calendar Year 2007* (San Diego: Jacobs Center for Neighborhood Innovation, 2008), 16.
7. Jennifer Vanica, interview with author, October 17, 2008; Tracey Bryan, e-mail message to author, August 29, 2008.
8. Jacobs Center for Neighborhood Innovation, *1997 to 2005*, 13.
9. Tracey Bryan, e-mail message to author, January 6, 2009.
10. Jacobs Center for Neighborhood Innovation, *This is Your Opportunity to Own a Piece of the Block*, CD-IPO sales brochure, 2006, 15.
11. Jacobs Center for Neighborhood Innovation, *Social and Economic Impact Report*, 18.
12. Jose Venegas (production director, Writerz Block), interview with author, June 9, 2008.

13. Vanica interview.
14. Jacobs Family Foundation and Jacobs Center for Neighborhood Innovation, *1997 to 2005*, 6; Bryan, e-mail message.
15. Jacobs Center for Neighborhood Innovation, *Social and Economic Impact Report*, 17–19; Vanica interview.

Chapter Five

1. Ford Foundation, "International Migration and Refugees: Information Paper" (unpublished report, Ford Foundation, 1980), app. 1; Ford Foundation, "Ford Foundation Refugee and Migration Rights and Policy Portfolio" (unpublished document, Ford Foundation, 2007), 3.
2. Foundation snapshot data are from Ford Foundation, "2007 Grantees," http://www.fordfound.org/impact/annualreports/2007/grants; Ford Foundation, *2007 Annual Report*, 2008; and Jeff Hernandez (grants administrator, peace and social justice program), e-mail message to author, March 30, 2009.
3. Jeffrey Passel, *The Size and Characteristics of the Unauthorized Migrant Population in the U.S.* (Washington, DC: Pew Hispanic Center, 2006), 3.
4. "International Migration and Refugees," 44–45.
5. Ford Foundation, *1978 Annual Report*, 1979, ix.
6. Ford Foundation, *1983 Annual Report*, 1984, 33.
7. Ford Foundation, *1982 Annual Report*, 1983, 21.
8. *Plyler v. Doe*, 457 U.S. 202 (1982), http://caselaw.lp.findlaw.com/scripts/getcase.pl?court=US&vol=457&invol=202.
9. Michael White, Frank Bean, and Thomas Espenshade, "The U.S. 1986 Immigration Reform and Control Act and Undocumented Migration to the United States," *Population Research and Policy Review* 9, no. 2 (May 1990), http://www.springerlink.com/content/l835748l60q61511/.
10. Ford Foundation, *1987 Annual Report*, 1988, 39; Ford Foundation, *1988 Annual Report*, 1989, 64.

Chapter Six

1. Bill Ong Hing, "Open Society Institute's Response to Welfare Reform: The Emma Lazarus Fund's Battle for Justice" (unpublished report, 1999), 1.
2. Daranee Petsod (executive director, Grantmakers Concerned with Immigrants and Refugees), e-mail message to author, July 14, 2008.
3. Institute snapshot data from interview with communications officer (U.S. programs, Open Society Institute), January 26, 2009;

the Communications Department of the Open Society Institute, e-mail message to author, January 29, 2009; Open Society Institute, "About OSI: OSI Offices," http://www.soros.org/about/offices; and Antonio Maciel (former director, U.S. Justice Fund, Open Society Institute), e-mail message to author, August 15, 2008.

4. Fund for Immigrants and Refugees, Donors Forum of Chicago, *Fund for Immigrants and Refugees: Final Report, 1997–2002* (Chicago: Fund for Immigrants and Refugees, 2002) 2–3, 32.

5. Hing, "Open Society Institute's Response," 40.

6. Michael Fix and Jeffrey Passel, "Immigrant Families and Workers: Facts and Perspectives," Brief No. 3 (Washington, DC: Urban Institute, September 2003), 1, 2, http://www.urban.org/uploaded pdf/310847_trends_in_naturalization.pdf.

7. Chung-Wha Hong (executive director, New York Immigration Coalition), "Celebrating Our Historic Victory for Immigrant and English Language Learner Students!!!" Memorandum to NYIC Education Taskforce and NYIC Members and Friends, February 2007.

8. Wendy Zimmerman and Karen Tumlin, "Patches Policies: State Assistance for Immigrants Under Welfare Reform," Occasional Paper No. 24 (Washington, DC: Urban Institute, 1999), 4–5, http://www.urban.org/uploadedpdf/occ24.pdf.

9. Hing, "Open Society Institute's Response," 29, 39, 41.

10. Grantmakers Concerned with Immigrants and Refugees, "Perspective on Immigration: An Interview with Bob Crane," *New Americans* 1, no. 2 (Fall 2001), http://www.gcir.org/system/files/NewAmericans1-2.pdf.

11. Thomas W. Donovan, "The American Immigration System: A Structural Change with a Different Emphasis," *International Journal of Refugee Law* 17, no. 3 (2005): 574–592, http://ijrl.oxfordjournals.org/cgi/content/abstract/17/3/574.

12. Jeffrey S. Passel, *The Size and Characteristics of the Unauthorized Migrant Population in the U.S.: Estimates Based on the March 2005 Current Population Survey* (Washington, DC: Pew Hispanic Center, March 7, 2006), 3, http://pewhispanic.org/files/reports/61.pdf.

13. Communications officer (U.S. programs, Open Society Institute), interview with author, January 26, 2009.

Chapter Seven

1. Foundation snapshot data are from Liberty Hill Foundation, "Liberty Hill Foundation: A Progress Report, July 1977" (unpublished report, Liberty Hill Foundation, July 1977), 2, 9, 18; and Margarita Ramirez

(deputy director of grantmaking, Liberty Hill Foundation), e-mail messages to author, January 5, 2009, February 24, 2009, and March 31, 2009.

2. Liberty Hill Foundation, "Liberty Hill Foundation," 2.

3. Clarke Fountain, "Review Summary: Song of the Canary (1979)," *New York Times*, http://movies.nytimes.com/movie/160973/Song-of-the-Canary/overview.

4. New Day Films, "Filmmakers: Josh Hanig (1952–1998)," http://www.newday.com/filmmakers/Josh_Hanig.html.

5. Torie Osborn (former executive director, Liberty Hill Foundation), interview with author, February 23, 2007.

6. Larry Gross (executive director, Coalition for Economic Survival), interview with author, December 6, 2007; Margarita Ramirez, e-mail message to author, November 13, 2007; City of Los Angeles, Department of City Planning, "Exhibit: Condominium Conversion" (unpublished document, January 2005), http://cityplanning.lacity .org/Forms_Procedures/6771.pdf;LosAngelesHousingDepartment, "Rent Stabilization Update: Tenant Relocation Assistance," October 2008, http://lahd.lacity.org/lahdinternet/LinkClick.aspx?link= Rent%2FWhat+New+Tenant+Relocation+October20082.pdf& tabid=36&mid=542.

7. African American Registry, "African American History: Rodney King Riots," April 1992, http://www.aaregistry.com/african_american_ history/850/Rodney_King_riots_erupt_in_Los_Angeles.

8. Liberty Hill Foundation, *1993 Annual Report*, 1994, 14.

9. Ibid.

10. Ibid.

11. Catherine Suitor (former development director, Liberty Hill Foundation), interview with author, February 23, 2007.

12. Community Coalition, "Accomplishments," http://ccsapt.charity finders.org/Accomplishments.

13. Joanne Kim (chief operating officer, Community Coalition), e-mail message to author, April 13, 2007.

14. SCOPE, "About Us: History," http://www.scopela.org/article.php? list=type&type=55; Asian Pacific American Legal Center, "Accomplish ments," http://apalc.org/accomplishments.htm; Margarita Ramirez, e-mail message to author, November 13, 2007.

15. "Biography," http://www.assembly.ca.gov/acs/makebio.asp?district=47.

16. Torie Osborn, "Notes from Los Angeles: Rebuilding a City One Block at a Time," *New York Times*, April 29, 2002, http://query .nytimes.com/gst/fullpage.html?res=9907E1DF103EF93AA15757C0 A9649C8B63&scp=6&sq=torie%20osborne&st=cse.

Chapter Eight

1. Marilyn Stein LeFeber (vice president, Mott Foundation), e-mail message to author, November 26, 2008.

2. Mott Foundation, *2005 Annual Report*, 2006, 2.

3. Foundation snapshot data are from Mott Foundation, *2000 Annual Report*, 2001, ii, iii, 3; Charles Stewart Mott, Expenditure of Funds— 1928; Mott Foundation, *2007 Annual Report*, 2008, 26, 35–36, 42, 43, 48; Eve Brown, e-mail message to author, May 6, 2008; Mott Foundation, *1999 Annual Report*, 2000, 55.

4. Mott Foundation, *1973 Annual Report*, 1974, 5.

5. Mott Foundation, *1971 Annual Report*, 1972, 10.

6. Mott Foundation, *1975 Annual Report*, 1976, 10.

7. Ibid. 8.

8. Mott Foundation, *1976 Annual Report*, 1977, 6; Mott Foundation, *1977 Annual Report*, 1978, 3.

9. Community development corporations (CDCs) are nonprofit groups that are accountable to local residents and engage in a wide range of physical, economic, and human development activities. CDCs rebuild their communities through housing, commercial, and job development and other activities. Definition adapted from NationMaster.com, "Community Development Corporation," http://www.nationmaster.com/encyclopedia/Community -Development-Corporation.

10. Mott Foundation, *1979 Annual Report*, 1980, 8, 26; Mott Foundation, *1980 Annual Report*, 1981, 56.

11. Definitions excerpted from *Funding Community Organizing: Social Change Through Civic Participation*, published by GrantCraft and The Linchpin Campaign, a project of the Center for Community Change. The full report can be downloaded at http://www.grant craft.org/index.cfm?fuseaction=page.viewpage&pageid=1091. Special thanks to Jan Jaffe for providing permission to use this excerpt.

12. Mark R. Warren and Richard L. Wood, "Faith-Based Community Organizing: The State of the Field" (Jericho, N.Y.: Interfaith Funders, 2001), presented on COMM-ORG: The On-Line Conference on Community Organizing and Development, http://comm-org.wisc .edu/papers.htm.

13. Mott Foundation, "Organization Profile Report for PICO" (database report, Mott Foundation, March 2008).

14. Results, "Children's Health Care," http://www.results.org/website/ article.asp?id=1561.

15. "Obama Signs Law Expanding Children's Healthcare," *Reuters*, February 4, 2009.

16. Robert Pear, "Obama Signs Children's Health Insurance Bill," *New York Times*, February 4, 2009.

17. Scott Reed (executive director, PICO), e-mail message to author, January 17, 2009.

18. Direct Action Research Training Center, "DART Facts," http://www.thedartcenter.org/facts.html.

19. Gamaliel Foundation, "Gamaliel Today," http://www.gamaliel.org/NewsRoom/NewsGamalielToday.htm.

20. Gregory A. Galluzzo, "Gamaliel and the Obama Connection," Gamaliel Foundation, http://www.gamaliel.org/Obama%20Gamalie%20lConnection.htm.

21. Robin Williams Adams, "Polk Indigent Care Plan Faces Deep Cuts," *Ledger*, July 30, 2008, http://www.theledger.com/article/20080730/NEWS/807290445.

22. Bruce Bussey (urban development manager, Pinellas County Community Development), interview with Susan Doherty, January 15, 2009.

23. Kavitha Mediratta and others, *Organized Communities, Stronger Schools: A Preview of Research Findings* (Providence, R.I.: Annenberg Institute for School Reform, Brown University, 2008), v.

Part V

1. Funding Exchange, "Member Foundations," http://www.fex.org/content/index.php?pid=31.

Chapter Nine

1. For more information on the founding of the Global Fund for Women, see Anne Firth Murray, *Paradigm Found: Leading and Managing for Positive Change* (Novato, Calif.: New World Library, 2006).

2. Snapshot data are from Shalini Nataraj (vice president of programs, Global Fund for Women), e-mail message to author, July 7, 2008; Global Fund for Women, *Annual Report, the First Two Years 1987–1989*, 1989; Heather Masaki (administrative associate to the vice president of development, Global Fund for Women), e-mail message to author, November 10, 2008; and Sande Smith (director of public education, Global Fund for Women), e-mail message to author, January 31, 2009.

3. Global Fund for Women, *Annual Report, the Third Year 1989–1990*, 1990, 5.
4. For more information on Semillas, visit www.semillas.org.mx.
5. Global Fund for Women, *Annual Report, the Fourth Year 1990–1991*, 1991, 11.
6. Global Fund for Women, *Annual Report, the Ninth Year 1995–1996*, 1996, 12.
7. For more information on Tewa, visit www.tewa.org.np.
8. Nataraj, e-mail message.
9. Emilienne de León Aulina (executive director, Semillas), e-mail message to author, June 2, 2008; Jacki Sands (marketing and communications officer, WHEAT Trust), e-mail message to author, November 11, 2008.
10. Rita Thapa, "E-Bulletin 28th Issue (April 2008) Special Issue on Victorious Candidates of CA Polls"; confirmed by Nataraj, e-mail message.
11. Emilienne de León Aulina, "Women Murdered in Cd. Juarez: How to Achieve Justice? A Civil Society Strengthening Process," November 2005, 1, http://www.unifem.org/attachments/events/Remarks_EmilienneDeLeon.pdf.
12. Emilienne de León Aulina, interview with author, May 28, 2008.
13. Maria-Isabel Rivero (press and outreach director, Organization of American States), e-mail message to author, May 28, 2008; Inter-American Commission on Human Rights, "Annual Report 2005: Report No 16/05 Petition 281/02 Admissibility, Claudia Ivette González, Mexico, February 24, 2005," http://www.cidh.org/annualrep/2005eng/Mexico.281.02eng.htm; Inter-American Commission on Human Rights, "Annual Report 2005: Report No 17/05 Petition 282/02 Admissibility, Esmeralda Herrera Monreal, Mexico, February 24, 2005," http://www.cidh.org/annualrep/2005eng/Mexico282.02eng.htm; Inter-American Commission on Human Rights, "Annual Report 2005: Report No 18/05 Petition 283/02 Admissibility, Laura Berenice Ramos Monarrez, Mexico, February 24, 2005," http://www.cidh.org/annualrep/2005eng/Mexico.283.02eng.htm.
14. Emilienne de León Aulina, e-mail message to author, August 25, 2008; Estados Unidos Mexicanos, Ley General de Acesso de las Mujeres a una Vida Libre de Violencia (General Law of Access of Women for a Life Free from Violence), Mexico, Camara de Diputados del H. Congreso de la Union, Nueva Ley DOF 01-02-2007, 1.
15. Murray, *Paradigm Found*, xxiii.

Chapter Ten

1. U.S. Department of Health and Human Services, "Katrina," http://www.hhs.gov/disasters/emergency/naturaldisasters/hurricanes/katrina/index.html; Sue Kirchhoff, "Rebuilding After Katrina to Take Monumental Effort," *USA Today,* October 5, 2005, http://www.usatoday.com/money/economy/housing/2005-10-05-katrina-housing-usat_x.htm.
2. Snapshot data are from Ezra Vazquez-D'Amico (associate, Rockefeller Philanthropy Advisors), e-mail message to author, January 16, 2009, and interview with author, April 2, 2009.
3. Rockefeller Philanthropy Advisors, "About RPA," http://rockpa.org/about_rpa/.
4. Ariane Wiltse, "Dispatch from New Orleans: Second Guessing Myself," blog entry, *Los Angeles Times,* July 3, 2008. http://latimesblogs.latimes.com/pardonourdust/2008/07/dispatch-from-n.html.
5. National Wetlands Research Center, "100 Years of Land Change for Coastal Louisiana," http://www.nwrc.usgs.gov/upload/landloss11X17.pdf.
6. Global Green, "Green Building," http://www.globalgreen.org/greenurbanism/.
7. Amy Liu and Allison Plyler, *The New Orleans Index: Tracking the Recovery of New Orleans and the Metro Area* (Washington, DC: Nonprofit Knowledge Works and Brookings Institution, 2008), 79, http://gnocdc.s3.amazonaws.com/NOLAIndex/NewOrleansIndexAug08.pdf. District 8 includes the Holy Cross Neighborhood and the Lower Ninth Ward Neighborhood. Number rounded to nearest whole and includes all households receiving mail.
8. Global Green, "Rebuilding New Orleans," http://www.globalgreen.org/neworleans/holycross/; "Rebuilding a Better, Greener New Orleans," *Today,* July 18, 2006, http://www.msnbc.msn.com/id/13892600/.
9. "Rebuilding."
10. *Rule: Department of Revenue Policy Services Division: Income Tax Credits for Wind or Solar Energy Systems,* LAC 61:I.1907, http://dnr.louisiana.gov/sec/execdiv/techasmt/energy_sources/Final%20Solar%20Rules%20as%20of%2010-28-08.pdf.
11. Blain Greteman, "Talkin' 'Bout My Generation," *Ode* 6, no. 7, September 2008, 24.
12. U.S. Army Corps of Engineers, "About Mr. GO," http://mrgo.usace.army.mil/default.aspx?p=MRGOInfo; Mathew Brown, "Shipping Interests Pushing for Mr. GO," *Times Picayune,* September 22,

2006, http://www.nola.com/news/t-p/frontpage/index.ssf?/base/
news-6/1158905741220990.xml&coll=1&thispage=2.
13. *Water Resources Development Act of 2007*, HR 1495, 110th Cong., 240,
http://frwebgate.access.gpo.gov/cgi-bin/getdoc.cgi?dbname=110_
cong_bills&docid=f:h1495enr.txt.pdf.
14. May Boeve (co-coordinator, Step It Up), personal communication
with author, September 17, 2008.
15. Step It Up 2007, http://april.stepitup2007.org/.
16. For information on the Lieberman-Warner Climate Security Act
(S. 2191), see http://lieberman.senate.gov/documents/lwcsaonepage
.pdf and http://www.pewclimate.org/analysis/l-w.

Chapter Eleven

1. "Interview—Luis Ubiñas," *Alliance*, September 2008, http://www
.alliancemagazine.org/node/1429.
2. Steven LaFrance, Andrew Robinson, Rick Green, and Nancy Latham,
"Funder Networks in Action: Data Highlights," Grantmakers for
Effective Organizations, March 2004, http://www.geofunders.org/
content.aspx?oid=64ff39bc-1eb3-4b10-a9de-298cae9d7976.

Afterword

1. Roberto Ungar, *What Should the Left Propose?* http://www.law.har
vard.edu/faculty/unger/english/wstlp.php.
2. Institute on Race and Poverty, *Racism and Metropolitan Dynamics:
The Civil Rights Challenge of the 21st Century* (Minneapolis:
Institute on Race and Poverty, 2002).

Appendix A

1. Adapted from GrantCraft, "Advocacy Funding: The Philanthropy of
ChangingMinds,"http://www.grantcraft.org/index.cfm?fuseaction=
Page.viewPage&pageID=763; also see Joan Minieri and Paul Getsos,
*Tools for Radical Democracy: How to Organize for Power in Your
Community* (San Francisco: Jossey-Bass, 2007), 187.
2. Direct citation of Lisa Ranghelli, *Strengthening Democracy, Increasing
Opportunities: Impacts of Advocacy, Organizing, and Civic
Engagement in New Mexico* (Washington, D.C.: National Committee
for Responsive Philanthropy, 2009), 6.
3. Final sentence provided by John Pomeranz (of the firm Harmon,
Curran, Spielberg & Eisenberg, and attorney for the Center for
Community Change), e-mail message to author, December 19, 2008.

4. Definition adapted from Ranghelli, *Strengthening Democracy*, 6; and Lisa Ranghelli, Andrew Mott, and Larry Parachini, "Strengthening Neighborhood Organizing in Hartford: A Report to the Hartford Foundation for Public Giving" (unpublished report, September 2004), 3, as provided in Sandy O'Donnell, Jane Beckett, and Jean Rudd, *Promising Practices in Revenue Generation for Community Organizing: An Exploration of Current and Emerging Fundraising and Grantmaking Practices in Community Organizing* (Washington, DC: Center for Community Change, October 2005), http://comm-org.wisc.edu/papers2005/beckett.htm.
5. Pomeranz, e-mail message.
6. Pomeranz, e-mail message.
7. Pomeranz, e-mail message.
8. Direct citation of Forum of Regional Association of Grantmakers, "Glossary of Philanthropic Terms: Funder Network," http://www.givingforum.org/s_forum/sec.asp?CID=2071&DID=5555#DtoF.
9. Adapted from Forum of Regional Association of Grantmakers, "Glossary of Philanthropic Terms: Operating Support," http://www.givingforum.org/s_forum/sec.asp?CID=2071&DID=5555#MtoO; and Pomeranz, e-mail message.
10. Pomeranz, e-mail message.
11. Direct citation of Forum of Regional Association of Grantmakers, "Glossary of Philanthropic Terms: Matching Grant," http://www.givingforum.org/s_forum/sec.asp?CID=2071&DID=5555#MtoO.
12. Adapted from Sarah Cooch and Mark Kramer, *Compounding Impact: Mission Investing by US Foundations* (Boston: FSG Social Impact Advisors and David & Lucile Packard Foundation, 2007), http://www.cof.org/files/images/ExecEd/FSGCmpndImpctReport.pdf.
13. Direct citation of Forum of Regional Association of Grantmakers, "Glossary of Philanthropic Terms: Payout Requirement," http://www.givingforum.org/s_forum/sec.asp?CID=2071&DID=5555#PtoR.
14. Adapted from Minieri and Getsos, *Tools for Radical Democracy*, 168.
15. Adapted from Forum of Regional Association of Grantmakers, "Glossary of Philanthropic Terms: Private Foundation," http://www.givingforum.org/s_forum/sec.asp?CID=2071&DID=5555#PtoR.
16. Pomeranz, e-mail message.
17. Adapted from Forum of Regional Association of Grantmakers, "Glossary of Philanthropic Terms: Operating Foundation," http://www.givingforum.org/s_forum/sec.asp?CID=2071&DID=5555#MtoO.
18. Pomeranz, e-mail message.

19. Adapted from Forum of Regional Association of Grantmakers, "Glossary of Philanthropic Terms: Site Visit," http://www.givingforum.org/s_forum/sec.asp?CID=2071&DID=5555#PtoR.
20. Adapted from Steven Lawrence, ed., *Social Justice Grantmaking: A Report on Foundation Trends* (New York: Foundation Center, 2005), ix.
21. Adapted from Philip J. Bostic, "Social Movement," Learning to Give, http://www.learningtogive.org/papers/index.asp?bpid=59.

Appendix D

1. Council on Foundations, "Nonprofit Infrastructure Organizations," http://www.cof.org/Network/content.cfm?ItemNumber=9846&navItemNumber=2226.
2. National Committee for Responsive Philanthropy, "Who We Are," http://www.ncrp.org/about-us.

Index

JEHT Foundation, 116
Jenifer Altman Foundation, 187
Jessie Smith Noyes Foundation, 58
Jewish Fund for Justice, 136, 158, 161
Jobin-Leeds family: Greg, 22, 23, 25–26, 28, 31, 33–34, 39–40, 41, 42; Maria, 22, 40, 41
Joe & Vi Jacobs Center, 84
Johnson, Charles and Bessie, 76–77
Johnson, Lyndon, 151
Joyce Foundation, 105
Joyce Mertz Gilmore Foundation, 105, 116, 119

K
Kamasaki, Charles, 97
Kettenring, Brian, 18
Keys, Alicia, 38
Kicklighter, Kurt, 78, 80–81
Kieschnick, Michael, 57
King, Rodney, 135
Kissling, Frances, 167, 170
Knight Foundation, 161
Koreatown Immigrant Workers Alliance (KIWA), 139
Korten, Alicia, xx

L
La Raza, 97
Labor: partnerships for living-wage campaign, 18–19, 20; transforming wages for, 7–8, 14
Lagarde, Marcela, 182
LaMarche, Gara, 107
Laws: Antiterrorism and Effective Death Penalty Act, 104; Illegal Immigration Reform and Immigrant Responsibility Act, 104, 111; Immigration Reform and Control Act, 97–99; Personal Responsibility and Work Opportunity Reconciliation Act, 104; Refugee Act, 96; Tax Reform Act of 1969, 146
Leadership: assessing grantee's, 109; cultivating women's, 181–182; finding, 30–31, 157, 206, 207; fostering within congregation-based

networks, 156–157; funding retreats for, 116; sharing family foundation, 67; strategies for building, 137; *See also* Advisory groups
Lederer, Laura, 167, 168
Leeds family: creating public charity, 30–31; Dan, 39–40; Gerry, 22–23; Greg Jobin-Leeds, 22, 23, 25–26, 28, 31, 33–34, 39–40, 41, 42; Institute for Student Achievement founded, 25; Lilo, 22–23, 25, 33; Maria Jobin-Leeds, 22, 40, 41; passion for equality in education, 22–23; political action by, 39–40; social justice philanthropy of, xx; vision of, 24–25, 41–42
LeFeber, Marilyn Stein, 163
Legislation: establishing rights for Mexican women, 182–183; on immigration, 96, 120; providing increased education funds, 40–41; responsive to Gulf Coast disaster, 205; supporting community schools, 145
Legler Benbough Foundation, 77
Lessons learned: Charles Stewart Mott Foundation, 163–164; community-driven development, 88; Discount Foundation, 21; Ford Foundation, 103; Global Fund for Women, 185; Gulf Coast Fund, 207–208; Schott Foundation for Public Education, 42; by Stranahan family, 63–64
Leticia A. v. Board of Regents, 97
Leveraging change: building interest in, 12–14; building support for education reform, 35–37; Discount Foundation's role in, 20–21, 215; finding potential grantees, 26–27; funding litigation, 27–29; including youth in, 64, 65–67; sponsoring public relations, 33–34; using assets for, 64, 88; Veatch Program's goal in, 17–18; via business sector, xxiv–xxv, 215; ways of, 214–215
Liberty Hill Foundation: about, xxii, 125–127, 214, 216, 217, 219; assuming leadership in community funding, 135–136; community funding board model, 133–134; effectiveness of,

BUILDING *the*
POWER
of MANY *for*

40

YEARS

CENTER *for*
COMMUNITY CHANGE

The mission of the Center for Community Change (CCC) is to develop the power and capacity of low-income people, especially low-income people of color, to change their communities and public policies for the better. Founded in 1968 to honor Robert F. Kennedy, the Center is one of the longest-standing champions for low-income communities of color. CCC strengthens community organizing groups and helps them unite across the dividing lines of race, geography, organizational affiliation, and issue priority to advance progressive public policy change. It is one of the few national social justice organizations whose leadership, staff, and board are in the majority people of color.

Through its Campaign for Community Values, CCC works with almost three hundred grassroots organizations nationwide to project shared values of the common good into the national debate—and into public policies on the economy, jobs, health care, immigration, and more. The Center cultivates the next wave of community organizers and nonprofit professionals for the social change sector by recruiting, training, and placing young people in paid learning opportunities with grassroots organizations. CCC works to generate new ideas and voices to energize the progressive movement and increase civic engagement among low-income people and people of color.

Although CCC is not a grantmaking organization, it has for many years provided technical assistance and small grants to grassroots groups through the C. S. Mott Intermediary Support for Organizing Communities program. In addition, CCC raises and regrants more than a million dollars to grassroots partner organizations each year.

Through its work in low-income communities, CCC has learned how essential—and challenging—it is to expand the resources available to community organizing efforts in the United States. This is the goal of the Linchpin Campaign, a special project of CCC. The Linchpin Campaign is led by Marjorie Fine, former executive director of the Unitarian Universalist Veatch Program at Shelter Rock and a longtime grantmaker and community organizer. The project seeks to persuade a wider range of donors and funders to support organizing, and to assist community organizing groups to communicate the impact of community organizing effectively.

Please contact Marjorie Fine at mfine@communitychange.org or (212) 643-3464, x101. For more information, please visit the Center's Web site, www.communitychange.org.

1536 U Street, NW – Washington, DC 20009 – *www.communitychange.org* – *tel (202) 339-9300 – toll-free (877) 777-1536 – fax (202) 387-4891*

About the Project Director

Marjorie Fine, who oversaw the development of this book, has over twenty years of experience leading grantmaking institutions. Most recently, Marjorie served for more than a decade (1993–2005) as executive director of the Unitarian Universalist Veatch Program at Shelter Rock, a national faith-based social justice grantmaker. Prior to her tenure at the Veatch Program, she was executive director of the North Star Fund, a public foundation serving the New York City progressive community.

Fine currently directs The Linchpin Campaign (TLC), a special project of the Center for Community Change (CCC), whose goal is to expand the resources available to community organizing efforts in the United States. TLC produced and copublished (together with Jossey-Bass) *Change Philanthropy: Candid Stories of Foundations Maximizing Results Through Social Justice.*

TLC also recently partnered with GrantCraft to produce a guide for funders titled *Funding Community Organizing: Social Change Through Civic Participation.* In addition, TLC has published *Untapped: How Community Organizers Can Develop and Deepen Relationships with Major Donors,* a downloadable manual for organizers and development directors.

Marjorie consults regularly with several national organizing and funder networks and is featured in many workshops and conferences on social justice fundraising and philanthropy. She serves on the boards of Interfaith Funders and the National Committee for Responsive Philanthropy. She is a Phi Beta Kappa, magna cum laude graduate of SUNY Buffalo, and holds a master of social work degree from Hunter College School of Social Work, with a concentration in community organizing and administration.

For more information about initiatives of The Linchpin Campaign, including *Change Philanthropy,* you can contact Marjorie Fine at mfine@communitychange.org or visit the TLC Web site at http://www.communitychange.org/our-projects/linchpin.

About the Author

Alicia Korten is the founder and CEO of ReNual (www.renual.com), a consulting firm working with foundations, socially responsible businesses, and nonprofit organizations to grow enduring institutions and initiatives. Alicia is fluent in Spanish and was a Fulbright Scholar to Costa Rica, at which time she wrote *Ajuste Estructural en Costa Rica* (*Structural Adjustment in Costa Rica*), a book on the impact of trade policies on the business sector, national finance, and environment in Costa Rica.

Korten has led strategic planning efforts and evaluations and has written publications for the United Nations, Ford Foundation, Inter-American Foundation, World Resources Institute, Share Foundation, Inter-Action, CARE-USA, Friends of the Earth, Association for Professionals in Infection Control Research Foundation, and many others.

Korten is a leader in the organizational storytelling movement and coauthored two chapters on branding and finance for *Wake Me Up When the Data Is Over: How Organizations Use Storytelling to Drive Results*. She has given keynote addresses and led public and private workshops on using storytelling to establish values-based organizations and strengthen strategic direction for the American Bar Association's Bar Leadership Institute, Smithsonian Associates Program, and Levi Strauss & Co., among others.